PRE-TITLE SEQU

FADE IN:

Over the past few years, a small English film production company called Hammer has become something of a worldwide cult. Numerous books have been written, TV documentaries produced, magazines published, film festivals thrown, all celebrating a dozen or so movies Hammer made over a specific period starting over 30 years ago in the late fifties. By the middle seventies the whole thing was over. Sure, Hammer still made films, but they weren't the same. They were just movies, some good, some bad. Similar to those they made before their so-called "golden years." I know because I worked on most of them. I was an assistant director and a production manager on 32 films made by Hammer before I started to write.

As one of the original employees of a cult company, I suppose that means I've become a cult figure. I get interviewed for obscure American magazines with strange titles like Little Shoppe of Horrors *and* Filmfax *and by people who are writing books about horror movies in general and Hammer horror movies in particular. I get letters asking for photographs of myself. I get invited to horror film festivals where, sometimes, I am asked to address the cult's acolytes. Once, in Hollywood, I was presented with a Golden Scroll of Merit for Outstanding Achievement by the Academy of Science Fiction, Fantasy and Horror Films. I've been on radio and TV talking about horror movies. Martin Scorsese is a fan, so too is Tim Burton. I don't know about Spielberg, but I like to think he is also. It's no sweat being a cult figure. Very few demands are made on my time which is something I've plenty of right now. So, if anybody asks me if I mind being a cult figure, I tell them it's okay by me.*

"Beginnings..."

The only part of my life that anybody out there is really interested in is my "Hammer Gothic" period. There was a life before Hammer and there most certainly has been a long, happy, productive life since, but I'll try to keep both those periods short. I promise. What I would like to do is to explain, as best I can, how I became a writer in general and a "horror film" writer in particular.

I read someplace recently that the older you get the worse your memory becomes. I've already forgotten where I read it, which pretty much proves my point. So when somebody suggested that I write this book, I had serious doubts. First the aforementioned memory thing. How am I going to recall events and personalities stretching back fifty years when I have a problem remembering last Wednesday? Then I realized that I don't remember last Wednesday because nothing much happened last Wednesday. Same with Tuesday and Thursday. Whereas in 1956, when I wrote my first movie, a hell of a lot happened. Same with 1950 when I got married for the

Posing with my first automobile, around 1953.

first time and emigrated to Canada, and 1946 when I worked at Ealing Studios, and 1943, during World War II, when I left school at 16 and got my first job in the movie business. Seems the further back I go, the easier it is to remember. I think there's a medical name for that condition, but I don't care to check it out.

Then there's the question of how do I know that my memory of things will be accurate. I mean, we're going back here more than fifty years. Reference books are great for digging out the facts and figures, but they don't help much when it comes to writing about personal stuff. How I felt about this, how I emotionally dealt with that. I have never been one to keep a diary other than "lunch on Thursday with Charlie" type journal. More a record of what is going to happen than the other way round. As for how I felt about lunch with Charlie, or even who Charlie was, forget it! As a result, large sections of this book might sound a little vague.

Another reason I hesitate to write my autobiography is that, in my opinion, to do so shows signs of arrogance. Who on God's green earth, with the exception of my nearest and dearest, could possibly be interested in my life? But it seems there are people out there who are interested. I was made aware of this when I received a letter from somebody who wanted to write my biography. I turned him down. Later I was talking this over with a friend who said that, like it or not, somebody, somewhere, someday is going to write my life story. If I won't give permission while I'm alive, they'll wait until I'm dead. Then they'll be able to say whatever they like and I won't

DO YOU WANT IT
GOOD OR TUESDAY?

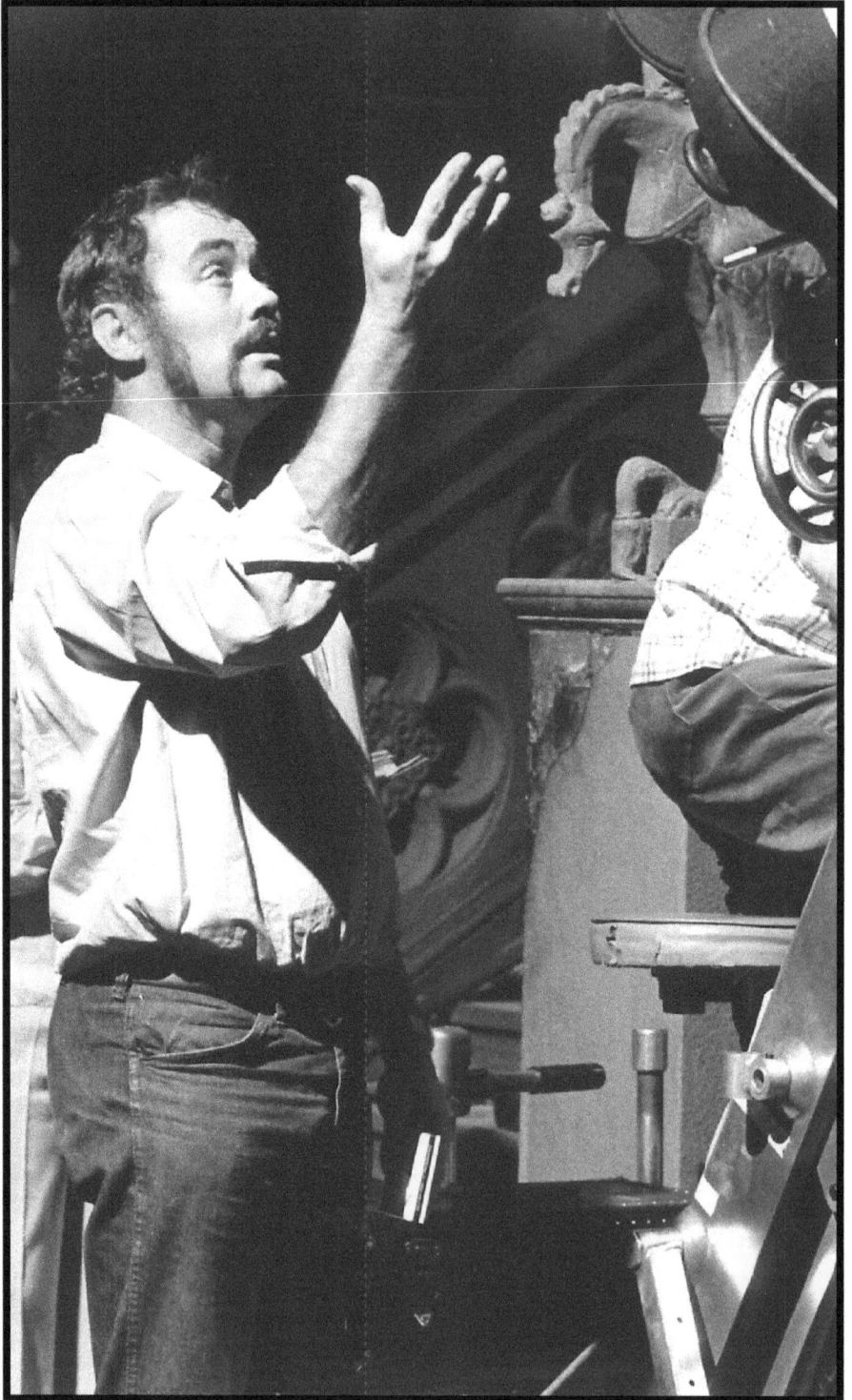

DO YOU WANT IT GOOD OR TUESDAY?

FROM HAMMER FILMS TO HOLLYWOOD! A LIFE IN THE MOVIES

An Autobiography by Jimmy Sangster

Midnight Marquee Press, Inc.
Baltimore, Maryland, USA

Frontispiece: Jimmy Sangster on the set of *Horror of Frankenstein*

ISBN 13: 9781887664134
ISBN 10: 1-887664-13-0
Library of Congress Catalog Card Number 97-070785
Manufactured in the United States of America

First Printing by Midnight Marquee Press, Inc., June 1997
Second Printing by Midnight Marquee Press, Inc. February 2009

This is for Claire and Ian

and, of course,

Mary.

TABLE OF CONTENTS

My son, Jim Sangster, Jr., poses with wife Joan and their children, Claire and Ian.

be around to refute anything. Either that or they'll write an "unauthorized" version which would be even worse. In that they can say practically anything they want and it's up to me to prove them wrong.

"Wouldn't you like your grandchildren to know something about their grandfather? Who he was. What he did," said somebody. I think that's what did it for me.

So, to my grandchildren and to anybody else interested enough to have begged, borrowed, bought, or stolen this book, I say read and, hopefully, enjoy.

FADE OUT:

Ruth and Dudley Sangster, my parents.

Do You Want It Good or Tuesday?

BANG, BANG, YOU'RE DEAD.

During the early part of World War II, my father kept two loaded guns in the house, both automatics. He only told us the reason when the fear of imminent Nazi invasion was long past. Apparently, the moment he saw German paratroopers climbing over the back fence, he was going to shoot my mother, my brother, and me. He was then going to take it out on a couple of Germans and save the last bullet for himself. No way was he going to allow any member of his family to fall into the hands of the dreaded Nazis. But the Nazis never came, and the guns, fully loaded, stayed in his bedside drawer. Except when my brother Peter and I were alone in the house and played with them.

We would rush around the house going bang bang until we discovered a better game. As you probably know, with an automatic pistol, when you pull back the chamber a bullet is fed into it from the magazine at the same time the one already there is expelled. Hold the gun sideways to one's opponent, pull back the chamber and, with any luck, he'll get whacked by the ejected cartridge. This action couldn't be performed with the safety catch on which was OK with us because safety catches were for sissies. Except one day I pulled back on the chamber with my finger on the trigger. This time the bang was for real. The cartridge Peter got whacked with was the empty casing of the bullet that had missed him by God knows how little. It took us over half an hour to locate where the bullet had gone. We finally found it. It had just missed the sideboard leaving a small hole in the wall. We tried digging for it. All that happened was the hole got bigger. Finally we peeled some wallpaper from the opposite side of the room and pasted the hole over. Then we put the guns back praying that my father would never bother counting the bullets left in the magazine. He didn't. It was just as well the Nazis never arrived. He'd have had a nasty surprise if he'd saved the last bullet for himself.

Act One. Scene One.
"Why not call him Kinmel...?"

While I can't imagine anyone being remotely interested in my prepubescent years, I believe it's mandatory for an autobiographer to let the reader know who he is and where he comes from.

First, my full name is James Henry Kinmel Sangster. I got the Kinmel because I was the first baby born in a small seaside town in North Wales called Kinmel Bay. The town fathers asked my parents if they'd kindly add the name to the James Henry they'd already chosen. Maybe they knew I was going to be writing my autobiography one day and I'd give the town a plug. My father was a real estate agent in the town. He was young and ambitious, and if cooperating with the senior members of the community would improve his business prospects, why not! So I got saddled with the name. I suppose I can be thankful I wasn't the first child born six miles to the West in the village of Llanelian-yn Rhos. In any event, my father's business prospects didn't improve and a year or so later we left Kinmel Bay forever.

Ruth and Dudley Sangster, my parents.

My brother Peter and I attended various day schools, and when I was seven (he was six) we were sent off to boarding school, Ewell Castle, in Surrey, a short drive from London. It was a ramshackle old pile supposed to have been built by Henry VIII in which to spend dirty weekends with Anne Boleyn, whose restless spirit was still supposed to walk the corridors at night. Whether she did or not, I have no idea. I know I never saw her. The school houses were historically named Castlemaine, Raleigh, and Essex after long-forgotten noblemen who had occupied the place at some time or other. Very grand, until you actually saw the place. Early grim and grimy. The cane was used regularly. I can still remember lining up outside the headmaster's office to be punished for some misdemeanor. I think it was smoking. Three whacks on each hand and three on the bum. And it hurt. But it didn't stop me smoking. I also

Do You Want It Good or Tuesday?

The Sangster family plus one cousin circa 1935.

ran away once, walking the twelve miles home. What I don't recall is why I did it. It certainly wasn't because I was unhappy or deprived or bullied. I think I was probably bored. In any event, when I finally got home I was coddled and comforted and put to bed in a pair of my father's pajamas which were far too big for me. The next day I was returned to school with an extra week's pocket money. Peter thought this was a pretty good deal so he ran away too. He got brought back the same afternoon and didn't get a cent.

We were at this school when war broke out in 1939. It was all very exciting at the time. Air raid drills, gas masks, foreign students disappearing back to their own countries, and food rationing. We must have had warning about the threat of rationing because I still have a letter I wrote to my mother from school.

> Dear Mummy and Daddy,
>   I do hope you are well thank you very much for the ointment and the comic the other day I bought two more lbs of sugar which brings our total up to 6 lbs between us if I am in time I will buy another two lbs next week Peter can't write because there is not enough ink in my pen for both of us but I expect he'll ask matron for a pencil or something well I am closing now goodbye love from Jimmy.

I wasn't too good on punctuation during my formative years.

We also had long, serious discussions as to how the war would be over by the end of the year. It wasn't, and having remained at school for another three years, my parents, in their infinite wisdom, decided we should be evacuated to Cardiff in the

Ruth Sangster

care of some relatives of my mother. We arrived in Cardiff the same week the city was blitzed by the Germans for three nights running. Those three nights we spent in a cupboard under the stairs. Even so, I enjoyed Cardiff. We attended Llandaff Cathedral school, where we both auditioned for the cathedral choir. My parents were very keen that we become choir members because it meant our school fees were waived. I was accepted but, unfortunately, before I became a fully fledged chorister, my voice broke.

Eventually we were shipped back home to Old Coulsdon, in Surrey, where we lived for the rest of the war. Here too we were shoved under the stairs whenever the air raid sirens sounded. By then, I had started going out with a girl named Elsie whose father was the Regimental Sergeant Major of the Irish Guards, which meant you didn't mess with Elsie. But if she happened to be visiting when the air raid started, she was ordered by my mother to get under the stairs with us. There were times I used to pray for an air raid. We were bombed out once. Later, when I'd started work and was staying with some maiden aunts in North London, I was bombed out again. Anyone asks me what I did in the war, I tell them I was bombed out a lot.

I'd wanted to be in the movie business for as long as I could remember. I've no idea why. That's just the way it was. I wasn't quite sure what I actually wanted to do, whether to be a lighting cameraman or a director or, as a last resort, a writer, just so long as I made a lot of money and became famous. I was an avid film fan. By the time I was 14 I had put together a huge collection of stars' biographies, credit lists, who was in what, who directed it, who was married to who, when they were born. God only knows where I managed to dig up all this information. There was a war on at the time, paper was in very short supply, so there were no fan magazines. Nevertheless, the material I'd collected filled two large ledgers and a couple of filing trays. I spent hours sorting, correcting, updating. At least I did until the house caught fire. The fire wasn't even caused by enemy action. Somebody upstairs left an electric burner on too close to an armchair. Eventually the chair burst into flame. We were all sitting on the front lawn watching our house burn down when an air raid warden told my father that he'd better do something about that fire pretty bloody quick or he'd be in deep shit for showing a light in the blackout. The fire brigade arrived eventually and proceeded to pour thousands of gallons of water onto the fire which eventually found its way down to the small room under the stairs, turning my collection into a soggy, unsalvageable mess. I decided there and then that showbiz wasn't for me. Then a couple of days later I saw *Gone With the Wind* and I was back on track.

The war was still on when I got my first showbiz job. I became a general dogsbody (gofer) and assistant projectionist at a grubby little office building in Wardour Street which was, and still is, the centre of the film business in England. That doesn't make it a glamorous thoroughfare like Broadway or Hollywood Boulevard pretends to be. It's just a narrow one-way street in Soho where homeless young people sleep in the doorways and movie companies have their offices.

I was employed by a company called Norman's Film Services. I was sixteen at the time, which would make it around 1943. All the able-bodied men were away fighting World War II, so, once I'd persuaded my parents to let me quit school, getting a job was no problem. The job itself wasn't much of a problem either. It mostly involved carrying cans of film from the vaults (which were on the roof) to the projection room, which was in the basement four floors down, then back again after the screening.

The only time I actually got to work the projectors on my own was the day my immediate boss, the chief projectionist, slipped across the road to a pub called The Intrepid Fox for a pint of beer (having first checked the book to make sure there were no screenings due). This time he miscalculated and I was called on to screen a documentary film for a group of potential buyers. I even remember the title, *Salute to the British Worker*, a dire little black and white film with a lot of emphasis on shirt-sleeved, flat-capped men giving their all for king and war torn country in shipyards and steel mills. Unfortunately I forgot to check that the film was correctly threaded onto the "take up" spool. I was so busy watching the screen through the projectionist's window, making sure my arc was trimmed and my rack was correct (that's technical stuff among us projectionists) that I didn't notice the film spilling out around my feet until it was up to my knees and seriously out of control. Fortunately my boss returned before it was over my head. My main memory was of him gathering up this highly inflammable film in armfuls, with a lighted cigarette waggling between his lips, as he called me a daft bugger. Not surprisingly, two weeks later I was out of work. A week after that I got myself another job. This time it was at a real studio, a place where they actually shot movies. Small movies, mark you, because it was a very small studio just round the corner from Abbey Road which the Beatles made famous. And seeing this was a proper studio, I was required to join the technician's union, the Association of Cine Technicians. Membership number 6001.

Nowadays there is strict job delineation. At least, there was last time I was on a film set which, I have to admit, was some time ago. God forbid a camera person should touch any sound equipment and everything grinds to a halt if a prop man tries a bit of carpentry. It wasn't like that when I worked at Carlton Hill Studios. I was hired and paid as a clapper/loader in the camera department, but I also worked in the sound department both on the camera (sound was shot on film in those days) and as a boom swinger, and I did a bit of production office work on the side. I worked from 7:30 a.m. to 6:30 p.m. for which I was paid $10.00 per week. But hey! My lifetime ambition was accomplished. I was in show business.

My job at Carlton Hill lasted around six months before they fired me! In fact I committed two sackable offenses. The first went undiscovered... or almost. There was a war on, everything was in short supply, including film cans. As a loader, every evening, after a day's shoot, I had to transfer the day's exposed film from the camera magazine into a film can for shipping to the laboratory. Before I could do this, I had to have a film can. So, in the pitch dark, I would open a fresh can of unexposed film, approximately 1,000 feet, lay it on the table, take the exposed film from the camera magazine and put it in the can, place the lid on the can, put the fresh film into the camera magazine, screw the lid back on and presto, a job well done. Then I'd go switch on the light. Only one day, as I started back to the bench having switched on the light, I saw a roll of 1,000 feet of film, the entire day's work, sitting there under the light. I'd forgotten to put the lid on the can. I must have stood there a full five seconds wondering whether it would be better to switch off the light or put the lid on the can or just slash my wrists here and now. In any event, I sent the film off to the lab, and the following day, when they were screening the day's work, I hid in the projection room ready to make a quick escape if necessary. It wasn't. The film was slightly fogged at the edges. That was it! No problem! The lighting cameraman told me not to leave the magazines hanging around on the set as it was obvious there was a light leak in one of them. I agreed to be extremely careful in the future, breathed a vast sigh of relief, and moved on to my next mistake, the one for which I got the boot. Quite justifiably.

The camera was large, cumbersome, and French. I think it was called a Debri. I've tried checking this out but these days nobody seems to have even heard of it any more. Newman Sinclair, Arriflex, Mitchel, Vinten, everybody remembers these cameras. Debri, forget it! The operator had to view everything through the film which meant he had to have a black cloth over his head to cut out any back light. After a couple of long takes he would emerge blinking from beneath the cloth with a red face and streaming eyes. But I wasn't the operator, I was clapper boy/loader. It was the latter that proved my downfall. There were two separate magazines, a feed and a take up. The film was loaded into the feed magazine which was fitted into one side of the camera, laced through the gate, and wound into the take up magazine on the opposite

My stint (I'm top row, fourth from right) in the RAF, 1945.

side. Very straightforward. Did it a thousand times. No problems. Unfortunately, in the winter, the studio was cold, so after lunch it was necessary to run the camera for a short time to warm up the motor. To do this you had to take the film magazines out. Anybody who knows anything about movie cameras has already worked out what happened next. To put it very simply, I reloaded the magazines the wrong way round. The 500 feet of film we had exposed during the morning went through the camera again. End result, half a reel exposed twice, half a reel not exposed at all. Day's work ruined. The studio liable for the entire cost. One camera assistant out of a job. I believe I had the temerity to feel hard done by. The arrogance of a teenager is quite amazing.

So I called an old friend and, without actually telling him what the problem was, I said I was looking for a change and perhaps he could put in a word for me someplace... anyplace. He talked to somebody who talked to somebody else and I went for an interview. Two weeks later I started work at Ealing Studios as a third assistant director.

For those who don't know, like me at the time, let me tell you what a third assistant director does. (Or what he did in those days.) He's always first to arrive in the morning to make sure the actors have arrived and are in make up or hairdressing or wherever. Then, during the day, he calls the actors onto the set when they're needed, he fetches their tea or coffee, he does small errands for them; he provides the same services to the director and to the assistant director and anyone else who needs them and, if he's any good, he does all this flat out. I'd arrive at the studios running and I wouldn't slow down until I was out of the gate on my way home. And I loved every minute of it.

After working on a couple of movies, just as I was starting to wonder whether or not I could reasonably be expected to be promoted to second assistant director, I received my draft papers calling me up for the Royal Air Force. Shit, the war was over, what did they need me for! Didn't they realize I was busy forging a career? But when you gotta go, you gotta go. So I went.

The Air Force was boring. The only benefit I received from the two years I wasted was a posting to India. And that was only in retrospect because while I was there I found it just as boring as the rest of my time in the service. I did get to see the Taj Mahal, and I was there during the partition which was a great moment in contemporary history. One night we went to bed in India. The next morning we woke up in a different country, Pakistan. The only impact it had on our life at the R.A.F base was we had to make do without electricity for a few days because the men who worked in the power station that supplied the base were mostly Hindu and the Muslims had slaughtered them on the stroke of midnight. The same thing was happening in reverse in India. We were confined to base for the next four weeks while carnage reigned all around us. A huge tragedy for which the British were mostly to blame. But, I am ashamed to admit, most of the drama passed straight over our heads. We were basically unaware of what was taking place and probably wouldn't have cared even if we had known. At that time all I could see was I was wasting time. All those guys coming out of the army and grabbing the good jobs back home. By the time I got back to England there'd be nothing left.

But, good or bad, everything comes to an end. I was demobilized, given a month's pay, an ill-fitting suit, and sent on my way. My parents had moved to a town on the south coast of England called Brighton and I moved in with them. There was a small studio there, smaller than Carlton Hill, where they were shooting an even smaller film based on a newspaper cartoon character named Jane. The lady of the title was forever getting into situations where she lost her clothes. Not all of her clothes. This was around 1948, and too much exposure was severely frowned upon. Who played the part of Jane, who was the producer and/or director, is way beyond my powers of memory. What I do recall is that they were shooting it on the cheap and were trying to do so without an assistant director. The union got to hear about it and threatened to close them down if they didn't employ somebody. I happened to be living almost next door to the place, the production manager was a drinking buddy of my father, so I got the job. From somebody I met on that job, I got my next. It was a medium-size movie, no big deal. But it led, eventually, to Hammer.

The movie was called *Third Time Lucky*. It starred Glynis Johns, and an actor named Dermot Walsh; it was directed by a very angry man named Gordon Parry and it was produced by an excitable Italian gentleman named Mario Zampi, more of whom later. The assistant art director, who seemed to do little more than rearrange the furniture, was a man named Ken Adam, who went on later to do all the early James Bond movies and to win two Academy Awards, one for *Barry Lyndon* and one for *The Madness of George III* (or *King George*, depending on which side of the Atlantic you are). Which just goes to show that when I was on the bottom rung of the ladder, I hung out with all the top talent.

Sometime during the shooting of the picture Mario Zampi was approached by Hammer and asked if he would like to produce their next movie for them, *Dick Barton Strikes Back*. They'd already made two previous Dick Barton subjects (Barton was a poor man's James Bond. A very poor man's.). Hammer, also known as Exclusive Films, had no regular production staff in those days and the idea was for Mario Zampi to move his crew onto the Hammer payroll as soon as he finished shooting *Third Time Lucky*. This he did, but the man himself promptly disappeared to Italy and the ship was left rudderless. To the rescue came Anthony Hinds, son of Will Hammer, armed with about as much knowledge of producing a feature picture as I had, and I was a third assistant. He learned fast. He had to. And he learned well, taking over the effective running of the production side of the company for the next twenty years or so. You'll be hearing a lot more of Tony later; he was an extremely important element in my career. Without Tony and, to an equal extent, Michael Carreras, son of the other boss, James Carreras, I probably wouldn't even have had a career. Certainly not the one I wound up with. Michael had just come out of the army and he was assigned to the *Dick Barton* unit as a location accountant. It was a job almost as low in the pile as mine. We both liked jazz, big band music, girls, and a drink now and then. We were twenty years old, single, and the world was our oyster. Best friend material for the next forty-five years.

Recent DVD release of the Dick Barton series.

We were on location in Blackpool for what seemed like forever and the interiors we shot in a tiny studio called Viking, just off Kensington High Street in London. More Dick Barton movies were planned, but Don Stannard, who played Barton, was killed in an auto accident after a garden party to celebrate the release of the first movie. The following day I had to go to the local morgue to identify the body. Also in the car, quite badly injured, was Sebastian Cabot, who played the villain in the film and went on to sitcom fame in America. Buster, as he was nicknamed, came back to England many years later to play in a couple of movies that I wrote and produced.

Between the time we finished shooting *Dick Barton* and the fatal garden party, Hammer had got themselves into gear and rented a house called Dial Close, at Cookham, high above the Thames. This was the first of the houses they rented to use as a studio. Here we shot a movie based on a radio character, a Sherlock Holmes-type detective named *Dr. Morelle*.

Let me deviate here for a moment, something I may do from time to time as I think of something I feel the reader would like to know. If anyone is really interested in the why's and wherefore's of *Dr. Morelle* or any other of the early Hammer films, I can only suggest they buy a copy of Tom Johnson and Deborah Del Vecchio's *Hammer Films: An Exhaustive Filmography* (published by McFarland). These two have itemized every movie Hammer ever made, complete with cast list, technical

On the set of *The Man in Black* (1950): Michael Carreras, Tony Hinds, Frank Searle, myself, Peter Bryan, C.B. Williamson, and Cedric Williams.

credits, story outline, and notes thereon. Another must for true fans of Hammer is the book *A History of Horrors* by Denis Meikle (published by Scarecrow Press, Inc.). When I first read these books I started to wonder why I was even bothering writing this autobiography.

During the shooting of the next 10-11 pictures, Hammer "moved house," as it were, three times. From Dial Close in Cookham, to Oakley Court near Bray, on the river Thames, from there to Gilston Park, another large country house which, until we arrived, was an unsuccessful private club (and may still be for all I know) where we shot four of them. Finally we moved to Down Place, also on the river, the house that eventually became Bray Studios.

Backpedaling slightly, Oakley Court was an extraordinary old pile. Built around 1860 in a style which can only be described as early ugly, it was owned by an ancient Frenchman, Monsieur Olivier. Every morning he would supervise the hoisting of the tricolour on one of the turrets. The furnishings could best be described as bizarre, along with the overall interior decoration, which we were not allowed to change. It was said by some you could arrive at the cinema in the middle of a movie and know it was a Hammer film because you'd seen the same set dressed the same way in their last three pictures. It's a hotel/restaurant nowadays, far more flamboyant than it ever was in Hammer's day, still hideously over dressed and vastly overpriced.

It was at Oakley Court that I was finally promoted to first assistant director. Tony Hinds, quite rightly, was a little wary about giving me the job. I was barely 22 and

Monica and I on our wedding day, 1950. "We had ten dollars in the bank."

it's a ball-breaking job if you're making five or six pictures a year. You're running a shooting unit at the same time as you're preparing for the next picture, due to start a week after this one finishes. But he finally took a chance on me. Jack Curtis, the chief electrician, Tommy Money, the property master, and Arthur Barnes, the production manager, formed a three-man delegation and told him that they would take care of me,

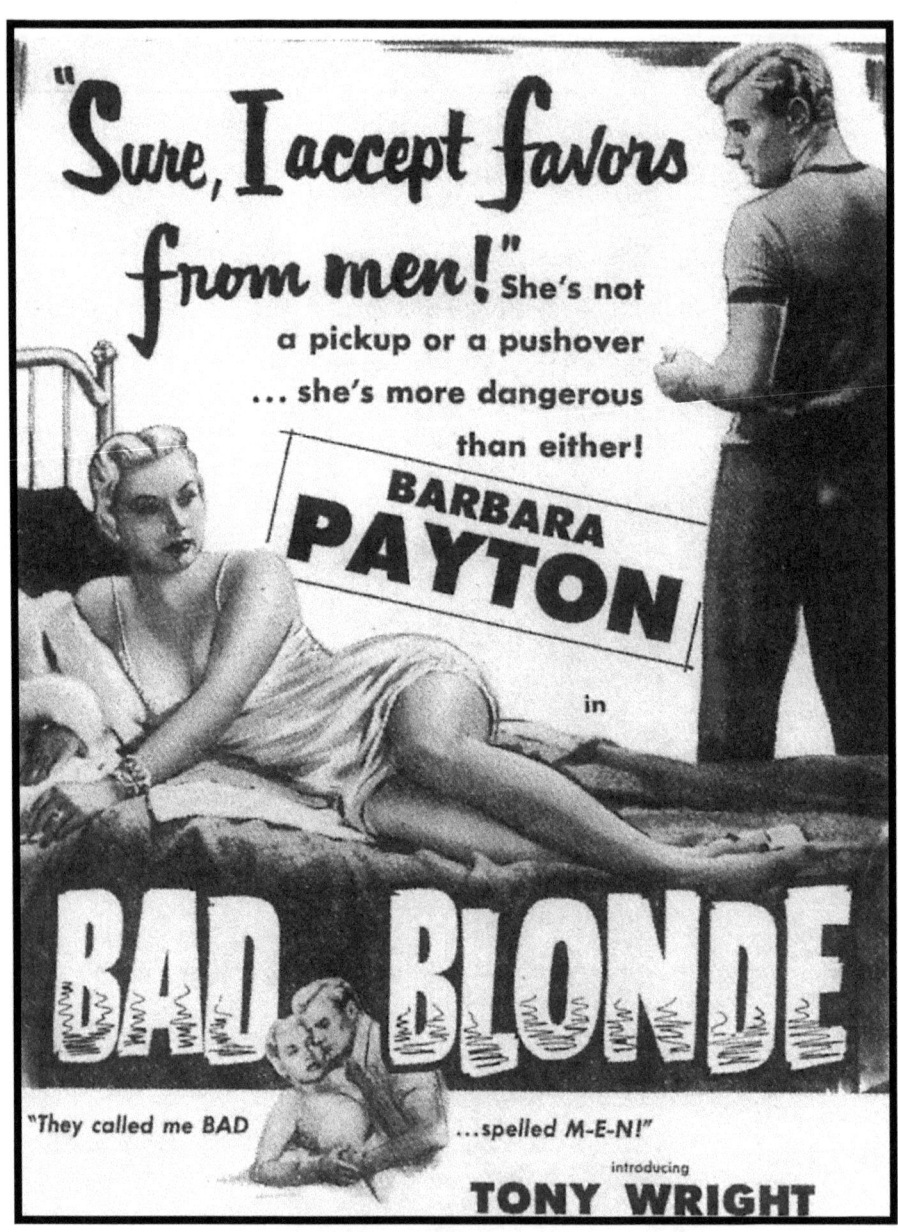

The Flanagan Boy (1953; US title; *Bad Blonde*); "I was about to start on a novel when Tony called and offered the job [of assistant director] to me."

make sure I didn't fall flat on my ass or screw up the shooting schedule. I might have stumbled a couple of times during the next few years, but I don't think I betrayed their confidence.

Not a great believer in false modesty, I don't mind admitting to having been a good assistant director. I later became production manager, a job which I hated and at which I was very bad... well, maybe not all that bad. On reflection, yes I was. I was terrible.

Do You Want It Good or Tuesday?

As for the 10-11 pictures. What can I tell you! It's only by reading *Hammer Films: An Exhaustive Filmography* that I mentioned earlier that I can even remember the titles of most of them, let alone the content. I can remember having a good time, of working very hard, of not making much money. It's a fact that when I married Monica, my first wife, who was hairdresser on all the early Hammer films, we had $10 in the bank.

Then, for reasons I don't know, Hammer went into temporary decline. They stopped production. After a couple of months I said that's it! The movie business is going to the dogs along with the rest of the country. Let's get out. Emigrate to Canada. In fact the country was still in pretty dire straits even this long after the war (around five years). Food was still rationed and there was a general shortage of everything, including confidence. So we packed our bags, paid our money, and emigrated to Canada. To Montreal, where the only job I could get was selling insurance while Monica worked in a department store. Very depressing! Especially so as I didn't actually manage to sell a single policy during the five months I worked there. Finally I wrote to Monica's father and asked if he could loan us the money to come home where I was prepared to go work for him as a bookmaker's clerk in Dorking, a small market town about twenty miles outside London. The money arrived, we fled Canada, and arrived home so broke I had to borrow cab fare to get from the railroad station to my in-laws' house. There, I duly went to work for my father-in-law's bookmaking company. If the idea of working in a bookie's office sounds dramatic, let me tell you it was no such thing. Unlike America, betting was perfectly legal in England. This was no glamorous Las Vegas-type set up. Just me, my father-in-law, and another guy in a room over a grocery store taking bets over the phone and working out the winnings at the end of the day.

I truly didn't intend to go back into the movie business, but I called Tony Hinds anyway, just to say hi! He asked what I was doing. I told him.

"Sounds interesting," he said and that was that.

I say I didn't intend to go back into show business. So what exactly did I plan to do with my life? I was around 23 years old with no qualifications other than the ability to work out the winnings on, for example, a twenty-five shilling each way accumulator bet on three races where the winning odds were 6 to 4, 3 to 1, and 5 to 2 on. No mean feat before the days of calculators. On the other hand, maybe I could become a writer. I'd always earned top marks at school for my English essay work. In which case, what was I going to write. I knew the movie business, so I'll write a screenplay. I did. It was called *The Camera*. I can't remember if it was any good or not. It certainly wasn't good enough to sell. I sent it to Tony Hinds who said "it showed promise." But promise doesn't pay the rent, so I tried my hand at short stories. I had one accepted by the London office of *Esquire*, but eventually turned down by the head office in New York.

I was about to start on a novel when Tony called me. Hammer was about to start shooting a movie called *The Flanagan Boy*. Tony wanted a man named Basil Keys as assistant director, but Basil couldn't or wouldn't do it. Basil was a top assistant director and I believe he had been offered the same job on a much bigger picture. The devil you know is better than the devil you don't, and Tony offered the job to me.

So, I put away my writing ambitions and, after a break of around six months, I was back in showbiz. And I've stayed there until this day.

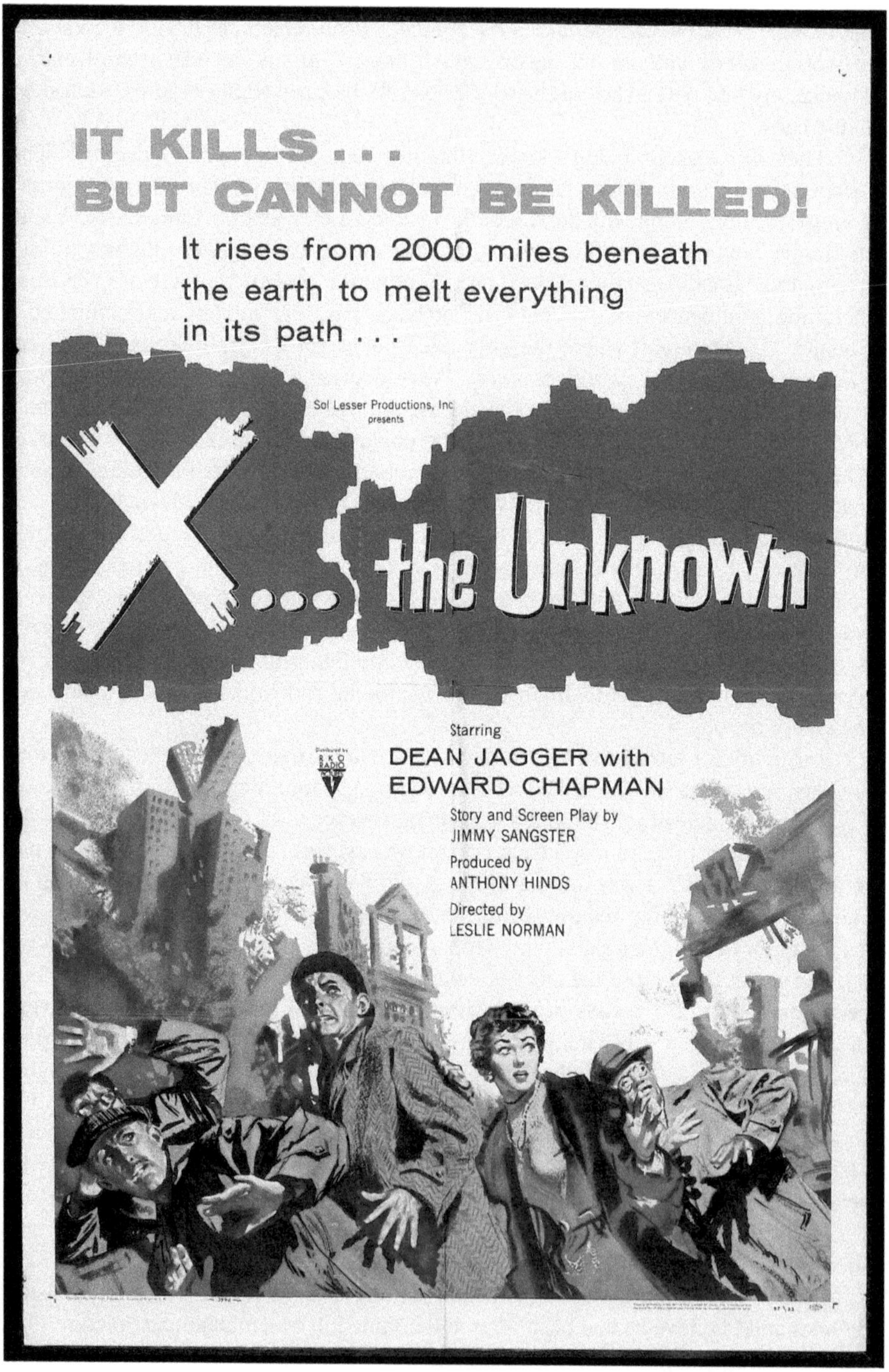

IT KILLS . . .
BUT CANNOT BE KILLED!

It rises from 2000 miles beneath
the earth to melt everything
in its path . . .

Sol Lesser Productions, Inc.
presents

X . . . the Unknown

Starring

DEAN JAGGER with
EDWARD CHAPMAN

Story and Screen Play by
JIMMY SANGSTER

Produced by
ANTHONY HINDS

Directed by
LESLIE NORMAN

Do You Want It Good or Tuesday?

THANKS FOR THE MEMORY... PLEASE!

I was listening to a talk on the radio the other evening where a group of people were each describing the same incident. Everybody's description was slightly different. Whether this was due to lapse of memory or just a different point of view doesn't really matter. I only bring it up to explain that perhaps some things you read in this book differ from what you might have read or heard on the same subject. If it does, bear with me. A lot of books and articles have been written about Hammer. You'd think that because I was actually there, I'd have an edge on the other writers. Not true. They seem to know far more than I do. I was being interviewed by a young American named Chris Koetting the other day. I played back the tape of the interview later.

CHRIS: What happened to the script you wrote for Hammer called Bride of Newgate Jail*?*

ME: My God! I'd forgotten all about it.

CHRIS: How about the movie you wrote The Gingerbread House*?*

ME: Never heard of it.

CHRIS: It was later retitled Who Slew Auntie Roo*?*

ME: Shelley Winters. Right?

CHRIS: Right.

It all came back to me. Lunching with Shelley Winters in the Polo Lounge of the Beverly Hills Hotel. Yes, she quite liked the script. Yes, she'd probably do the picture and, please, would I drive her home after lunch.

You've reached the big time, Jim, I told myself. Movie stars are lusting after your body.

She told me, as I dropped her off at her house, that her car was in for a checkup, goodbye, and thank you for lunch. At least she did the movie. Shelley Winters might have a completely different version of that day or, what is more likely, she's forgotten about it altogether.

I guess what I'm trying to say here is that I am writing about things which took place up to fifty years ago, about people and events which, at the time, were of passing interest only. Sometimes not even that. The fact I can remember some of them at all is quite an achievement.

Act One. Scene Two.
"Not all of it was fun..."

Back from Canada. First job. *The Flanagan Boy*, followed by a whole bunch of equally unmemorable movies until, finally, after working for Hammer as second assistant director on seven and first assistant on twenty-two movies, I was promoted to production manager. That's when the good times stopped. It's a thankless job basically. One is removed from the centre of action. The production manager is the man who runs the whole thing. If anything goes wrong, it's his fault. If nothing goes wrong, big deal! The director finds a location he wants to use, the production manager

All Earth Stands Helpless! "THE CREEPING UNKNOWN"

Starring BRIAN DONLEVY · MARGIA DEAN
with JACK WARNER · DAVID KING WOOD
Screenplay by RICHARD LANDAU · Produced by ANTHONY HINDS
Directed by VAL GUEST · Released thru UNITED ARTISTS

has to arrange permits, transport, hotels, feeding for up to sixty people. The picture looks like it might be creeping over budget, it's the production manager who gets a flea in his ear first. Trouble on the set... send for the production manager. Maybe it's not like that any more. It's a long long time since I was directly connected with the actual physical production of a movie. All I can remember was that I stopped enjoying going to work.

Flashes of memory. My office had a window that overlooked Tony Hinds' office. Tony, the producer on most of these movies, was wired through to the shooting stage where he could listen to everything that was happening on set. Occasionally I would see Tony scoot out of his office, leap into his car, and drive off in all directions. When that happened I knew for sure that within two minutes the third assistant would be tapping on my door and announcing that there was trouble on the set and could I please sort it out.

I don't blame Tony one little bit. He believed if he wasn't around, the problem would eventually sort itself out without him. It nearly always did, but I was the one who had to do the sorting. But I couldn't complain. That's what I was being paid for.

Another flash of memory. As production manager I did a couple of nights second unit location on the first of Hammer's science fiction movies. It was called *The Quatermass Experiment* (*The Creeping Unknown* in the US). The plotting of the film required that huge amounts of electricity be redirected to the scaffolding inside Westminster Abbey where the multi-tentacled monster has taken refuge. Shots were required of various landmarks being blacked out as the supply is diverted. One of these landmarks was Battersea Power Station on the South bank of the river Thames. Back then it wasn't the empty shell it is now, it was a functional supplier of electricity to a good part of London. I arranged with the night man in charge that he would switch off the power station floodlights at exactly midnight, while we photographed it from the opposite side of the river. We synchronized our watches, I gave him the equivalent of $50 and joined the crew where we had set up the camera. At thirty seconds to midnight we rolled the camera and exactly on time the floodlights illuminating the power station went out. I was about to tell them to cut the camera when other lights started to go out all along the river frontage. Obviously I'd over tipped the guy. He blacked out most of London south of the river and didn't switch the power back on until fifteen minutes later, by which time we'd packed up the camera and moved on. There was a short paragraph about the affair in the newspapers the next day, "mysterious blackout south of the river."

In all I was production manager on seven pictures over the next couple of years. There was one starring Paulette Goddard, an Academy award nominee way back when and an ex-Mrs. Charlie Chaplin, a polite, ice cold lady who never complained about anything up front but who would bitch to her driver all the way home. He, in turn, would report everything she said to me the following day. I would take care of whatever it was that she was bitching about without ever having to discuss it with her. I learned much later that she was well aware that the driver was telling me everything. It was her diplomatic way of getting what she wanted without confrontation. This turned out to be her last picture. She went back to Los Angeles and, sensibly, retired from the business.

The same driver I mentioned above, Len Ingram, told of the time he dropped one of our actors off at the apartment we were renting for him in London's West End. The actor was going out to dinner later and asked Len to wait with the car while he did a quick change. This was in the days before they cleared the hookers off the streets, and one of them propositioned Len who was waiting in the car. More out of curiosity than anything else, Len asked her how much she charged. She told him and he said it was far too expensive.   "You can afford it luv," said the hooker. "A big car like that, you must have plenty money."

"I'm only the chauffeur," said Len.

"Then put your fucking cap on," said the indignant hooker.

We did a movie with Lloyd Bridges called *Deadly Game*. I remember this one mainly because I was always finding Lloyd wandering around the studio grounds looking for locations that he felt would open the picture up. As usual, we were on a very tight budget. God forbid we should leave the studio lot even though the grand finale was supposed to be taking place in the main square of a small Spanish pueblo. Put a couple of bullfight posters on the side of the house, stick tortoiseshell combs in the leading lady's hair, rattle a castanet and, olé, who needs to go to Spain. Lloyd Bridges might have, but Hammer, no way! I only mention this because these budget restrictions had a lot of bearing on the stuff I later wrote.

I did two more movies as production manager. One was a silly little woman's prison story called *Women Without Men*, only memorable in that it was directed by Elmo Williams from Hollywood who had won an Oscar for editing *High Noon*. Poor Elmo, he should have stuck to editing. The other was a science fiction subject called *X-The Unknown*, my first screenplay.

"All the science fiction stories I've read, the threat comes from outer space. How about one where it's from inner space... the earth's core."

The whole thing came about by accident. I've told the story many times, but bear with me because this is my autobiography so I'm going to tell it again. *The Quatermass Experiment* had just come out and was wowing them at the box office. Because it was based on Nigel Kneale's hugely successful TV series, in England it had a pre-sold audience. But it was a good enough movie to make it on its own legs. Hammer was as surprised as anyone at its success and they decided they just had to make a follow up in the same genre. Problem was there wasn't anything immediately available.

We were sitting 'round the office one day, Tony Hinds, Michael Carreras, and myself and I said,

"All the science fiction stories I've read, the threat comes from outer space. How about one where it's from inner space... the earth's core."

"What happens next...?" Tony asked.

"Search me. I'm not a writer," says I.

"Maybe if..." says Michael.

"Better still..." says Tony.

"And then..." says I.

Anyway, bottom line, in about thirty minutes we had the bare bones of a story. It seems that I had come up with a couple more ideas than the other two because Tony told me to go write it.

"I'm a production manager, not a writer," says I.

"Maybe you'll write better than you production manage," said Michael, always the optimist.

"You always fancied yourself as a writer," said Tony. "So go write. If we like it we'll pay you. If we don't, tough shit. You're still on the payroll as a production manager so what have you got to lose."

Or words to that effect.

He was absolutely right, so I borrowed a typewriter and went to work on a treatment. A treatment can mean different things to different people. To some writers it's just an extended storyline, to others it's a detailed blueprint of what the script is going to be. I've always gone for the second. My treatments can run to forty or fifty pages. They're basically the script without the dialogue.

I worked hard writing this, my first treatment, and I enjoyed doing it immensely. The thought that someone could actually make a living doing something that was such fun seemed almost ludicrous. Still, I figured, as I typed FADE OUT, THE END, maybe the whole thing is a disaster and everyone will hate it.

They didn't. Tony offered me the same deal. "Go write the script. We like it, we'll pay you. We don't, we won't."

As far as I was concerned, with the treatment, the real hard work had been done. The characters had been defined, the scenes blocked and, most important of all, the construction of the piece had been laid down. And that's where it's at, all you potential screenwriters out there, the three most important elements of a screenplay, construction, construction, and construction. It's the foundation, the framework, the scaffolding, whatever, of the whole thing. If you haven't got a strong, basic construction you're never going to have a halfway decent script. I was lucky. I got it right first time. I delivered the script after three weeks, they liked it, and they paid me. Not much, but hey, suddenly I was a movie writer.

There's a line in *X—The Unknown*, where the lead, played by American actor Dean Jagger, says, "Let's not conjure up visions of nameless horrors creeping about in the night."

But that was exactly what I set out to do. Conjure up nameless horrors. Things that go bump in the night. Something nasty in the woodshed. Put a lot of people into dire peril, especially helpless, innocent little children, but make sure none of them actually get hurt. Threaten the end of the world unless our hero can come up with the solution before ninety minutes are up. Have him stymied at every turn until, finally, in the last few minutes, he pulls it off. Hopefully everyone leaves the theatre having been scared witless, which is the reason they paid their money in the first place. Do all that and you can consider yourself a horror film writer.

The critics liked it.

"Gripping science fiction..."

"The picture builds up big suspense and ends spectacularly."

"Good, grisly fun."

"Vastly entertaining."

In the end, I liked it too. I say "in the end" because while it was actually being shot I positively hated it. I was still on Hammer's payroll and I took over the job of production manager. I should have quit while I was ahead. But I didn't. I budgeted

We shot the interiors at Bray Studios and the exteriors at the Gerards Cross Sand and Gravel Pits. *Pits* **was the operative word.**

my script, scheduled it, and the late, great Joseph Losey was signed to direct it. He was still a refugee from McCarthyism and had signed on under the name of Joe Walton.

The picture was cast. Dean Jagger from Hollywood. Leo McKern in a small role, Anthony Newley in an even smaller one. Sets were built, locations were chosen and prepared. Then, one week before shooting was scheduled to start, Joseph Losey was suddenly off the picture. There are two versions of what actually caused him to quit. The public story was that he caught pneumonia. I believed it at the time, firmly convinced that he'd been determined to catch something to get himself off the picture. The other, more likely version is that Dean Jagger, the American star, refused to work on a movie directed by a man on the Hollywood blacklist. In either event, there we were, one week from start date with no director. Tony Hinds called Ealing Studios, who had a number of directors under contract and they were only too happy to loan us one.

Leslie Norman arrived to find a script already written, the picture cast, and all the sets and locations built and selected. I didn't appreciate it at the time but it was a terrible position for a director to be put in. I say "at the time" because exactly the same thing happened to me many years later. But even that didn't excuse the fact that the man was a natural born bully. He was unhappy on this particular job and, by God, he was going to make sure everybody else was unhappy too. He succeeded admirably. He also made a good movie. It's just a pity he was such a shit about it.

We shot the interiors at Bray Studios and the exteriors at the Gerards Cross Sand and Gravel Pits. *Pits* was the operative word. It rained for the first three days and we spent the next three digging out the equipment. Absolutely nothing went right from the beginning to the end of the shoot. Halfway through I got sick. I didn't so much get sick as make myself that way. I tried everything, including paddling in the river

It rained for the first three days and we spent the next three digging out the equipment. Absolutely nothing went right from the beginning to the end of the shoot.

with my shoes and socks on hoping I'd catch a very bad cold or, if I was really lucky, like Joe Losey, pneumonia. I didn't get either. What I did get was a small dose of food poisoning. Maybe it was psychosomatic food poisoning, but whatever it was, I got it. I called Tony Hinds who was the line producer and told him sorry, I won't be coming to work for the next few days. He immediately got sick too. Maybe he caught it from me over the phone. Anyway, he disappeared and Michael Carreras stepped in. The one good thing about that period was that just before we started shooting, my son James was born.

So I became a writer! My first screenplay. At least, my first full-length screenplay. It constantly slips my mind that about a year earlier I'd written a short film (26 minutes) that Hammer had made called *Man on the Beach*. It starred Donald Wolfit and Michael Medwin. This one had been directed by Joseph Losey. It really does slip my mind. As far as I'm concerned, *X—The Unknown* was my first writing credit. Just to fill my cup to overflowing, *Variety*, the American trade magazine said it was "a highly imaginative and fanciful meller."

But before it even hit the screen, Hammer asked me to write a script based on Mary Shelley's *Frankenstein*. That's when I thought maybe I'm destined to be a writer after all. And I bought a typewriter from Tony Hinds' brother just to prove it to myself.

Baron Frankenstein (Peter Cushing) was a well-educated, brilliant, seemingly charming man who was guilty of the ultimate evil. (*The Curse of Frankenstein*)

PLEASE CAN I HAVE YOUR AUTOGRAPH... WHOEVER YOU ARE?

As I said way back at the beginning of this book, I have fans. They emerge mostly when there is some kind of horror film festival being staged. I don't mean they hibernate between festivals, but that's the only time I'm aware of them. Recently there was a big Hammer Festival in London, a whole month of Hammer movies. On the opening night, I arrive. Almost immediately I have an autograph book shoved under my nose.

"Please Mr. Hinds, can I have your autograph!"

I asked him if he wanted me to sign his book with Tony Hinds' name or mine. He wanted to know who I was. I told him, and he gave me permission to sign my own name.

The same evening a polite gentleman came up to Mary, my wife, and asked for her autograph. Under her maiden name, Mary Peach, she was an actress of some importance, having starred opposite Rock Hudson in Gathering of Eagles *and played opposite Laurence Olivier in a TV version of* Cat on a Hot Tin Roof.

"Do you know who I am?" she asked.

He thought about it for a moment and eventually he shook his head.

"Who would you like me to be?" she asked.

He looked bemused.

"How about Doris Day?" suggested Mary.

He wasn't impressed. He shook his head again. "Never much liked Doris Day," he said.

"How about Katharine Hepburn?" Mary asked.

He thought about it for a moment. Then he nodded. "Yes please," he said. My wife signed his book "Katharine Hepburn" and he went away happy.

Act One. Scene Three.
"No villagers please...!"

I was still on the payroll as production manager. After the debacle over *X—The Unknown*, which, due partly to the weather and partly to Leslie Norman, went ferociously over budget and schedule, I was surprised they even let me into the office. I was breaking down and budgeting a script when Tony Hinds asked me if I'd like to have a crack at writing the *Frankenstein* movie. There was none of this "if we like it we'll pay you" nonsense this time. They offered me a fee up front, just like a grown-up screenwriter. It was £450, around $2,000 in those days. It wasn't much money, but I'm not complaining. As for why Tony picked me, I can only quote something I read in Denis Meikle's book on Hammer.

"I wanted Jimmy Sangster because he was a friend. And because I knew he'd do what I told him."

I guess now is as good a time as any to talk about the writing of the Gothic horror movies which, I'm first to admit, are my main claim to fame. My only claim. These days I get invited to Film Festivals along with others who were connected with the

"THE CURSE OF FRANKENSTEIN" WILL HAUNT YOU FOREVER!

The creature created by man and forgotten by nature.

From WARNER BROS. in **WARNERCOLOR**

Not recommended for people of nervous disposition.

ALL NEW AND NEVER DARED BEFORE!

PLEASE TRY NOT TO FAINT

STARRING
PETER CUSHING · HAZEL COURT · ROBERT URQUHART and CHRISTOPHER LEE
Screen Play by JIMMY SANGSTER · Directed by TERENCE FISHER · Executive Producer MICHAEL CARRERAS

Hammer Horror scene, people like composer James Bernard, director Freddie Francis, actor Christopher Lee. I'm sure more of us would be invited but we're a bit thin on the ground now.

Sometimes I go, mostly I don't. It depends on the venue, and on whether or not the organizers are prepared to pay my business class air fare. I'm too old to fly economy any longer. I travel business class even when I'm buying my own ticket. When I'm at these festivals I get asked by Hammer fans, most of whom are young enough to be my

Peter Cushing as Baron Frankenstein in *The Curse of Frankenstein*.

grandchildren, what was the hidden meaning of this scene, what was the undercurrent of that; was I trying to tap the audience's secondary emotional level when I had Peter Cushing say so and so; and wasn't that last scene terribly anti-Freudian. Why did you write it like that?

My answer is always the same. I wrote the way I did for wages. That's how I made my living in those days. Same reasons I worked earlier as a production manager and before that as an assistant director. There's no deep-seated, suppressed psychological motive in my writing Gothic horror movies. If the first movie I'd written had been a comedy, then I would have probably have stuck to that genre and you wouldn't be reading this book. In fact, if one counts them up, out of the forty-five odd movies I wrote, only five were "Gothic" horrors. A couple of *Frankensteins* and three *Draculas*, one of them under a *nom de plume* (John Sansom). Maybe some people classify *The Mummy* as a "Gothic" horror. So be it. Throw a couple more in for good measure and we come up an absolute maximum of ten. It's frightening to think that any notoriety I have is based on these ten scripts because I'm convinced that some of the stuff I wrote later was far better. Those too I did for the wages.

But like it or not, the Gothics are what interest the fans and so over the last couple of years I've tried to sort out in my own mind the reason for their successful longevity. Maybe some of the things the critics say about them are true. But then how can one treat seriously the comments of the people who are supposed to know about such things when one pronounced *The Curse of Frankenstein* "...among the half-a-dozen most repulsive films I have encountered..." while another said it was "...intelligently written, beautifully photographed... one of the most polished horror movies ever made..." And just in case that should go to my head, somebody else said "...surprisingly tacky." What I'm trying to say here is either you were for it or against it. There was very little middle ground.

I set out to write it with a variety of restrictions. Stay as far away as possible from any of the previous *Frankenstein* movies. This was because as soon as the project was announced, Universal started gnashing their teeth and threatening to beat us to death with their legal cudgels. Never mind that the original Mary Shelley novel was in public domain, they had made the movie, and God forbid we should infringe their "copyright." They needn't have bothered waving the big stick at us; I didn't want to remake the Universal movie, I wanted to make my own. I was more interested in Baron Frankenstein than the monster. The monster couldn't help doing monstrous things. Having the hands of a famous sculptor isn't going to be much good if his brain is full of broken glass before it's even put in his reconstructed head. On the other hand, everything monstrous that the Baron did was well thought out. Done for a reason. A much more interesting character.

Restriction number two in the scripting was, as in most Hammer projects, to do with the budget. We've only got ten cents to spend, so keep it tight. Every other *Frankenstein* movie, before or since, has had a bunch of irate villagers descending on the castle. Villagers cost money, so eighty-six the villagers. Talk about them if you like. Threaten to get their help. Hear them baying in the background. But keep them off screen. Also keep the sets to a minimum, have as few locations as possible, and certainly no more than thirty minutes' drive from the studio. No special effects please, and not too large a cast. Oh yes, one other thing, design the script so that the director can shoot it in four weeks maximum.

While all this placed certain restrictions on the writing, it wasn't as difficult as it might sound. I'd been assistant director and a production manager for Hammer most of my working life. I'd worked on half a dozen movies in one capacity or another with Terry Fisher, and I knew exactly how long it would take him to shoot a certain sequence, I knew how much it should cost.

Back to the character of Frankenstein for a moment. A well-educated, brilliant, seemingly charming man who is guilty of the ultimate evil. Not the evil of creating a

The Curse of Frankenstein—Peter Cushing as the Baron and Christopher Lee as the monster

monster, because in that, his intentions were purely scientific. It wasn't his fault it all went wrong. His was the evil of cold-blooded murder, first victim the professor for gain and second the maid, to keep her quiet. And when he is confronted with these crimes, he really cannot see what all the fuss is about.

I watched this movie the other day, the first time I've seen it for I can't remember how many years. If it hadn't been for my name, writ large on the screen, I would never have known I wrote it. It is an admirable example of how fashions change. There would be absolutely no way that a movie like that could or would be made today. Take the first "horror" element. The Baron says to Paul, "...let's go steal a body from the gibbet." So they go steal the body. Big deal! Nobody threatens them, there's no danger, no tension, and there's very little shown anyway. Okay, so later Frankenstein removes the head, but in the print that I recently watched, you didn't see anything of that either. Today, you'd have a detailed anatomy lesson in slow decapitation. I have to say I prefer my version.

Another deviation I made from the original was not having the Baron there when the monster actually comes to life. He pulls all the levers, throws all the switches, and finally gives up and goes to get help. Then, fortuitously, lightning strikes the equipment and, hey presto, the monster lives. Later he wanders off into the forest and encounters the blind woodcutter and the boy and is eventually shot by Paul. Frankenstein and Paul bury him deep in the woods. The next thing we know is Frankenstein has dug him up

From Hammer Films to Hollywood! A Life in the Movies

39

and brought him back to the castle. Nobody has ever asked me how he managed to do that all on his own. For this I'm grateful, because I don't have an answer. Maybe I did forty years ago when I wrote it. Maybe Terry asked me how this could be. And maybe then I was able to come up with a satisfactory explanation. At least as far as Terry was concerned. But for the life of me I don't remember what it was.

One thing I do remember well is the "pass the marmalade" line.

INT. HALL. CASTLE FRANKENSTEIN—NIGHT

A scene is played between Victor Frankenstein and the maid, Justine. She is angry that the girl, Elizabeth, has moved in and reminds Victor that he said he would marry her. Victor laughs at the idea. Then she tells him she is pregnant. What's more, unless he marries her she'll tell the authorities about what he's doing in the laboratory.

It's at that moment that Victor gets the idea of killing her. He tells her that the only thing that will convince the authorities is proof. This ensures that she will go up to the laboratory.

INT. LABORATORY—NIGHT

Sure enough, later that night, as Victor leaves the lab, Justine creeps in. She wanders around for a few moments eventually finding her way into the inner sanctum where the monster is kept. She becomes aware of the monster, who goes for her. She runs for the door. But before she can reach it, Victor slams and locks it from the other side and then stands listening to her dreadful screams as the monster kills her. And, incidentally, his unborn child.

INT. BREAKFAST ROOM. CASTLE FRANKENSTEIN—DAY

Victor and Elizabeth having breakfast, all very civilized. First line from Victor, "Pass the marmalade."

The line was put there for a good reason. I'm a great believer in giving the audience a breathing space. If you frighten them or show them something horrible, give them a chance to settle down again afterwards. And the best way to do that is to give them something to laugh at. "Pass the marmalade," a simple ordinary line, delivered in complete contrast to what had gone before, brought the house down. I think Terry waited too long to have Peter deliver the line, but that is just my personal opinion. There's very few of my scripts subsequently that don't use what Tony Hinds and I came to refer to as the "pass the marmalade" syndrome.

What more can I say about *The Curse of Frankenstein*! Many things have been written about Christopher Lee's interpretation of the monster, some good, some bad. Allow me my two cents' worth. I think he was first class, especially in the scene where he had been partially trained by Frankenstein, like a puppy dog would have been. Peter Cushing as the Baron was immaculate, as always, and Terry Fisher did his customary efficient job. This was his first Gothic horror. It was everybody's first. I think Phil Leakey's makeup for Chris Lee was excellent and James Bernard's musical score set

Production Designer Bernard Robinson was one of the true stars at Hammer.

the pattern for all the others he subsequently scored. One of the real stars, one that remained in the Hammer firmament for many years, was Bernard Robinson. He too was under the Hammer's budget restrictions.

"Build us a castle halfway up a mountain, but keep it cheap."

Thanks to Les Bowie's matte work, this wasn't too difficult. The hard part came when he was also asked to build a grand entrance hall, a living room, a laboratory, a couple of bedrooms, and the roof of the castle for the finale, and given next to no money to do it. But whatever people may say about the Hammer Gothics, and they say plenty, nobody could ever accuse them of looking cheap. This was mainly due to Bernard.

Unfortunately, I don't have any gossipy tales about what happened on the set from day to day because I wasn't on the set. Sure, I visited a couple of times. Once to do a rewrite of a particular scene and once purely socially. But that was it. By the time *Frankenstein* actually went into production, I was no longer on Hammer's permanent payroll. I had become a freelance writer. Like my first introduction to scriptwriting, this also happened mainly by chance.

I'd just finished writing *Frankenstein* when *X—The Unknown* hit the screens. The press was very good and I got a call from a company called Warwick Films run by Irving Allen and Cubby Broccoli. They'd recently burst onto the scene making a couple of big action movies starring Alan Ladd. They split up a couple of years later and Cubby joined forces with Harry Saltzman where he made a couple of hundred million dollars out of the Bond movies. When he died recently his death was a headline story in the

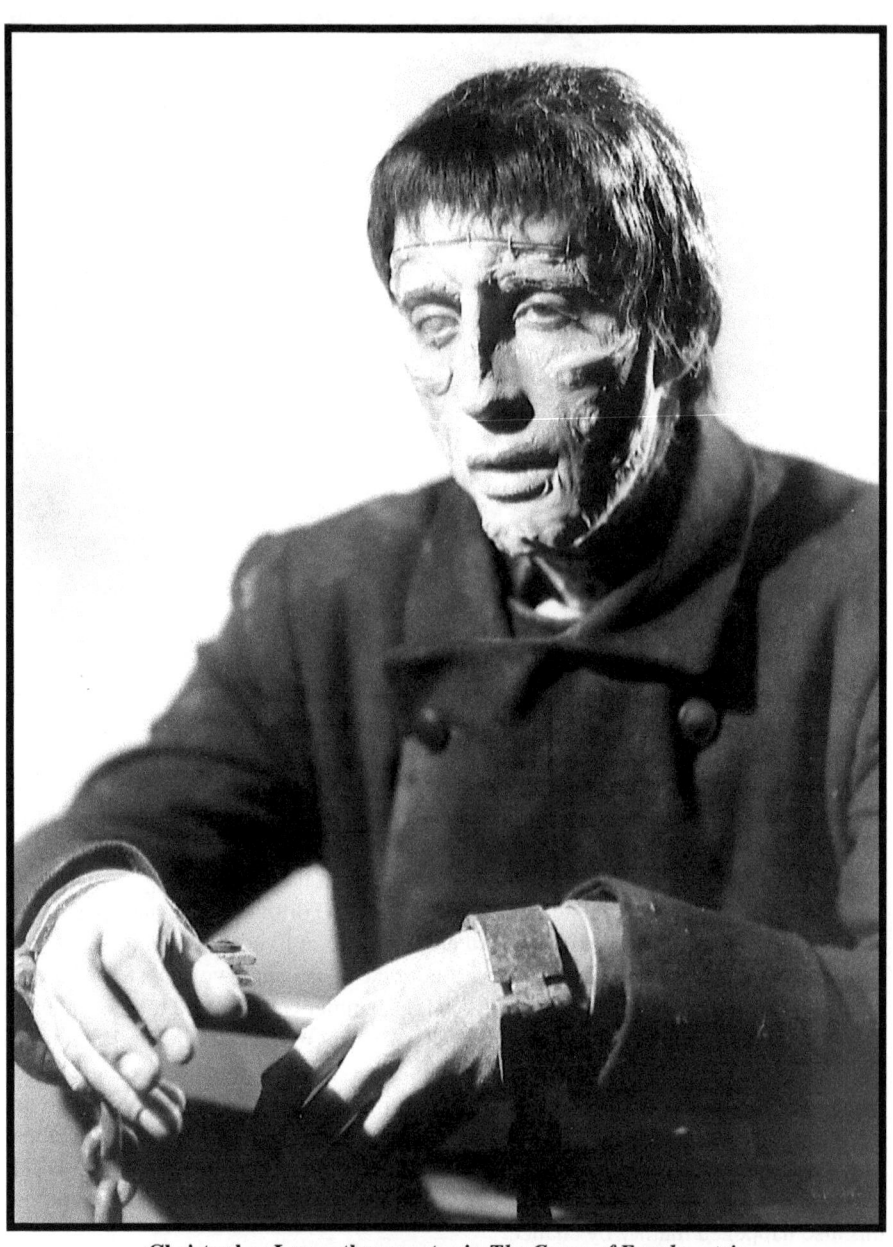

Christopher Lee as the monster in *The Curse of Frankenstein.*

newspapers. He was a nice man, much respected for his business acumen and his generosity. He was also a very good judge of people, which he demonstrated when he described the onetime James Bond actor, George Lazenby, as a putz.

But all that was later. Right now he and Irving wanted me to write a script from the novel *The Day of the Triffids*. In my opinion, John Wyndham was one of the best sci-fi novelists writing at the time and I felt duly honoured and a little bit intimidated that I was about to start messing with his book.

I went to a meeting with Cubby and Irving and told them I'd need ten weeks to write the script. They were horrified. Nobody takes that long. (In fact it takes me on average four weeks to write a first draft.) What I didn't tell them was that I was still a production manager at Hammer and I was going to have to do some heavyweight juggling with my time.

Fortunately at Hammer I wasn't working on an actual production at that moment. Nevertheless there were still jobs that had to be done around the office like breaking down and scheduling a couple of scripts which might or might not get made. *Curse of Frankenstein* was one of them. And it was this that I was supposed to be doing when Michael Carreras walked into my office one day and caught me writing *Day of the Triffids*.

I felt like a schoolboy who'd been caught cheating. I shoveled paper and pencil into the desk drawer and tried to look as if I was working out the cost of a four-day location in Basingstoke. Needless to say, it didn't work. Michael wanted to know what I was doing and I told him.

First, bless him, he congratulated me on getting the assignment. Then he got down to the nitty gritty. He told me I must make up my mind what I wanted to be, a production manager or a writer. I had a new baby, a new mortgage on a modest little house in Ascot, and I wasn't about to give up a regular weekly wage for the perils of freelance scriptwriting. I told Michael I wanted to be a writer but I wasn't going to take the chance. So he made me an offer I couldn't refuse. He guaranteed to buy from me one script a year for the next three years. I won't even tell you what he agreed to pay. These days I spend twice that on one week's vacation. But back then, believe it or not, it was just enough to enable me to keep up the payments on the house and the car and feed the wife and child. But only just.

So that was it. After ten years I left Hammer's permanent payroll. They even gave me a gold cigarette case to mark the occasion. Old Will Hammer, Tony's father, appeared from out of the woodwork and presented it to me himself. They'd had it inscribed. "Congratulations on serviving (sic) 10 years with Hammer." That was the only time I ever met the old boy even though I'd been working for him indirectly for ten years. A hello, goodbye relationship.

As for *The Day of the Triffids*, the cause of the upheaval, Warwick never shot it. The movie was made years later by another company. They didn't use my script, which was just as well because I don't think it was all that good. Actually, the version they made wasn't very good either. It starred Howard Keel, whose only reason for being in a movie is, in my opinion, to sing a couple of songs. Whether a couple of songs would have improved *The Day of the Triffids* I don't know. I seriously doubt it. John Wyndham's two great sci-fi books *Triffids* and *The Kraken Wakes* were best left in novel form.

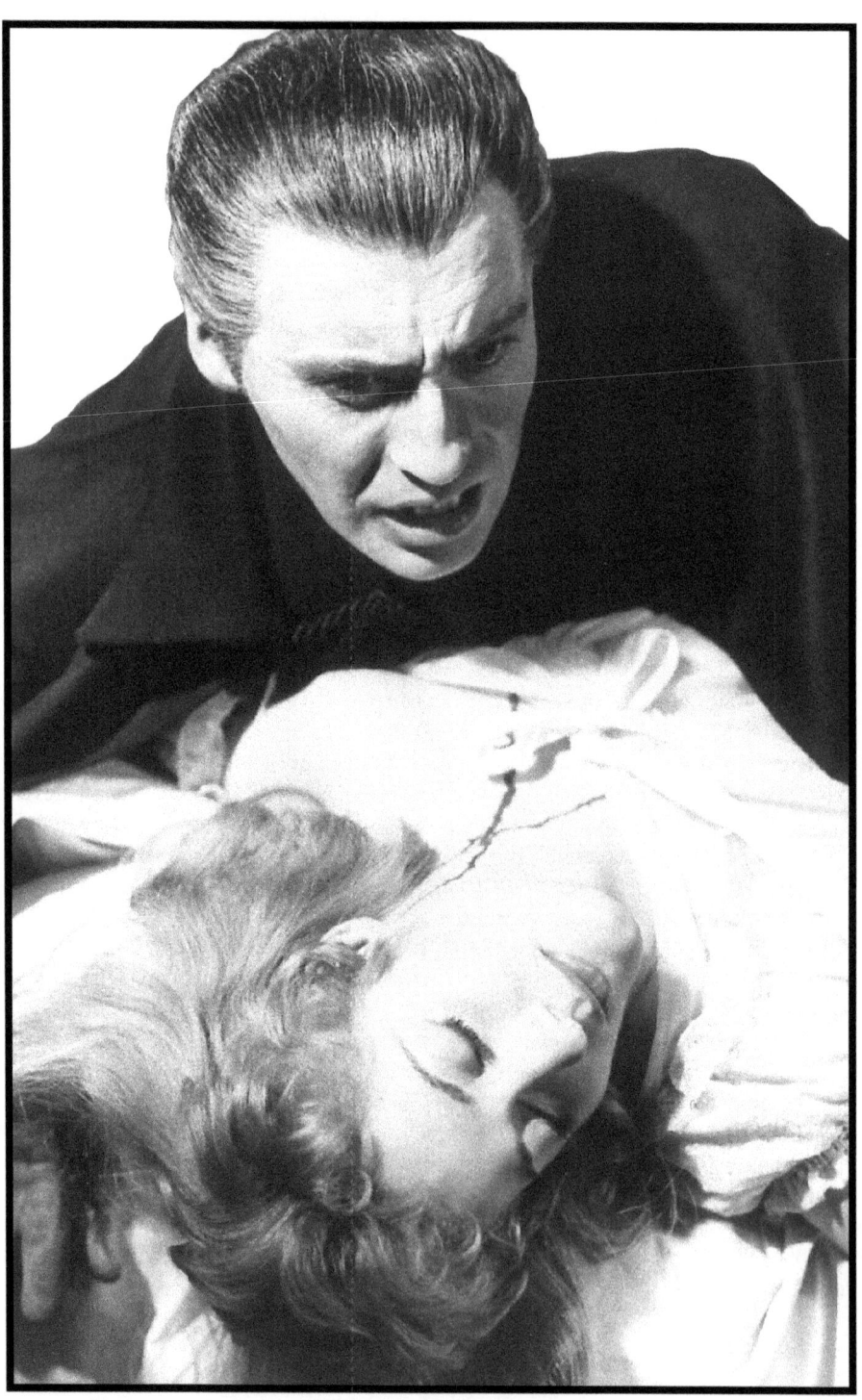

The sets were great and Christopher Lee was very good, even if he hasn't stopped bitching about the part ever since. (*Dracula*)

Selection of reviews for Dracula *(1957):*

> *"I regret to hear that it is being shown in America with emphasis laid on its British origin, and feel inclined to apologize to all decent Americans for sending them a work in such sickening bad taste."*
>
> *"I came away revolted and outraged."*
>
> *"There should be a new certificate to replace the X. S for sadistic and D for disgusting."*
>
> *"I can't remember being so revolted by a film."*

Selection of reviews for Dracula *(1996):*

> *"Romantic cinema that transcends genre... unimpeachable and unsurpassed."*
>
> *"A model of lucid economy... a fine film."*

Who says things don't improve with age?

Act One. Scene Four.
"My Daddy works for a living..."

So here I was, secure in my modest Ascot house with wife and child and typewriter, a fully fledged author. I had a movie showing (*X—The Unknown*), another in post production (*The Curse of Frankenstein*) and I was writing a script for a big independent company (*Triffids*). I finished and delivered *Triffids*. They thanked me politely, gave me my last pay check, and I sat back waiting for my next assignment. Nothing! No ringing of the telephone, no banging on the front door. After about a week I started picking away at the typewriter. And that's what I did for the next six months. I wrote a four-part television serial, one-hour episodes, each one ending with a cliff-hanger to make sure the audience tuned in next week. Four one-hour scripts ran to close to 250 pages. I stuck them in an envelope and mailed it off to one of the newly created independent ITV companies. Then I wrote an original screenplay. It didn't sell. Another TV play, likewise. *X—The Unknown* had received good notices and was doing fairly well at the box office, but still nobody employed me. I took to sulking in the garden a lot. A neighbor's child was talking to Monica one day and asked what I did for a living. She told him I was a writer.

"My daddy works for a living," said the little brat.

Michael's one-script-a-year deal didn't kick in until next year and the situation became serious. I borrowed money from everybody I could, including my agent, a dear old guy named Alroy Treeby who worked for an agency called Film Rights. Shows how things have changed. Go try borrowing money from your agent nowadays. I recently delivered a spec script to my agent in Los Angeles. A couple of days later I got a call. He liked it and wanted to send it out. Please, will I let him have ten copies. He was perfectly happy to have them printed at the office, in which case, where did I want him to send the bill.

From Hammer Films to Hollywood! A Life in the Movies

45

I talked over our financial situation with Monica and we decided that I'd made the wrong decision when I gave up my production manager job and that I should forget all this nonsense about being a writer and ask Michael and/or Tony for my job back. Beg if necessary. I duly called Michael and made an appointment to see him a couple of days later.

The following day, so help me, I get a call from the TV company. They'd received my four-episode TV script. They liked it and wanted to buy it, but unfortunately, when I sent it to them I hadn't given them my return address. That's why it had taken so long for them to get back to me. They made me an offer. It wasn't much, but enough for me to pay back my agent and provide for the family for a few more months. So I accepted. Then I called Michael and canceled the appointment I'd made. I was a writer again.

The TV serial was called *Motive for Murder*. There were a few weeks of rehearsals, some of which I attended, duly making the revisions everybody asked for and finally it was transmitted. In those days stuff went out live. What you saw was what you got. In other words, straight from studio floor to TV screen. If an actor fluffed a line or tripped over the furniture, then it was seen by a million or so people. In my case, the director mistimed the opening episode and, just as we were building up to the cliff-hanger, the last three minutes of episode one, they cut the show and up came the commercials. The following week episode two started with the hero escaping from a dangerous situation that nobody had seen him getting into. Very confusing.

The perils of live drama were many. My wife, Mary Peach, can tell stories to curl your hair. The time that Finlay Currie, a grand auld Scottish actor, opened the wrong door on the set, and, walked into a closet. Or the time Mary herself was supposed to make an entrance through a certain door but couldn't because one of the cameras was blocking the other side.

My show was a reasonable success. Or, as they say in America, it got the numbers, because they asked me to do another later. But it didn't really matter because once *Frankenstein* opened, I was off and running.

And about here, the problems are going to start. Up to now I have used other people's books on Hammer as works of reference. If I've gotten anything wrong, blame them. But now I'm on my own because I'm about to start writing about the world other than Hammer. Certainly a large percentage of what I did was for Hammer, but there were a lot of other people I worked for over the next few years.

Research has never been a strong point with me. I don't like it. If whatever I'm supposed to be writing about isn't in the *Encyclopedia Britannica* then forget it. I think I'm the only person in the world who has actually gone out and bought (as opposed to being sold) this venerable work of reference three times. Twice in England, once in Los Angeles. Very occasionally I'll take a trip up to the local library which has a good reference section, but beyond that, no way. A friend who lives a couple of houses away says I should get onto the internet. He tells me there's all kinds of stuff out there once you learn how to find it. But I'm not comfortable with computers. I once lost seventy pages of a novel I was writing. Truly lost them, never to be recovered. That was three weeks hard work. I was so fed up, I gave up on the novel. Now I approach my computer very carefully. I think I'm reasonably secure with the word processor program, but filing is a problem, and forget doing the family accounts. So the thought of laying myself open to surfing the internet (whatever that might mean) is quite frightening. I know that fifteen-year-old kids are computer proficient enough to hack into the high

THE BLOOD IN HIS VEINS ONCE FLOWED THROUGH HERS

now she's one of the dead-alive brides of **DRACULA!**

ALL NEW!
TECHNICOLOR

Hammer Film Productions, Ltd. Presents

HORROR OF DRACULA

DON'T DARE SEE IT...ALONE!   THE TERRIFYING LOVER WHO DIED...YET **LIVED!**

starring
PETER CUSHING · MICHAEL GOUGH and MELISSA STRIBLING with CHRISTOPHER LEE as DRACULA

also starring

Screenplay by JIMMY SANGSTER From the novel by BRAM STOKER Directed by TERENCE FISHER Executive Producer MICHAEL CARRERAS Associate producer ANTHONY NELSON-KEYS Produced by ANTHONY HINDS
A UNIVERSAL-INTERNATIONAL RELEASE

security systems of the CIA or Bank of America. All I can do is take small comfort in the fact that they probably don't know what 11 multiplied by 11 is if they don't have their calculator with them. What I am saying is that from here on, the facts may be a little frayed around the edges.

One thing I do know for sure is that the next movie I wrote for Hammer was *Dracula*. It was retitled *Horror of Dracula* for the American market. I can only assume that it was in case the American cinemagoer didn't know who Dracula was and the distributors wanted it made clear that this was a horror movie.

I was at a film festival in Nancy, France a couple of years back and they screened the French version. Needless to say, I didn't understand much of it, French not being a strong point with me. Added to this, the print was old and scratched. However, after the screening a couple of young people who couldn't even have been born when we made the movie came up to me and said it was a masterpiece. I kid you not. Their

Peter Cushing as Van Helsing in *Dracula*.

very words. Okay, so it was a pretty good movie. The sets were great and Christopher Lee was very good, even if he hasn't stopped bitching about the part ever since. But masterpiece! Come on!

Do You Want It Good or Tuesday?

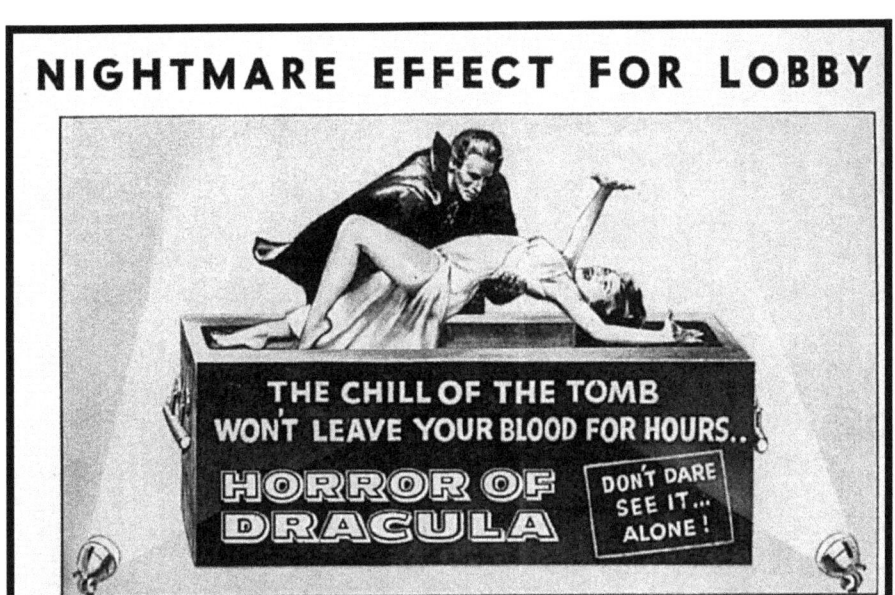

More about Christopher, while I'm on the subject. He's a fine actor with a great screen presence. He's made well over two hundred movies. He's recognized worldwide. So why does he denigrate some of the early Hammer movies he was in? He says the first *Dracula* was an okay movie and he was okay in it. It was an okay movie, and he was sensational in it. In my opinion, and I'm not the only one, it made him a star. If, as he's been reported as saying, he didn't think much of some of the other Hammer movies he appeared in, why did he appear in them? Denis Meikle says in his book it was as a personal favor to Jim Carreras, they were golfing buddies. So okay! Do the favor, if that's what it was, but stop bitching about it. Maybe I'm over-reacting. I'm sure he'll tell me if I am.

As for being considered a "masterpiece," I think one should look at it in perspective. While it was being shot, and for the next few years, *Dracula* was just another movie. Hammer's attitude was, okay, *Frankenstein* had gone down well, let's have a bash at another classic horror tale, and *Dracula* was it. If memory serves, this was the first of my three-picture option that Michael had given me, which means the script cost Hammer £750 which is around $1,200 at today's rate of exchange

When it finally hit the screen, most of the critics didn't think much of it. As I wrote in the introduction to this chapter, some of the descriptive adjectives were pretty violent.

"...sickening bad taste."

"... revolting and outrageous."

"...disgusting."

I don't agree with the critics. I didn't then and I still don't. I don't think it was revolting, disgusting, or outrageous. I know that the boundaries of what is considered "bad taste" have broadened considerably since we made *Dracula*. But even by 1958 standards I don't think it warranted such epithets. The battles we had with the British

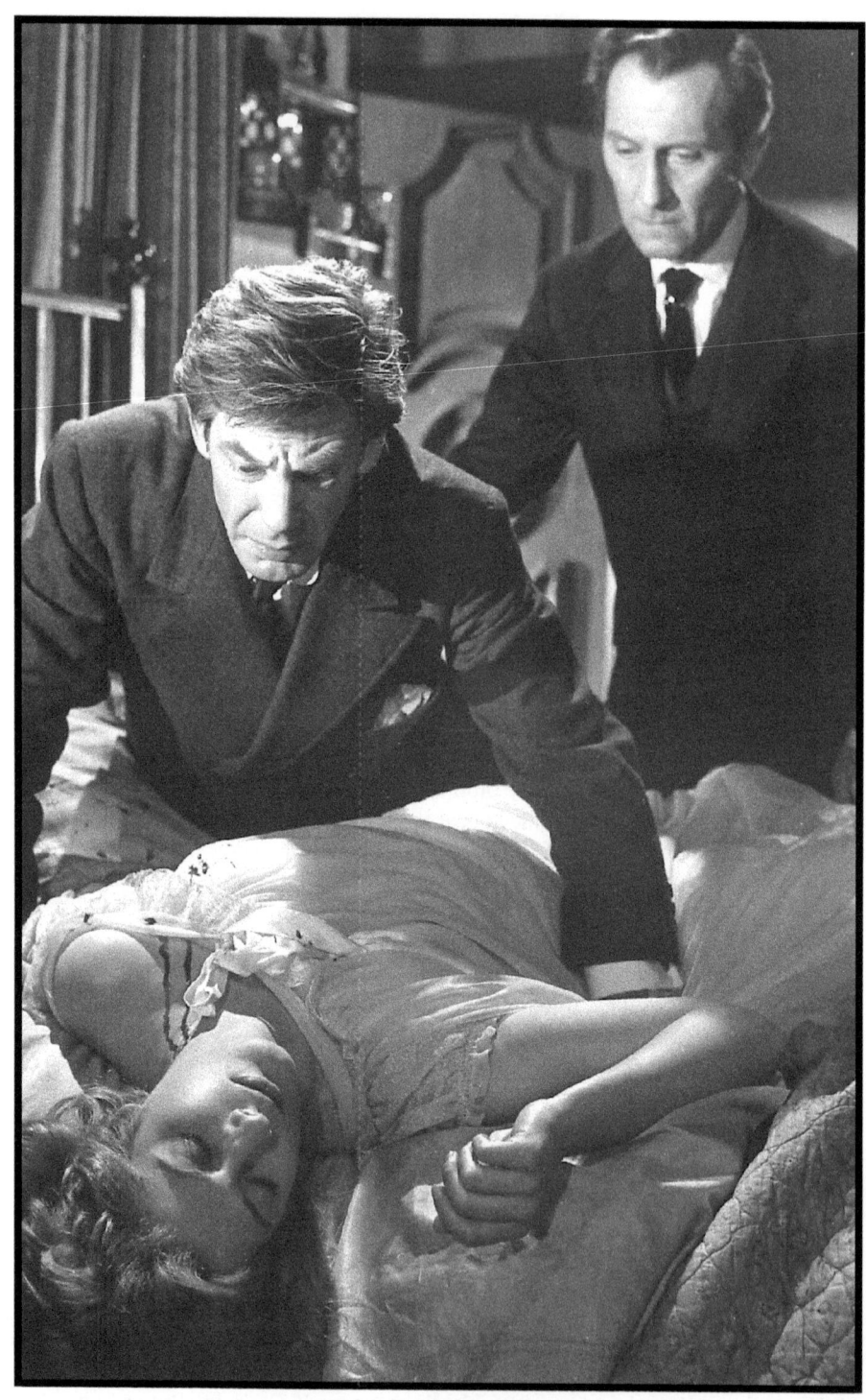

I don't think [*Dracula*] was revolting, disgusting, or outrageous.

Do You Want It Good or Tuesday?

Board of Film Censors were ferocious. They started long before shooting commenced. One of the BBFC's readers referred to "the uncouth, uneducated, disgusting, and vulgar style of Mr. Jimmy Sangster." In fact, Mr. Jimmy Sangster wrote a lot of stuff into the first draft that he knew the censor would demand be cut, in the hope that some of the slightly less "horrific" be allowed in. Tony Hinds, bless him, went ahead with the script as he wanted to shoot it and ended up battling desperately with the censors over the final version. Eventually, but reluctantly, they issued us a certificate. This, combined with the reviews (...revolting ...disgusting) brought the audience flocking and the picture was a huge financial success.

A number of people have questioned my deviations from the Bram Stoker novel. One person actually asked me if I had ever bothered to read it. I'd like to say now that I did read it. Twice, as a matter of fact. And the reasons for the changes I made were pretty much the same as for *The Curse of Frankenstein*, mainly financial. In the novel, Dracula comes to England by sea. There was no way that Hammer was going to go for that.

"A boat, for Christ's sake! At sea! Are you crazy!!!"

So we settled for a journey on a horse-drawn carriage, crossing a border manned by one customs/immigration official. That they could shoot in the grounds of Bray Studios.

Next came the transmogrification scenes. Does he or does he not have the ability to change himself into a bat? If he does, better not to show it because we can't afford to do it properly. My attitude was if we couldn't show it on screen, better off to do without it. So I wrote it out. Not so much wrote it out as never wrote it in. I also left out the fly-eating Renfield character. While I was writing the script I had problems fitting him into the basic construction. I realized then something that has stuck with me ever since. If a character isn't slotting in smoothly, then he shouldn't be there.

The basic storyline of the Bram Stoker book remained intact. Breaking it down into a three act structure one has:

...act one, a vampire is introduced in his castle which, for...

...act two, he eventually leaves to prey upon a family before returning home in...

...act three, where he meets his just deserts.

Once more Bernard Robinson built wonderful sets which Jack Asher photographed beautifully. And once more, Terry Fisher came up trumps, from the initial introduction of the Count where he sweeps down the great staircase to politely introduce himself to Jonathan Harker, to the well-staged finale sequence between the Count and Van Helsing. It was one of those productions where everything worked out exactly as everybody wanted it to... except the censor.

Once again we set out to make what was, in effect, a modest little movie. Once more it turned into a blockbuster. It made a star of Christopher Lee and, I suppose, to some extent, it made a star out of me, albeit in a completely different firmament inasmuch as it led directly to my next writing job, a script which, with stunning originality, was entitled *Blood of the Vampire*.

Robert Baker and Monty Berman were a couple of nice guys who ran a company called Tempean. Over the next two or three years I wrote five movies for them, starting with the aforementioned *Blood of the Vampire*. Its only claim to fame was the fact that it starred Sir Donald Wolfit, one of the last great thespians (as opposed to actors). I've

Christopher Lee in *Dracula*.

Do You Want It Good or Tuesday?

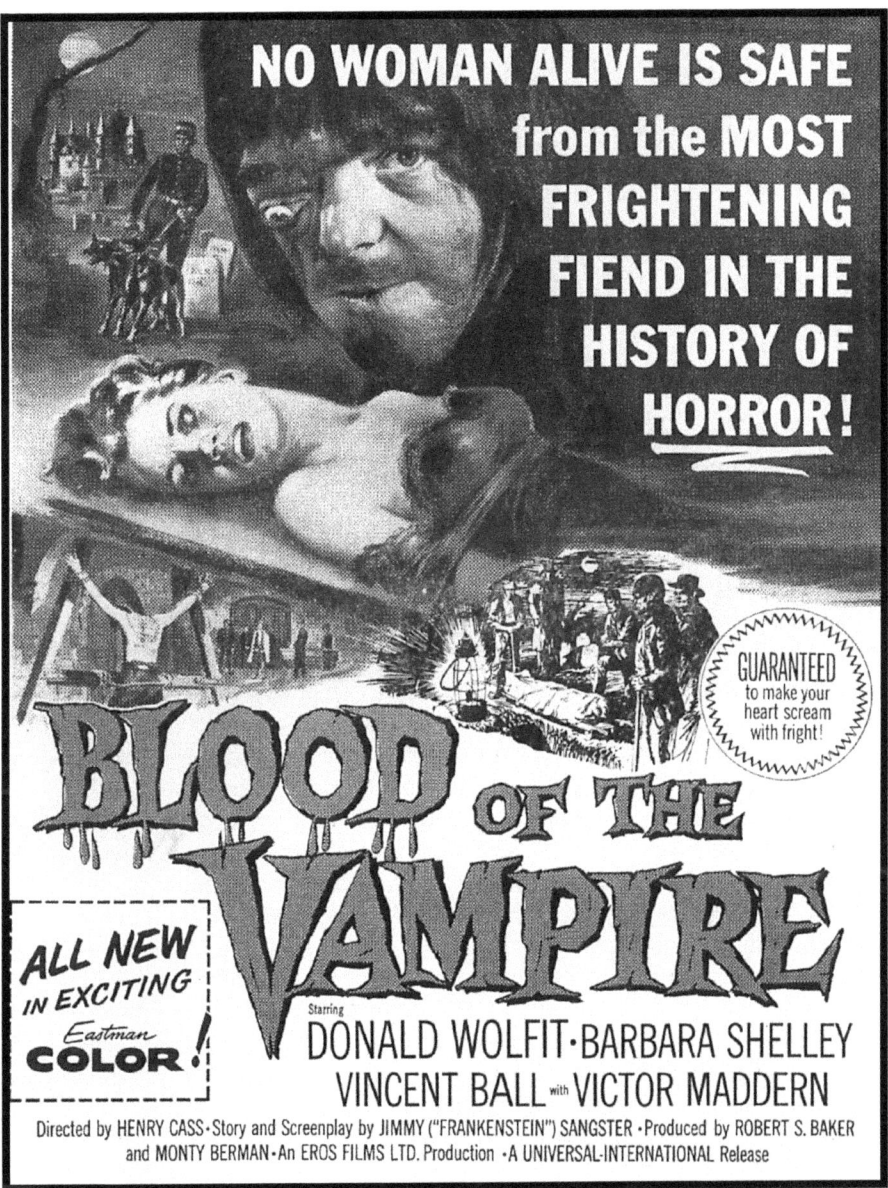

NO WOMAN ALIVE IS SAFE from the MOST FRIGHTENING FIEND IN THE HISTORY OF HORROR!

GUARANTEED to make your heart scream with fright!

Blood OF THE VAMPIRE

ALL NEW IN EXCITING *Eastman* COLOR!

Starring
DONALD WOLFIT · BARBARA SHELLEY
VINCENT BALL with VICTOR MADDERN

Directed by HENRY CASS · Story and Screenplay by JIMMY ("FRANKENSTEIN") SANGSTER · Produced by ROBERT S. BAKER and MONTY BERMAN · An EROS FILMS LTD. Production · A UNIVERSAL-INTERNATIONAL Release

heard tell that the old actor character in the play and movie *The Dresser* is based on Sir Donald. If he isn't, he most certainly could have been. I have very little recollection of the film itself except that Sir Donald was so far over the top he was practically out of reach. But the producers must have been happy with it because later they asked me to do another. It was called *The Trollenberg Terror*. (It was retitled *The Crawling Eye* in America.) It starred Forrest Tucker from Hollywood and a very pretty, pleasant young English girl named Janet Munro who later, like her American namesake, died in rather strange circumstances (did she fall or was she pushed?). Most of the movie took place up a mountain in Switzerland and I didn't get to go on location. Come to think about it,

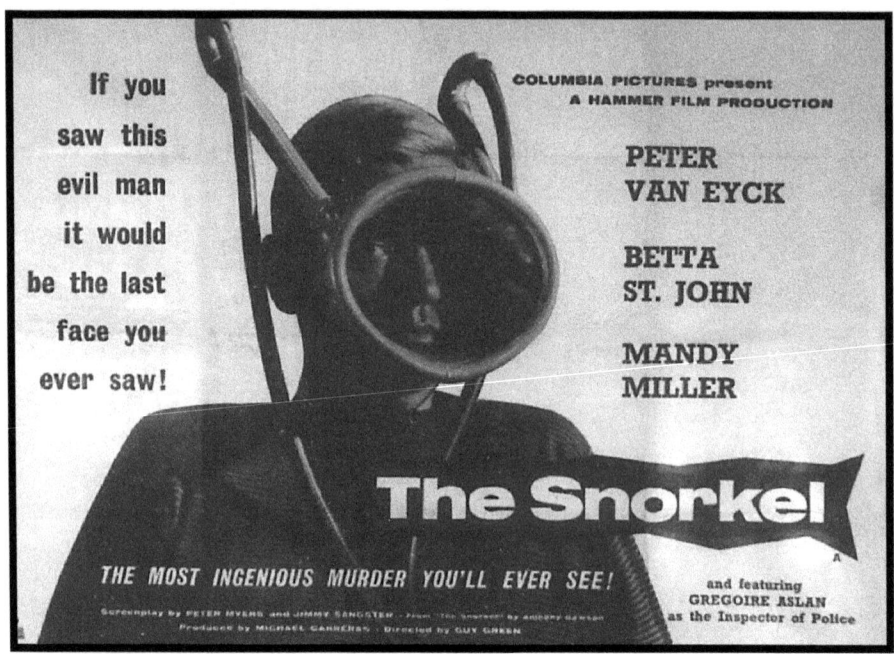

If you saw this evil man it would be the last face you ever saw!

COLUMBIA PICTURES present
A HAMMER FILM PRODUCTION

PETER
VAN EYCK

BETTA
ST. JOHN

MANDY
MILLER

The Snorkel

THE MOST INGENIOUS MURDER YOU'LL EVER SEE!

and featuring
GREGOIRE ASLAN
as the Inspector of Police

Screenplay by PETER MYERS and JIMMY SANGSTER · From "The Snorkel" by Anthony Dawson
Produced by MICHAEL CARRERAS · Directed by GUY GREEN

I don't think anybody else did either. Tempean was a bit like Hammer when it came to spending money. They probably shot their locations in a local gravel pit painted white. I'd ask Monty, but I bumped into him the last time I was in London and he didn't even remember my name, so I don't think there would be much point.

But between *Blood of the Vampire* and *The Trollenberg Terror*, quite a bit happened. First I did another Hammer picture called *The Snorkel*. I shared a writing credit for this one with a guy named Peter Myers whose original script I rewrote.

Let me digress for a moment. Checking through my credits I see that I am credited with co-writing any number of scripts. This conjures up visions of a couple of guys sitting around batting out a story, trying out the dialogue on each other, and generally working together. Not true! At least it's not true with me. I have never worked with another writer. I wouldn't even know how to begin. Anytime my name appeared with somebody else it meant that we both tackled the same script but at different times. Maybe the director wanted rewrites and the original writer was no longer available; maybe the producer wanted rewrites and figured the original writer couldn't handle them. These days, the stars invariably ask for rewrites. Anybody did that in my day, they'd have recast the picture.

But back to *The Snorkel*. Michael Carreras was the producer. Guy Green, an Academy Award-winning cinematographer for *Great Expectations*, was director. But before Guy started, Michael wanted to get the main location tied down. Most of the action took place in and around a villa on the Mediterranean riviera. It was impossible to

design and build the interior sets until the exterior had been selected. So Michael set off, by car, via Paris, to the Mediterranean. And in case the script would need adjusting to allow for the physical properties of the location, he took me, the writer, along with him.

We were in Paris for a couple of days en route. I'm not sure why, other than we had a hell of a good time. There were no French freeways in those days or, if there were, we missed them as we headed out of Paris. It took us two days to reach the coast and another three to decide there was no suitable location in France. So on to Italy.

We finally found what we were looking for in San Remo. It was a lovely old villa built into the side of a hill with terraced gardens leading down to the sea.

"Perfect," said Michael. "But we're going to need to change a couple of the entrances and exits in the script. And that scene where Paul climbs along the outside of the house, we'll need to move that. That means when the girl Candy finds out that..."

He stopped, looking at me. I was standing there nodding my head in agreement.

"So take some notes," he said.

"I forgot to bring a pencil," says I.

Michael went bananas!

"I bring my writer a thousand miles, give him one of the best times he's had in his life, and he forgets to bring a fucking pencil!"

Maybe it doesn't sound all that amusing in the retelling. But we dined out on that story, Michael and I, for years afterwards.

As for the movie, it wasn't at all bad. One thing that tended to spoil it for me (I had a similar problem years later with a movie called *The Nanny*) was having to soften the ending for the American market. The young girl, Candy, played by Mandy Miller, has been pursued through the picture by the villain, played by Peter Van Eyck, who has previously murdered her mother and now tries to kill her. Eventually she turns the tables on him and leaves him trapped under the floorboards in the deserted villa where he is certain to die a terrible death within a few days. The Americans thought this was too heavy and I was forced to write a scene where Candy informs the local police where they can find her mother's killer.

After *The Snorkel*, I wrote a movie for 20th Century-Fox based on a novel entitled *Intent to Kill*. This too was directed by an ex-cinematographer, Jack Cardiff. In fact he was photographing a blockbuster movie on location in Munich when I took the first draft of the script out for him to give me notes on. The movie was called *The Vikings* with Kirk Douglas, Janet Leigh, Tony Curtis, and Ernest Borgnine. Dick Fleischer was directing. This was bigtime Hollywood stuff going down here. Hanging out with that lot I felt I'd truly arrived. *Intent to Kill* was eventually shot at Shepperton Studios and turned out to be not at all bad.

Because of *Intent to Kill*, Fox, as was their wont, signed me to a seven-picture writing/producing contract over the next few years. The company chief in England at the time was a man named Bob Goldstein. He asked if, as my first movie under the contract, I'd like to write a script based on a novel they'd bought, the title of which escapes me, dealing with a bounty hunter who goes off after his prey, catches him, but before he can be deliver him back to justice and collect his pay check, the outlaw dies. They're to hell and gone out in the desert and after a couple of days the body starts to rot so our hero decides to cut off the head and just take that in. This he does, but he encounters all kinds of dire problems on the way. It was a good story and I got to go to South Africa to scout out some locations.

It was round about that time that I wrote my next Hammer film, *The Revenge of Frankenstein*. James Carreras, the man who made the deals and, in the final analysis, decided what Hammer would or would not make, had been quite overwhelmed by the

Myself, director Jack Cardiff, and producer Andy Worker on the set of Fox's *Intent to Kill* **(1958).**

success of the first *Frankenstein.* He came up with the title *The Revenge of Franken-stein* and he had an extremely talented artist design a blood curdling poster which he took to Los Angeles, where he announced that this was going to be Hammer's next movie, starting shooting in a few weeks. Everybody wanted in on the act. The money appeared, Jim Carreras returned to London and presented me with the poster. Please would I write a movie to fit, and hurry up because he'd promised delivery within an impossibly short space of time.

Jim Carreras, known as the Colonel, later Sir James, was an extraordinary man. He was the ultimate salesman. He knew very little about the physical business of movie making. During the many years I worked for Hammer I was only aware of him visiting the studios on four occasions. One of the reasons for this was that, not fully understanding the technicalities of movie making, he'd get upset at the number of people on the company payroll standing around, apparently doing nothing. There is always a good percentage of the crew sitting around. The set has been lit, so the electricians are redundant until the next set up, the carpenters and the painters are off in a corner playing cards... whatever, the camera isn't turning and the sound man's doing a cross-word. But, surrounded by all this inactivity, the director is huddled in a corner of the set telling the actors what he wants from them. Jim Carreras didn't appreciate this. All he could see was a lot of high-priced individuals wasting his money.

TOMORROW IS FRIGHT-DAY!

Look once at history's newest and most horrifying Frankenstein – and be terrified forever!

Take your tranquillizers with you when you see this brand new billion-volt shocker!

SUPERNATURAL TECHNICOLOR!

WHAT IS *YOUR* TERROR-RATING? Can you keep your eyes open...your pulse normal...your heart from pounding? Can you keep your seat?

"THE REVENGE OF FRANKENSTEIN"

starring PETER CUSHING · EUNICE GAYSON · FRANCIS MATTHEWS · MICHAEL GWYNN · Written by JIMMY SANGSTER
Produced by ANTHONY HINDS · Directed by TERENCE FISHER · A HAMMER FILM PRODUCTION · A COLUMBIA PICTURE

First I had to work out a way of resurrecting Baron Frankenstein after his execution in *Curse*. No problem. Don't kill him in the first place. After that, unlike the first movie, I had to start from scratch inasmuch as I didn't have a storyline to follow. It was a fun picture to write. But then most of them were. Once again, Tony Hinds was the producer so he was the man I had to deal with. Michael Carreras is named as executive producer, but he was busy having a frantic time producing a movie called *Ten Seconds to Hell*. Robert Aldrich was the director and, from what I heard, was behaving like the pint-size maniac he often turned into if he wasn't getting his own way. Michael told me that Aldrich actually threatened to beat him over the head with a bottle of Scotch at the "start the movie" party. Nothing like that ever happened at Bray. Apart from anything else, we couldn't afford Scotch.

I have been asked many times about the difference between working for Michael and Tony. To me, there was no difference. Most of the time the two of them were interchangeable, Michael would produce while Tony was the executive producer and vice versa. I suppose, in hindsight (a land where we're all brilliant), Tony liked the Gothics more than Michael. This is partially evident in their own writing, inasmuch as Tony, under the name of John Elder, went on to write any number of Gothic horrors, *The Curse of the Werewolf*, *Kiss of the Vampire*, etc. while Michael, either under his own name or that of Henry Younger, stuck mainly to the non-Gothics like *One Million*

Peter Cushing reprised the role of Baron Frankenstein in *The Revenge of Frankenstein*.

Do You Want It Good or Tuesday?

Years B.C., *Slave Girls*, and *Creatures the World Forgot* (although he did write *The Curse of the Mummy's Tomb*).

Denis Meikle calls *The Revenge of Frankenstein* "Jimmy Sangster's most accomplished work." While I'm flattered, I don't necessarily agree. Maybe he's right as far as the Gothic horror genre is concerned, but I'm convinced that stuff I wrote later was far better. Still, I never argue with people who say complimentary things about me.

The script contained its "pass the marmalade" material. The plotting was reasonably convoluted, and this time we left the ending open so that the Baron could appear in subsequent movies. As with most of the Gothic horrors I wrote, *The Revenge of Frankenstein* was directed by Terry Fisher. A lot has been written about Terry. Allow me to put in my two cents' worth. He was a kind, gentle, and talented man and I was extremely fortunate to have him direct some of the movies I wrote for Hammer. I remember well two of the pictures he made before he started with Hammer. *The Astonished Heart* with Noel Coward in this adaptation of his own play. And *So Long At the Fair*, which remains one of my favorite storylines of them all. (Don't tell anyone, but I've used it a few times myself.)

I think Terry was as surprised as I was at the cult status achieved by the early Hammer Gothic horrors. He was a working director who came to Hammer quite early on and directed around a dozen unremarkable movies before he did *Frankenstein*. I was his assistant on most of them. He was extremely good at his job. The crew liked and respected him and would do their best to cover for him on those mornings he would arrive at the studio in a London cab, having been out all night God knows where. On those days we'd have a slow start, but by 10:30 a.m. we were always in top gear again. It didn't happen often and nobody really worried about it. He always finished his pictures on schedule and budget and, with a great deal of help from the cameraman and from Bernard Robinson, he always managed to make them look far more expensive than they actually were.

And that was it for me and *Frankenstein*. Others were made, but I wasn't involved again until something like ten years later when I had already moved to America. That was *The Horror of Frankenstein*, more of which later.

I wrote another movie for Bob Baker and Monty Berman, *Jack the Ripper*, which was reasonably satisfying as a horror movie mainly due to an extremely gory ending where the suspected Ripper hides at the bottom of an elevator shaft, the elevator comes down, and what's left of him squelches up through the floor boards.

My next assignment for Hammer was a script based on the Barre Lyndon play, *The Man in Half Moon Street*. It had been made into a movie once before, in 1944, a movie which, unfortunately, I never got to see. In fact, it wasn't until I read Denis Meikle's book that I even knew there had been a previous movie. Needless to say, that title meant very little to a movie audience so I changed it to *The Man Who Could Cheat Death* which at least gave some idea of what the picture was about. There were shades of *Jack the Ripper* here too, inasmuch as the lead character prowled the streets at night searching for young women as victims, except the locale was Paris as opposed to London. The lead was designed for Peter Cushing who, when he read the script, decided he didn't want to do it. According to Tony Hinds, who should know, Peter never considered I was much good as a writer in spite of the fact he starred in six or seven of my movies. God only knows what he thought of me as a director when

This lady of the night has taken her last walk!

The swinging purse ... the swaying hips ... the sensuous body ... then, the sudden glint of a knife ... a choked scream ... fleeing footsteps *and over and over he would repeat his brutal, compulsive act of killing!*

JOSEPH E. LEVINE
PRESENTS

JACK THE RIPPER

starring
LEE PATTERSON · EDDIE BYRNE · BETTY McDOWALL · EWEN SOLON · Screenplay by JIMMY SANGSTER · From an original story by PETER HAMMOND and COLIN CRAIG
Produced, Directed and Photographed by ROBERT S. BAKER and MONTY BERMAN · A Mid-Century Film Production · A PARAMOUNT PICTURES RELEASE

THE MOST DIABOLICAL MURDERER IN ALL
THE ANNALS OF CRIME! HE BAFFLED
THE GREAT SCOTLAND YARD!
THE FILE ON JACK THE RIPPER
HAS NEVER CLOSED.

Do You Want It Good or Tuesday?

INCREDIBLE HORROR!

Fantastic Eternal-Youth Operation! His Victims—Beautiful Girls from all Over the World! Draining Life-Fluid from the Young! Innocent Men Turned Inhuman! "Dungeon of the Damned!"

SEE THE TERRIFYING SECRET...THE HIDEOUS OBSESSION OF

The Man Who Could Cheat Death

TECHNICOLOR®   A HAMMER PRODUCTION

From the producers who gave you "THE CURSE OF FRANKENSTEIN" and "DRACULA!"

starring ANTON DIFFRING · HAZEL COURT · CHRISTOPHER LEE
Produced by MICHAEL CARRERAS · Directed by TERENCE FISHER   A PARAMOUNT RELEASE
Screenplay by JIMMY SANGSTER · From a play by Barre Lyndon

I finally got around to directing him many years later in *Fear in the Night*. His part went to an actor named Anton Diffring, best known for his portrayals of Nazi officers and, I have to admit, it showed. One expected him to shoot out his arm and snap "heil Hitler" throughout a large part of the movie. Christopher Lee played a "straight" part for a change, and the lovely Hazel Court, who had become something of a Hammer stock player, got to show her tits in a scene which was designed for overseas screening only. According to the English censors in those days, bloody carnage was okay, but God forbid anybody should see a bare breast. Terry Fisher did his customary efficient job, getting the best out of the cast and script, but somehow, the picture never really made it. The critics were pretty brutal.

"Too wooden and stylized..."

"...ham and ketchup."

"Substandard..." and "...a flop."

Nobody was particularly happy with the picture, but, as a bonus for me, somebody paid me quite good money to write a novelized version of the script which I did in two weeks flat.

By now, I was riding high. Monica and I bought a large house on three acres of land in Northwood, just outside London. We built a house in a village called Les Arcs de Provence in the South of France; I had the first of a long line of Bentleys in the garage, and I wrote *The Mummy* for Hammer.

This one wasn't based on a novel by Mary Shelley or Bram Stoker. It was a movie based on a movie. Not a sequel so much as a remake. According to Denis Meikle's book, I based the script on three different Mummy films, all made by Universal, *The Mummy*, *The Mummy's Tomb*, and *The Mummy's Ghost*. I certainly remember seeing one *Mummy* film before I started writing my script. Maybe Denis is right and I saw three, but from this distance, they blend into each other. I would probably have been better

Peter Cushing and Yvonne Furneaux in *The Mummy*.

off not seeing any and coming up with a story of my own, but Hammer had been told by Universal (who was putting up the money) to come up with a remake, so that's what they got. The best thing about the final movie was Christopher Lee's performance. He brought energy and sensitivity to the part, no mean feat when he was required to spend half the movie swathed from head to foot in dirty bandages. Peter Cushing gave his customary polished performance and Terry Fisher did what Terry always did, namely turn out a creditable movie. This time, the critics were kinder.

"Spectacular..."

"Highly entertaining..."

And, most important of all for Hammer, "A sure-fire box office hit."

I took time off from Hammer after *The Mummy* and wrote a "tits and swords" for Baker and Berman called *The Hellfire Club*. It was a fun story loosely based on fact, very loosely. Just outside London in a town called West Wycombe is the ancestral home of the Earls of Dashwood. A couple of hundred years ago the family were heavily into politics and they formed a club for like-minded aristocrats. Their base was in a series of caves in the grounds of Dashwood Hall. Along with the politics they were also suspected of dabbling in devil worship. Maybe they did, maybe they didn't. The two certainly are compatible these days. But for the purposes of my script, they most decidedly did. Like I said, it was very loosely based on fact.

I also wrote another TV series, a four-parter. It was called *The Assassins*, and pretty good it was too. Unfortunately TV companies didn't keep tapes of their shows in those days, so it's gone forever. I say "unfortunately," but maybe it's for the best because now, when I say it was good, there's very few people out there who can give me an argument because they can't check it out on their VCR.

Then came *The Brides of Dracula* for Hammer. Its gestation was long and complicated. In fact, I'd written the first draft much earlier under the title *Disciple of Dracula*. Tony Hinds had asked me to write a *Dracula* sequel, but "let's not go overboard with Chris Lee." Tony felt he was playing hard to get. In fact this was exactly what he was doing, moving to mainland Europe where he hoped to build an international reputation based on his huge success as Dracula. And who could blame him. Nobody likes to be typecast, and although he reprised the part many times later, right then he wanted to break away. So, on Tony's instructions I wrote the "Christopher Lee" part down and made the character of Baron Meinster as the principal vampire. It turned out that Chris Lee was playing even harder to get than Tony thought and he flatly refused to do the picture. So I was paid and it was shelved. But like all good vampire legends, it was destined to be reborn.

Tony Hinds was practically bludgeoned by Universal to come up with a sequel to *Dracula*. All he had was my old script, but I wasn't around to update it, so he turned it over to Peter Bryan, who had worked on a number of early Hammer films as camera operator and had later turned to writing, having just scripted *The Hound of the Baskervilles*. Peter had a go at the rewrites, but Peter Cushing, who was of course to play Van Helsing, didn't like the end result and turned the part down. Finally Tony turned to yet another writer, Edward Percy, who contributed his two cents' work and the movie was shot.

The critics, on the whole, didn't like it.

"A horrible bore..."

The most evil, blood-lusting Dracula of all!

BRIDES of DRACULA

TECHNICOLOR®

100 YOUNG GIRLS IN A LONELY SCHOOL... DOOMED BY THE INHUMAN FIEND!

Starring PETER CUSHING · FREDA JACKSON · MARTITA HUNT · YVONNE MONLAUR
Screenplay by JIMMY SANGSTER, PETER BRYAN and EDWARD PERCY · Directed by TERENCE FISHER
Produced by ANTHONY HINDS · Executive Producer MICHAEL CARRERAS · A Hammer Film Production · A Universal-International Picture

"...the cast is too good for its material."

And from the doyen of critics, Bosley Crowther of *The New York Times*, "There is nothing new or imaginative."

Fortunately the public didn't agree with the critics and a number of box office records were broken. Johnson and Del Vecchio, in their *Hammer Films*, consider it, "...one of Hammer's best horrors and one of the great vampire movies."

I followed this with another film for Baker and Berman. Strictly non-horror this one. It was called *The Siege of Sydney Street* and is memorable, at least to me, inasmuch as I played the part of Winston Churchill (who had been home secretary at the time of the actual siege). It was also memorable because Bob and Monty shot the picture in Dublin because the Irish capital looked more like London than London.

Sometime during this period I had another Joe Losey experience. I'd written a movie for a man named Jack Greenwood who ran a company called Merton Park Studios. It was an original screenplay and I rather liked it. Jack Greenwood liked it too.

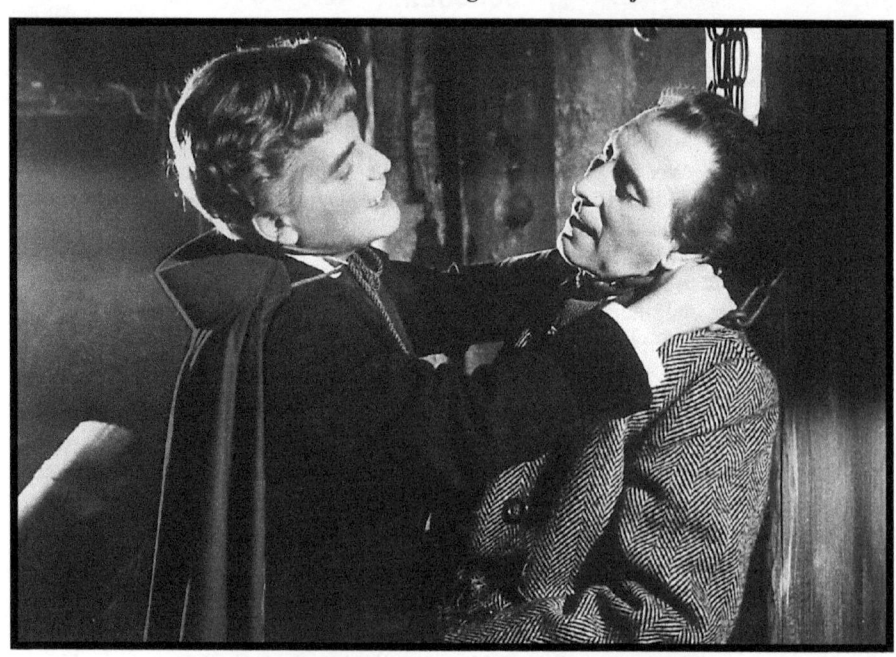

David Peel and Peter Cushing in *The Brides of Dracula*.

David Peel and Peter Cushing in *The Brides of Dracula*.

Do You Want It Good or Tuesday?

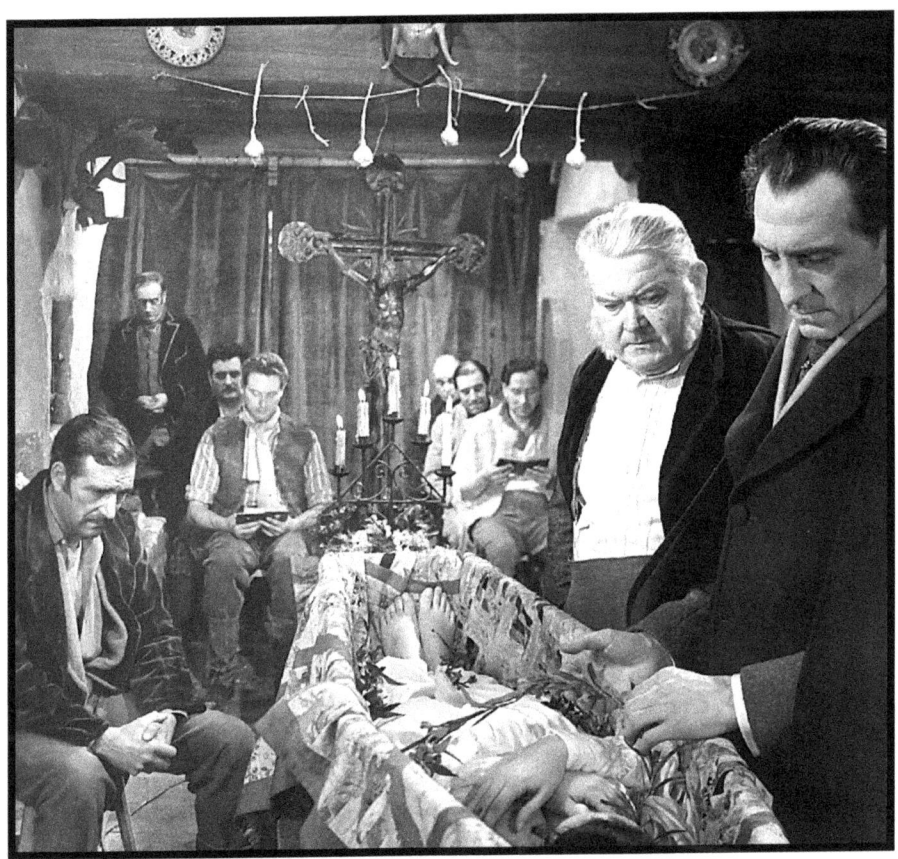

Peter Cushing as Van Helsing in the Dracula-less *The Brides of Dracula.*

Unfortunately Joe Losey didn't and, as he'd been engaged to direct, what he said was law. He wanted changes made, quite substantial changes as a matter of fact. But they didn't come to me to make them. The first I knew of what had happened was when I saw an ad in one of the trade papers for *The Criminal.* Screenplay by Alun Owen from a story by Jimmy Sangster.

I called Jack Greenwood in a high old state of dudgeon.

"How dare they!" "...without giving me the option." "...never been treated so badly..."

Stuff like that. In the end I said take my name off it altogether, which they did very quickly before I could change my mind. The movie went on to screen at the Edinburgh Festival and was considered quite a good picture. I agree. It was a good picture. But to this day I think I was screwed over the credit. I'm sure Alun Owen won't agree, and Joe Losey's dead so he can't vote one way or the other, so what's the point of bitching about it any more. Anyway, from now on I was going to be producing as well as writing. Just let anybody try messing with my credits again.

With Liliane Brousse on the set of *Maniac*.

Do You Want It Good or Tuesday?

ALL THE WORLD'S A STAGE.

I'm sitting in a London club late one night with a friend, Ken Hyman. Both our wives are out of town and we're having a drink. Apart from us there's hardly anybody in the place.

"Oh shit," says Ken suddenly. He's looking past me. "Here come three wannabe actors. None of them are going to make it and right now they're broke and they're going to try bumming a drink."

They were, and they did. Michael Caine, Terence Stamp, and Donald Sutherland.

Act One. Scene Five.
"What's not to be happy...?"

I became involved with a producer named Sidney Box. A charming man whose sister, Betty, was a big time producer in her own right. Sidney had been in the business a long time. As well as being an independent producer, he also headed up Gainsborough Studios during their heyday when they were making "tits and swords" pictures starring James Mason, Margaret Lockwood, Patricia Roc, and Stewart Granger. There's a bunch of names to boggle your mind. Big stars of their day, all of them.

I'd written an original screenplay on spec entitled *Taste of Fear*. In case anybody doesn't know, "on spec" means that nobody was paying me to write it, the idea being that when it was finished, I'd shop it around. It was a new experience for me at the time. The last dozen movies I'd written had all been commissioned. I learned later that the latter was the exception. Nowadays, especially, ninety percent of screenwriting is done on spec, and about one percent of that actually finds a market. It's a tough world out there and I'm quite content not to be a part of it any more. Having said that, I have to admit to this day I have three "on spec" scripts at one or the other of my agents, all, apparently, unsellable.

To get back to *Taste of Fear*. Without wanting to blow my own trumpet too loudly, I have to admit to it being a pretty good script, something I was quite proud of at the time. Needing to broaden my horizons and do something away from the Gothics and away from Hammer, I sold it to Sidney Box and he asked me if I'd like to produce it. I jumped at the chance. The deal was set a couple of days before Sidney went off to America on a business trip. On his way back, he had a heart attack. It didn't kill him, but it laid him pretty low. Because of this all his projects were taken over by his brother-in-law, Peter Rogers, the hugely successful producer of the English series of comedies, the *Carry On* films. Peter was a busy man in his own backyard and he needed Sidney's stuff like a hole in the head. I could see that *Taste of Fear* wasn't going to get made under his auspices, so I offered to buy it back for the same amount of money that Sidney had paid me. Peter was delighted. I made one condition. He would have to give me two weeks before we completed the deal. I needed that time to see if I could re-sell the script.

With Susan Strasberg at the London airport.

I took it first to Baker and Berman. They loved it, but "no," they wouldn't accept me as producer. So I took it to Michael Carreras, where I should have taken it in the first place. Michael loved it too, and he was willing to let me produce. Columbia was putting up the money and Mike Frankovich, the boss man, queried this with Michael. Who needs Sangster! Michael told him that either I produced or it was a no deal and, anyway, with him peering over my shoulder the whole time, how could things go wrong. That was it! Deal made and all of a sudden, I was a producer.

In general, there are two kinds of producers in the movie business. There are the deal makers, the guys who buy a script, and then raise the money to make the picture. Then, when they have put the package together, they hire somebody else to actually physically produce the picture. This is the second kind of producer, a nuts and bolts

On the set of *Taste of Fear* (US title, *Scream of Fear*) with Susan Strasberg. Strasberg was Columbia's choice for the lead.

man who knows about scheduling and budgeting. Meantime the first guy takes the title of Executive Producer and hovers in the background like some kind of overseer. There's a third type too, the studio executive who is ostensibly in charge of every movie made by his organization. Most of these know less about actually producing a movie than any other accountant or, as is the case in Hollywood these days, any other agent. Motto for the day. "Be nice to your agent going up because he'll probably be running a studio when you're on your way down."

I was the second type of producer, the nuts and bolts guy. This meant that Hammer would ask my opinion on casting and/or the director and/or script changes and most of the time they'd go along with me. But bottom line, they had the final say. If I'd said I wanted an extra week in the South of France on location at a cost of umpty thousand dollars, they would have said no way. If I'd have said I wanted my girlfriend to play the lead, also no way. Unless, in this case, she'd been Susan Strasberg.

Susan was Columbia's choice. She'd played Anne Frank on Broadway and had just done a couple of movies. She was, at that time, a reasonably hot property. Daughter of the acting guru Lee Strasberg, I figured we were going to be in a lot of trouble on the set waiting while she searched for inner motivation before screaming her head off in terror at finding her father's dead body in the deep freeze. But she was a pussy cat from start to finish with one exception, the day that her mother came on the set.

With Michael Carreras on location in Nice filming *Taste of Fear*.

Paula Strasberg, Lee's wife and apostle, one time mentor to Marilyn Monroe, was as wide as she was tall, dressed in what looked like a sack and wore dark glasses practically all the time. The day she came on the set Susan went to pieces. Paula sat in a chair at the edge of the set, and every time the director said "cut," Susan would look toward her for approval. If Paula shook her head, Susan would ask the director if she could do another take. After an hour of this, the director dragged me off to a corner and said if I didn't get rid of that witch he was going to quit. So I got rid of her. I can't remember what I said to her, what excuse I used, what lies I must have told, but whatever it was, it worked.

The rest of the cast were first class, Ronald Lewis and Anne Todd and Christopher Lee. A lot of critics said Christopher was wasted in the part, that it was bad casting. They missed the point. I cast Christopher because he was the perfect red herring. Everybody would think he was the villain just masquerading as the sympathetic family doctor when, in fact, he was exactly as he appeared, and rather boring to boot.

I enjoyed producing *Taste of Fear*. I had a good director, Seth Holt. He could have been a great director if he hadn't abused himself so much. But that was later. Right now he was behaving himself extremely well and he did a top class job. We did a two- week location in and around Nice on the French Riviera and shot the interiors at Elstree Studios. There had been a fire at Bray which, as it happens, was rather fortuitous because Bray was too small for the set that Bernie Robinson wanted to build. Kubrick

was shooting *Lolita* there at the same time and I used to sneak on the set and watch him at work. He wasn't quite the legend he is now, but he was still a pretty impressive character. And if black and white was good enough for Kubrick, it was good enough for me. I begged Michael to let us shoot the picture in black and white and, after a battle royal with Columbia, he agreed. Doug Slocombe, the cinematographer who later went on to photograph the *Indiana Jones* movies, did a first rate job behind the camera and we had a good score by Clifton Parker. It turned out to be one of the few pictures I can look back on and say I'm pleased and proud that I made that.

I read somewhere recently that Hammer has sold the remake rights of all their pictures to a Hollywood company, which has announced that *Taste of Fear* is one of the movies it intends to remake. All I can say is "over my dead body!" Considering the length of time it takes some Hollywood companies to get into gear, it probably will be.

We were still cutting *Taste of Fear* when Hammer thought they might like to dip their feet into the American TV market. They set out to make a TV pilot entitled *Visa to Canton*. Around 80 minutes screentime, designed for 90 minutes on air in America. Richard Baseheart came over from LA to star and Michael Carreras was the producer/director. I had nothing to do with this movie and I only bring it up because it is the reason I wrote my next Hammer subject.

Bernard Robinson built a very large, very expensive set on the lot at Bray for *Visa to Canton*. It represented a large merchant ship moored dockside somewhere in China, Canton I imagine. The whole thing was so impressive, not to mention expensive, that someone at Hammer said we've got to use it in our next picture. What next picture? We don't have a script that calls for a Chinese dockside. Never mind, we'll get Sangster to write one. So they came to Sangster who'd just bought a house he couldn't afford and needed the money, and Sangster said sure, I'll write you a script. I should have kept my mouth shut. *The Terror of the Tongs* was probably the second or third worst piece of writing I ever did.

The old adage that you can't make a good picture from a bad script is admirably demonstrated here. Mind you, I don't think the assembled company would have made a good picture even if the script had been good. Apart from the line producer, Ken Hyman, I don't think they were too sure what they were doing. As for Ken, he went on to produce *The Hill*, *The Dirty Dozen*, and other blockbusters. He also became head of production at Warner Bros., one of the top posts in the movie industry. I think the fact his father had just bought the company helped him get the job, but nevertheless, he did it very well. Then the company was sold and Ken became head of production at MGM, another illustrious post. But everybody was so busy buying and selling movie companies in those days the mortality rate among the top echelon people was horrendous. MGM was sold and Ken was out again. To hear him tell the story it sounds like he lasted at MGM around fifteen minutes. He invited me to tea one time when I was in Los Angeles. It was just after he'd started the job at Warners. He was ensconced in Jack Warner's old office, as large and as opulent an office as I'd ever seen. I think he wanted to prove to me that in spite of all my efforts with *The Terror of the Tongs*, he'd managed to make it to the top anyway.

James Carreras called me into his office one day and asked me if I'd like to take the first print of *Taste of Fear* to New York to hand it over to Columbia? Wow! I was going to get to go to America. I got myself a visa, packed my bag, and waited for the off. Then I got a call from Michael. He was going to come with me. Great, I thought! What I didn't find out until many years later was that James Carreras had changed his mind about sending me and told Michael to go instead. Michael said he wasn't going to go in my place because very likely Jimmy Sangster would never talk to him again and probably quit Hammer forever. I don't know whether I would have done either of those things. But we never had to find out because James relented and told Michael to take me along if it would make him and me happy.

It did make me happy. My first trip to the States. New York, a side trip to Houston to visit with my brother whom I hadn't seen for ten years, a stopover in Las Vegas, the whole thing ending up in Los Angeles. I mean, what's not to be happy about!

I've been to New York many times since then. But nothing beat that first sight of Manhattan as we crossed the river from the airport around seven in the evening. We checked into our suite at the Hampshire House hotel on Central Park South, one of the

With Michael Carreras en route to New York.

largest hotel suites I've ever been in, to this day. Three bedrooms, an enormous living room overlooking the park, a dining room, and a kitchen. I got the second bedroom, which held the largest bed I'd ever seen. I couldn't wait to wallow around in it. I discovered later the apartment was owned by Greer Garson and her husband, their New York pad, which the hotel rented out when they weren't in residence. We unpacked and that night we hit the town.

Michael had a business date he wanted to cut as short as possible so he told me to wander into this bar around ten-thirty, pretend surprise at seeing him, and then stick with him because that was the only way he was going to get rid of his company. So I arrived

Anthony Nelson Keys, producer of *The Pirates of Blood River*, deputizes as clapper boy. Kerwin Mathews and Marla Landi wait patiently.

at the bar, duly expressed surprise at Michael being in New York, and sat myself down. I don't know what Michael was getting at but he introduced me as Lord Northwood (I had a house in Northwood) and for the rest of the evening there was a lot of bowing and scraping and I was referred to as milord. Joey Bushkin, the pianist, was playing at the club and came to join us at our table. Later he took us across the street to have a very late night snack with Gerry Mulligan who was off to play a session someplace downtown. We went with him. We got back to our grand suite at 8:00 a.m. in time for us to shave and shower before going to meet the big wheels at Columbia. After a screening, which we slept through, and a couple of meetings, I was back at the hotel packing my bag to leave for the airport to catch my plane to Houston, Texas. I never did get to wallow in Greer Garson's bed. I told her about it a couple of years later. I don't think she got the joke.

The side trip to Houston was pretty predictable. I visited the grave of my parents who had died there in the mid-fifties, I had a row with my brother about nothing at all. Then I hopped an aeroplane to Las Vegas where Michael met me. All I can really remember about that trip was that due to heavy connections through Columbia we were considered VIP guests. "Your rooms are comped. Any show you guys wanna see, just name it! You want credit at the tables, you got it. You want broads, you got them too."

RANSACKING A LOST TROPIC ISLAND... FOR A FABULOUS IDOL OF GOLD!

The Pirates of Blood River

COLOR

starring KERWIN MATHEWS · GLENN CORBETT · CHRISTOPHER LEE and MARLA LANDI

Screenplay by JOHN HUNTER and JOHN GILLING · from a story by JIMMY SANGSTER · Produced by ANTHONY NELSON KEYS · Directed by JOHN GILLING · A HAMMER FILM PRODUCTION · A COLUMBIA PICTURES RELEASE

We didn't want to see a show and neither of us were gamblers (later I became a gambler), and one look at the "broads" on offer was enough to put you off sex for life. So our Vegas trip was a bit of a disappointment. Come to think of it, I've been to Vegas literally dozens of times and it's always been a disappointment. Even the time I went there to get married for the second time. Come to think on it, especially the time I went there to get married. More of which later.

From Las Vegas, on to Los Angeles and a bungalow at the Beverly Hills Hotel. I mean, Howard Hughes and Elizabeth Taylor stayed in those bungalows. There we were, a couple of young upstarts from London living way above our station. The first night there we joined some Columbia personnel for dinner at a place that later became my favourite restaurant in Los Angeles, the Cock 'n Bull. It's gone now, like so many of the fun things. After dinner we went to a movie theatre on Wilshire Boulevard to watch a world championship fight transmitted live onto the main screen from Las Vegas. In the couple of days we were there we toured the Columbia lot on Gower Street (where I later had an office), ate like pigs, drank too much, and altogether had a great time. As we climbed on the aeroplane for our flight back to London, I promised myself that one day I was going to come back here.

Back in London I wrote a pirate picture for Michael. At least, I thought I wrote a pirate picture. It's been on my CV (resume) forever. *The Pirates of Blood River.* Screenplay by Jimmy Sangster. Now, after all these years I discover that I didn't write it at all. The credits read screenplay by John Gilling and John Hunter from a story by

Jimmy Sangster. Why is that, I wonder? It wasn't because I wasn't capable of writing a pirate picture. I did one for Hammer the following year called *The Devil-Ship Pirates*. Maybe I did a first draft and John Gilling, who directed it, wanted changes and I was too busy to make them. That sounds good so I shall stick to it. But to all those people I've lied to over the years, I apologize.

What I do remember is the genesis of the script. Michael told me he wanted to make a pirate picture, would I be interested in writing it. There was one small problem however, Hammer couldn't afford a boat. At least, not one that would actually float. A pirate movie without a boat? Like Robin Hood without bows and arrows. What one might call a challenge

I've always been a fan of the "desperate hours" type movie where a gang of criminals hole up in an apartment or house, taking the family who live there as hostage while they plan their eventual getaway. I can remember at least six movies based on that premise. So why not make it seven? Have a bunch of pirates hole up in this small village while they repair their boat which has been shot up during the Spanish Armada battle. They don't manage to get it fixed before the good guys overpower them, so there was no need to have anything that floated. Hammer liked the idea. Half a boat was built on dry land at the side of a reservoir close to Bray Studios. In spite of the fact that hardly any of it was in the water, the bloody thing managed to topple into the reservoir halfway through shooting, taking half the crew with it and nearly drowning a couple of them.

Sometime around here I was summoned to the offices of Harry Saltzman, who, with Cubby Broccoli, was busy making the Bond movies. He didn't want me for a Bond movie, but would I be interested in scripting and eventually producing a novel he'd just bought the movie rights to entitled *The Ipcress File*? I went home, read it, came back, and told him I'd love to. We talked about director and cast. I suggested the young actor who had recently appeared in a movie called *Zulu*, Michael Caine was his name. As for director, I suggested another new kid on the block, Sidney Furie. Harry wasn't over excited, but he made a couple of notes. Then my agent started to negotiate my deal. The money was okay, but there was no way Harry Saltzman was going to commit to a timeframe. He wanted me to deliver the script, then hold myself available for a production date which could have been next week or next year. It was a deal that was impossible to sign. So I dropped out of the picture. Harry went on to make the movie using both Sidney Furie and Michael Caine. I don't know why I bother to tell this story except maybe to demonstrate that my instincts were pointing in the right direction. A similar "timeframe" thing happened to me later with Anthony Newley. He was a big star at the time, about to make the movie of his musical hit *Stop the World I Want to Get Off*. He needed a line producer, would I be interested? Again the money was fine, but once more, nobody was able to give dates. I could have been sitting on my ass for a year doing nothing. I turned the job down and made a cowboy movie instead.

Michael Carreras decided he'd like to strike out on his own so he formed a company called Capricorn and set out to make a Western. There was already a script, written by an American, but Michael, who was going to direct, wanted some rewrites. Would I like to do them and, why not sign on as producer at the same time. I quite liked the idea of a location in southern Spain and a few weeks at the studio in Madrid, so I agreed.

The Savage Guns. The first western shot in Spain. We found locations outside Almeria where we built a ranch complex and we brought in from America Richard

Relaxing at home in 1960.

Baseheart, Alex Nicol, and Don Taylor, all of whom had worked for Hammer before, all good friends. And because this was a Spanish co-production, we had a group of Spanish actors to balance the books. Fernando Rey is the only name I can recall although there were a couple of Spanish actresses along for the ride. I suppose here, as in other places in this book, I could go along to the public library and look it all up in the reference books. But you know my attitude as far as research is concerned and, quite honestly, who gives a damn? About the only thing I can remember about this picture was that we had a fine old time making it. There weren't any hotels in Almeria in those days, at least none that anybody would want to stay in, so we rented a large house, fully staffed, and we shared, Michael, me, and the cast. Somewhere down the line we made friends with a couple of American servicemen from a nearby Air Force base who used to shop for us at their PX, bringing us all the stuff you couldn't buy in Spain in those days. Later we shot the interiors at a studio in Madrid.

The movie didn't turn out very well, which was a pity in more ways than one. First, nobody wants to make a bad movie, and second, it was the first picture Michael shot under his own aegis, his attempt to break away from Hammer and the influence of his father. If it had been a big success, who knows, the final history of Hammer might have been completely different.

With Michael Carreras on location in Arles, France filming *Maniac*.

It was around that time I met an American guy, Bruce Newberry. He had bought the rights to the Bulldog Drummond novels, would I be interested in writing an original script based on this character? Would I also be interested in producing it? I was interested. I wrote it, gave it the title *Deadlier Than the Male*, and the money was found to make it. Then we hit a snag. The money people were not willing to entrust their investment to Bruce and me. They suggested a more experienced production team would be safer. Maybe they were right. Bruce had no movie experience and I'd only acted as a line producer up to now, always with somebody peering over my shoulder to make sure I didn't go crazy. I certainly wouldn't have entrusted my money to us two.

The picture was turned over to Betty Box (Sidney's sister) to produce and Ralph Thomas to direct. Richard Johnson played Bulldog Drummond. (More like Spaniel Drummond in my opinion.) There was a good villain played by Nigel Green and a couple of sexy ladies, Elke Sommer and an Italian starlet whose name I've forgotten. Rank distributed the movie and, to this day, thirty years on, I still get the odd cheque in the mail representing my 10 percent share of the producer's profits. I have been a profit participant in over a dozen movies and this is the only one that has ever shown me any money. What about all those Hammer movies I can hear you asking. Forget it! Like most companies, Hammer can come up with more reasons a movie didn't go into profit than I've had hot dinners.

Time gets jumbled about now. I went to Hollywood again on the Bulldog Drummond script. And again for Sidney Box, who'd obviously recovered from his heart

Do You Want It Good or Tuesday?

Freddie Francis, Don Weeks, and myself on the set of *Nightmare*.

attack, to talk with Universal about financing a picture that I'd written for Rock Hudson to star in. Hudson had just come to the end of his long-term contract with Universal and asked for so much money to do the picture that Universal said no way and backed out.

And somewhere in here I wrote another original for Hammer which I called *Maniac*. Michael liked it and decided he wanted to direct, and was that okay with me? What was I supposed to do! Say no you can't! Actually, I was delighted. The movie was set in the Camargue, in southern France on the Mediterranean. It's a vast, flat area, a nature reserve where the pink flamingoes flock and where they breed fighting bulls. A truly wonderful place. The nearest town is Arles where we shot a couple of sequences in the Roman Amphitheatre. They still have bullfights there. Or they did until recently. Maybe Bridget Bardot has put a stop to all that. It was while we were shooting in the amphitheatre that our leading lady, Nadia Gray, asked if she could bring a visitor onto the set. We told her okay just so long as he didn't get in the way or ask dumb questions about how to make a movie, at least not while we were working. Anything he wants to know, I said, I'll tell him later. It turned out to be Orson Welles, who was absolutely charming and didn't once tell us what we were doing wrong.

By now I'd slipped into a different phase. No more Gothic horror, let's do psychological thrillers instead. First there had been *Taste of Fear*, now *Maniac*, shortly followed by *Paranoiac*, *Nightmare*, and *Hysteria*.

With Jennie Linden on the set of *Nightmare*.

Paranoiac was memorable only because it was the first picture I did with Freddie Francis. I only wrote this one. Tony Hinds produced it while Freddie directed. It was based on the novel *Brat Farrar* by Josephine Tey, of which Hammer had owned the film rights for a good few years. For some reason it had never got made until now. Oliver Reed starred, and very good he was.

Next up for Freddie and me was *Nightmare*. Early on, during the casting, we thought we'd got very lucky indeed. There was this wonderful young girl who came to see us. She read for the lead part and we signed her on the spot. A week later we get a call from her agent, please can we release her from her contract, she's been offered a part in another movie. No way, was Freddie's and my reaction. Let them postpone the other movie until we've finished ours. No can do. The other movie is already shooting,

Do You Want It Good or Tuesday?

they realize they've made a mistake with the casting, they've fired their leading lady, and they want to start over. Then the girl herself got on the phone. "Please, please!" So, what the hell! Who needs an unhappy leading lady? Reluctantly we let her go.

There's only so much **SHIT** a girl can take!

Jennie Linden in *Nightmare*.

This is Julie Christie who went into *Billy Liar*, the movie that gave her instant and well-deserved stardom. Meanwhile we recast the part with Jennie Linden, who was first class, but Julie Christie she wasn't.

Nightmare was the first of two of my psycho-type movies that Freddie directed. The other was *Hysteria*. *Nightmare* I remember as being all fun; *Hysteria*, I remember as being no fun at all. I have to define the word "fun" used in this context. Making even the most modest movie can be a very complicated, complex process involving as many as a hundred people. The logistics of getting everybody to the right place at the right time, making sure they're fed and watered, that all the equipment turns up, that they don't get too cold or too hot or too wet, that we don't run into too much overtime because it's expensive... I could go on and on. Suffice to say, producing a movie can be a ball-breaker especially if, on top of everything, the director is inclined to be over-demanding, which is a polite way of saying difficult. Maybe he wants a crane for a certain shot when he doesn't really need one, maybe he feels the scene would be better if it was played in a boat in the middle of the Thames on a windy day or, worse still, a windy night. Some directors will dig in their heels. "That's the way it's gonna be and bugger the expense and inconvenience."

Leslie Norman was like that, Freddie Francis wasn't. At least, he wasn't with me. "Can we afford to do it this way?" he would ask.

"No," I'd reply, more often than not.

The overall memory of *Hysteria* is of an unhappy movie.

So he'd do it another way. Maybe he bitched about it when he got home, but I don't remember him and me ever having a cross word.

So *Nightmare*, happy picture, *Hysteria* unhappy. With all the same ingredients, how come? Cast problems was how come. The male lead in *Hysteria* was played by an American actor, Robert Webber. He was a very good actor indeed. He'd never become a "star," but he was always working. You might not remember the name, but you'd recognize the face straight away. The female lead was an actress named Lelia Goldoni, who was relatively new in the business. For some reason Webber took an instant dislike to her and proceeded to put her down whenever he could. This destroyed whatever confidence she might have had, which affected her performance. It wasn't her fault and Freddie and I did everything we could to set things right. But Webber was a mean-minded guy. Whenever the two of them were on set at the same time, it cast a pall of gloom. I'm sure we had some light moments, but the overall memory is of an unhappy movie.

Later I wrote a movie called *Traitor's Gate*, about the stealing of the crown jewels from the Tower of London. It was produced by a German company and Freddie directed, having spent a Christmas with us in our house in the South of France while we pretended to be working on the script. I never saw the finished product, but I couldn't have liked the script I wrote all that much because I insisted on my *nom de plume*

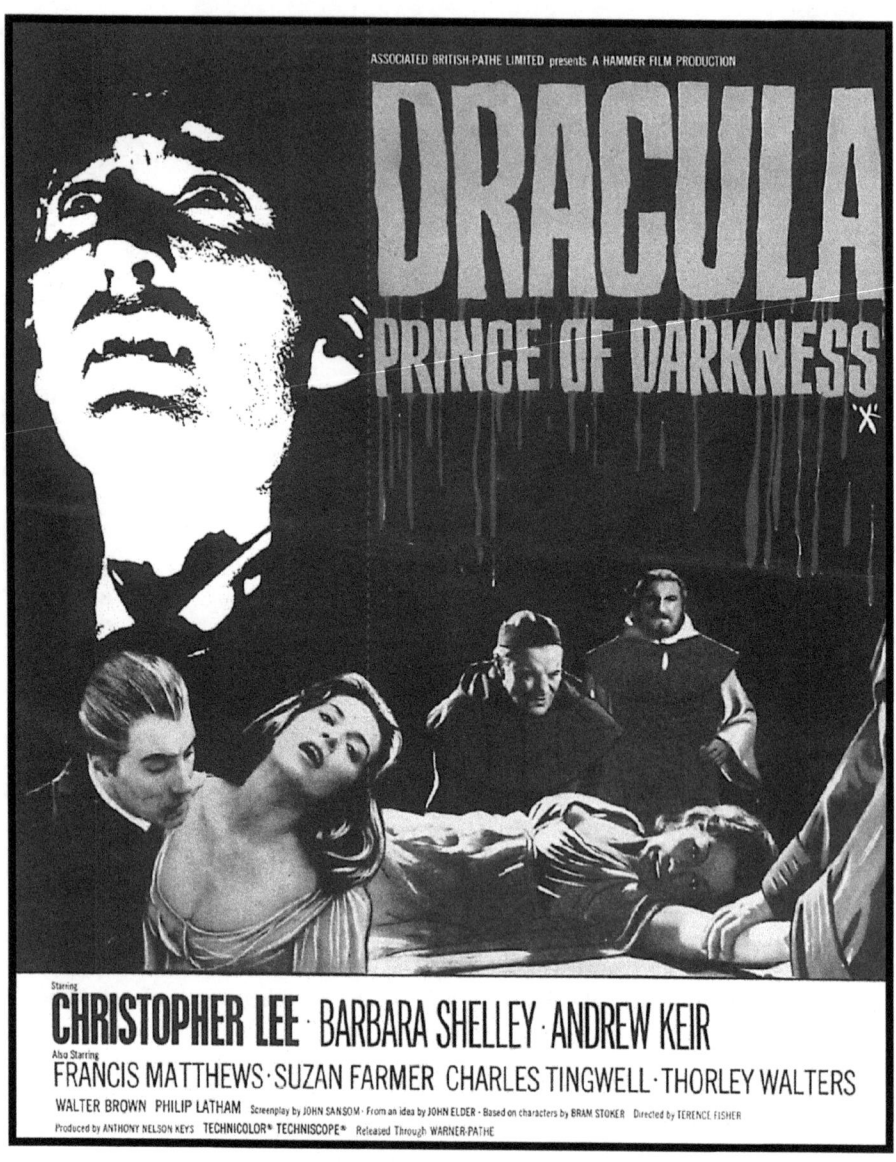

credit, John Sansom. But *Traitor's Gate* notwithstanding, I'm a great fan of Freddie's. I remember the first time I visited his house in London a couple of years ago. There on the bookshelf in the living room are his two Oscars. One for photographing *Sons and Lovers*, the other for *Glory*. One Oscar is flash enough, but two! Forget it!

I wrote another Dracula movie. *Dracula—Prince of Darkness.* Rather, I rewrote it. It was an old Tony Hinds script which he now handed to me to doctor. I wasn't too pleased with the work I did so I asked for my *nom de plume* John Sansom to be used on the credits. Obviously Tony wasn't too happy with what went on the screen because he also used his *nom de plume* "from an idea by John Elder."

The most memorable thing about the movie was the fact it brought Chris Lee back to the role of Dracula after nearly nine years. Sure, he'd worked for Hammer during that time, but this was his first reprise of the role which had originally brought him stardom. This was a "non-speaking" part for Christopher. Legend has it that when he told Peter Cushing that there were no lines for him in the Jimmy Sangster script, Peter replied that he shouldn't look a gift horse in the mouth. Another story has it that Christopher himself thought the lines so bad he flatly refused to say them. Whether I wrote dialogue for the part of Dracula, I honestly don't remember. It's quite possible that I didn't. After all, in the original, he only said around half a dozen words. To top it all, to this day I have never seen this movie. But the critics quite liked it.

"The latest *Dracula* is the best they (Hammer) have made up to now..."

"...extremely well made example of classic, ghoulish horror."

"I didn't see the picture," may sound strange to the uninitiated. I assure you it's perfectly true. As a writer, I delivered my finished script and then went on to something new. Around six months later the picture would hit the screen. By then I'd forgotten I'd even written it. Not being a particular fan of horror movies, I just never got around to going to see it. This occurred on at least half a dozen of my movies including *Crescendo*, another psycho thriller I wrote for Hammer a couple of years later. On this one I shared the screen credit with Alfred Shaughnessy, whom I didn't even meet for another twenty years. I believe the movie was a disaster. But before I did *Crescendo* I wrote and produced what I consider the best movie I was ever involved in.

20th Century-Fox presents

BETTE DAVIS iN THE ANNIVERSARY

Bette Davis adds another portrait in evil as the most merciless mother of them all

...and remember, Mum's the word for depravity!

SUGGESTED FOR MATURE AUDIENCES

Also Starring SHEILA HANCOCK · JACK HEDLEY · CHRISTIAN ROBERTS · JAMES COSSINS · ELAINE TAYLOR
Produced by JIMMY SANGSTER · Directed by ROY BAKER · Screenplay by JIMMY SANGSTER · Color by DeLuxe · A Seven Arts-Hammer Production

FROM ENCYCLOPEDIA BRITANNICA

Davis, Bette b. April 5, 1908 Lowell, Mass.
Motion picture actress for over 45 years best known for her brilliant and intense characterizations of sensitive, neurotic women. Her mannered acting style is based on such gestures as a defiant toss of the head, a dramatic lift of the chin, and a distinctive vocal inflection...

FROM THE DIARY OF JIMMY SANGSTER

...especially when she was telling me that she wasn't happy and please will I fire the director.

Act One. Scene Six.
"Greer Garson slept here..."

The Nanny was originally a novel by Evelyn Piper. I never met Ms. Piper but I am forever grateful to her for writing the book. Hammer bought it without much idea what they were going to do with it. I think they gave it to me hoping I'd turn it into one of the psycho-type horror movies I'd been doing for the past couple of years. But as far as I was concerned, it didn't fit into that category.

I wrote the first draft, we made a couple of small changes and then got in touch with Seven Arts in Los Angeles which, by then, owned a large part of Hammer. The company was owned and run by Eliot Hyman, Ken's father, and Ray Stark who later went on to own most of Columbia, or at least behave as if he did. Seven Arts suggested Greer Garson for the part of the Nanny. They forwarded her a script; she read it and didn't say no. She didn't say yes, either. First she wanted to meet the writer/producer to talk over the script.

She didn't want to see me in New York or Los Angeles. She wanted me to visit with her in Santa Fe, New Mexico where her husband, Buddy Fogelson, owned a spread called the Forked Lightning Ranch. I flew to New York where I spent the night in the apartment owned by Seven Arts and used mostly by Ray Stark. He'd left a lot of mail lying around the place and, being nosy, I got to read an awful lot of semi-libelous material about who said what to who and who made a deal with whatsisname and how so and so was screwed over such and such. Fascinating stuff. The next day I flew on to Santa Fe where Greer Garson and her husband met me at the airport. They drove me to the ranch, had me shown to my room, and told me I was expected for afternoon tea at 4:30 p.m. Sure enough, that's what we had. I can't swear to it, but I think there were cucumber sandwiches. I told her of my first trip to New York when I had almost slept in her bed. Her husband was so rich and they had so many homes, I don't think she even remembered she had a place in New York. That night we went to a restaurant in Santa Fe where we were treated like royalty. In fact the Fogelsons were the nearest thing Santa Fe had to royalty at the time. They owned this huge spread just out of town and she was on the board of the University and they had financed a couple of buildings on campus. Apart from that, she was a movie star right out of the old school. Mrs. Miniver, Mrs. Chips, Madame Curie, Mrs. Parkinson. Five times nominated for the best actress award, winning it once.

The following morning we went through the script briefly. She was polite, said she liked it but was a little worried about what it might do to her "image." I didn't like to mention that as far as the current cinema audience were concerned, she no longer had one. It was a long time since she had made a movie. They loaned me a Stetson and a pair of cowboy boots, and after a picnic lunch somewhere out on the range or the prairie or whatever they called it, I was driven to the airport where I caught a plane back to London.

I told them at Hammer that I thought Greer Garson was all wrong for the part. "Tough!" they said, meaning that if Greer Garson wanted the part, then she's got it, whatever the writer/producer might have to say. A couple of weeks later we got a message from Los Angeles. Sorry, Miss Garson doesn't want to do the movie. How about Bette Davis? Now they were talking.

We'd already hired Seth Holt to direct but now, for the first time, we were faced with an actress who had "director approval." So Seth and I duly flew to Los Angeles where Seven Arts had booked us into the Bel Air Hotel on Stone Canyon Road in Bel Air where Bette was living at the time. The morning after we arrived we walked a few hundred yards down the road, rang the front doorbell of an extremely modest little house, and madam herself answered the door. We were asked in, we introduced ourselves, and were duly auditioned. At least, Seth was auditioned. I just sat there.

What did he think of this picture and that performance? Did he agree that William Wyler was one of the best directors of all time? What was his opinion of *Whatever Happened to Baby Jane*? In *The Nanny* script, how would he handle the scene where so and so does such and such, and, dragging me into the discussion, didn't he think the penultimate scenes were a bit over the top? Impressive stuff to someone who was used to having actors who, when offered a part, asked when does shooting start, how much do I get paid, oh, and maybe I could have a look at the script.

After half an hour we went back to the hotel. As far as I was concerned, that was it. The following day I caught a plane back to London leaving Seth in Hollywood to get drunk with some old buddies he hadn't seen for some time. Five days later we get a call: Miss Davis would be happy to accept Seth Holt as director, when does shooting start, how much do I get paid, oh, and I'd like a couple of changes to the script.

She arrived in England two weeks before shooting started. She came in on one of the ocean-going Queens. Seth and I drove down to Southampton to meet her. We had rented for her a huge house in Elstree quite close to the studios and she was accompanied by her son, around ten years old, and a rather strange lady companion/gofer type person named Viola Rubber. Contrary to what has been said, especially by actress Sheila Hancock, who appeared with her in a later movie of mine, she never had a "great entourage." One person was provided for in her contract, and that's what she had. Viola Rubber on this, the first movie I made with her, and some delightful middle-aged guy whose name I've forgotten on the second. But then Sheila Hancock was always prone to exaggeration both on and off the screen.

Bette Davis in *The Nanny*. Tough. Demanding. A perfectionist. She was all these things.

I've also read something that Seth Holt wrote about the picture. "Davis got the flu during shooting, and sometimes she'd stay away altogether, holding up shooting while she sent in day-to-day reports on her condition."

If memory serves me correctly, Bette didn't have one single day away during shooting. If she had, we wouldn't have finished on schedule, which we did with a little time to spare.

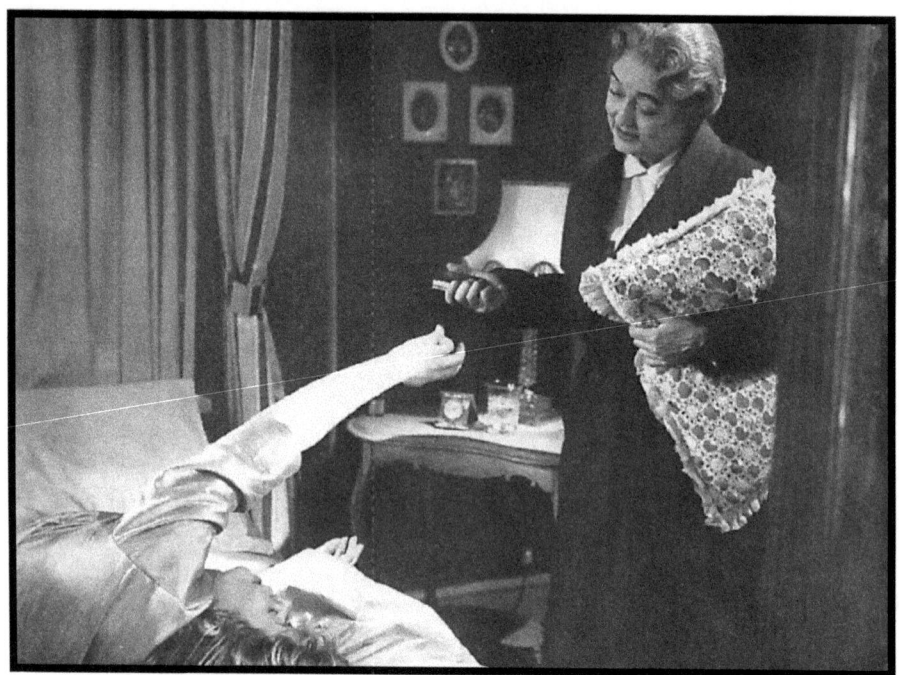

I consider *The Nanny* the best movie I was ever involved in.

Tough. Demanding. A perfectionist. She was all these things. Awkward bitch too, on occasion. But she never asked for anything that she didn't consider was to the benefit of the movie as a whole. If it could be proved to her otherwise, fine, she'd withdraw her demand.

She would invariably preface her request with the phrase, "I've starred in sixty-two movies and..."

It's difficult to argue with somebody who has been nominated for an Academy Award ten times and won it twice. You've got to believe they know what they're talking about. On the first day of shooting there was a bedroom scene between her and Wendy Craig, who played her employer, the mother. Wendy is in bed and Bette is sitting on the side of the bed talking to her. As usual, Seth shot the two-shot first and then went in for the close-ups. Wendy first, because to shoot Bette's we had to pull out the back of the set and bring in a false ceiling, maybe twenty minutes' work. After work was over for the day I get a call in my office, Miss Davis would like a word in her dressing room. There she offered me a large drink before saying, "I have starred in... etc. etc. and the director always does my close up first."

I explained about the work we had to do on the set before we could get 'round to her shot and I apologized for offending her, but it might happen again. "You think I'm being an awkward bitch, don't you," she said. I did, but I didn't say so. "Don't you understand that the person who does the first close up controls the scene." I didn't. But later I thought about it. She was right.

A couple of other things bugged her. First was the fact that everybody could get a drink at lunchtime. In America, the studios are dry. In England they're not. She would scowl at the beer and wine on the tables where our people were eating lunch. Never

Do You Want It Good or Tuesday?

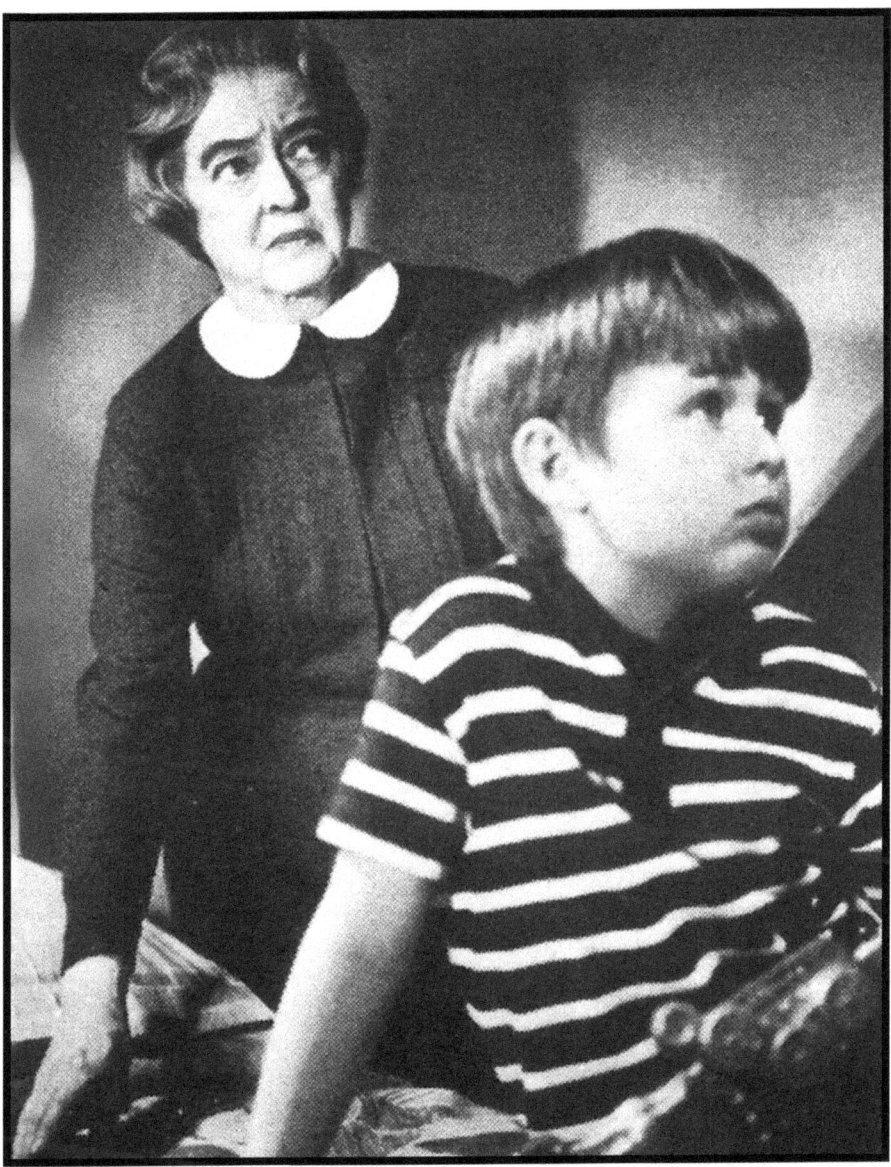

It's difficult to argue with somebody who has been nominated for an Academy Award ten times and won it twice.

mind that she invariably drank herself legless after shooting finished, during the working day, zilch. Time keeping was very important to her also. If the daily call sheet said Miss Davis on set at 9:30, she would be there, on the set at exactly 9:30. Nobody would have to call her from her dressing room or give her five minutes' warning. And God forbid the set wasn't ready for her when she turned up. It certainly kept the assistant director on his toes when he was making out the call sheet.

In fact, whatever Seth Holt might have recalled, shooting on this picture went pretty smoothly. Apart from Bette confiding in me one day that she thought Seth was "a mountain of evil," she respected him as a director. We had a first rate cast with Wendy Craig and the late Jill Bennet and a young boy, William Dix, playing the protagonist. It was his first role and he was excellent. It was a good picture, one of the few that I am proud to have made.

It could have been better. Seth had just finished supervising the director's cut when we get a call from the Fox offices in Soho Square that Seymour Poe, the head honcho of Fox's world-wide distribution, a very important person indeed, wanted us to screen the picture for him. We explained there were no music or effects, no opticals, and it was a pretty dirty print to boot. Not to worry, bring it over around 10:30 when Mr. Poe and his good lady will take a look. Seth and I duly delivered the film and sat in the front row while Poe and his wife sat at the back. The screening finished and we looked back toward Poe, hopefully to take our bow.

"What happened to the ending?" he wanted to know.

If you haven't seen the movie, and there's no reason why you should because it's a long time ago, the concluding scene is when the Nanny character realizes suddenly that she is in fact guilty of the crimes the little boy has been accusing her of all through the movie. Riddled with guilt she goes to her room and starts to pack. Her life has finished. End of picture. At least, that was the end of the picture as written and as we had shot it. But not for Mr. Poe. "You can't end a movie that way. It's too downbeat. Have everybody leaving the theatre in a bad mood. Cheer 'em up, for Christ's sake. Give 'em a happy ending."

We were forced to recall Wendy Craig and William Dix, rent studio space, build a set, and spend two days shooting a new scene I had to write. A kiss, kiss, hug, hug, Nanny will get her just deserts type scene.

Much later when Bette saw the movie in Los Angeles, she called me. She was furious. "You shouldn't have let yourself be bullied that way," she said. "You should have called me. I've starred in sixty-two movies and..."

That was Bette Davis professionally. Socially was a different matter altogether. She was a lonely and not very happy woman. It was essential for her to be the center of attraction at any social gathering. If you behave badly enough, shout loudly enough, this isn't too hard. Monica decided she'd like to give a dinner party for her at our house where Bette behaved so badly that Denise, our au pair girl, who was doubling as maid that evening, got so scared she dropped the coffee tray. One Friday night Monica and I managed to put together a small group and, with Bette, we went to Danny La Rue's night club. Just before the cabaret started a couple of the Beatles arrived. Bette said she was going to get their autographs for her daughter. She returned to our table a couple of minutes later almost apoplectic.

"Little bastards didn't know who I was," she said. And she bitched about it loudly all through the cabaret, which she hated.

She could also be extremely intimidating. One day at the studio I got a call from comedian Frankie Howerd. I'd never met the man, but I was a great fan. He introduced himself before asking if he could possibly come down to the studio one day and have lunch with Bette Davis. No, he didn't know her, but he'd always worshipped her from afar. I checked with Bette who had never heard of him.

"What's he do?" she wanted to know.

I told her he was a comic, both stand up and actor, an extremely funny man. "At least we'll get a couple of laughs over lunch."

"Gay?" she wanted to know.

"I've no idea," said I.

"Take my word. He's gay. They adore me," she said.

Anyway, she agreed he could drop by for lunch, which he eventually did. Introductions were made, we ordered our food (no booze), and I sat back to enjoy the crosstalk between superstar and supercomic. Bette opened the dialogue. "They tell me you're a comic," she said. "Make me laugh!"

Poor Frankie Howerd. He seized up completely. He managed to say about three words during the entire meal, and left before the coffee.

Also, somewhere down the line, Bette began to come on a little strong to me personally. I'd like to say I was flattered, but I wasn't. It wasn't an easy situation to handle.

She would take to calling me at home in the evening and asking me to come 'round to her place where she wanted to talk about the following day's work or bitch about what happened today. I would duly drive the thirty-five minutes to her place where she would answer the front door herself, Scotch on the rocks in hand, Viola and young son having been packed off to bed. She would have her say about the work problem, then she would ask me to have another drink and I would have to start ducking and weaving. I was desperately unoriginal in my evasion.

"I'd love to but I love my wife too much..." was my standard line.

It worked. She respected the institution of marriage. At least she did until her next try. Needless to say, I told Monica about this. She was very magnanimous about it. Not as difficult as it sounds, because Bette really wasn't very fanciable at that time. If I'd had Sigourney Weaver or Michelle Pfeiffer as my star, things may have turned out differently. But then neither of those two would have made a pass in the first place and I would have been far too chicken to have made the first move. The day I put Bette on the plane home the Sangster household breathed a vast sigh of relief. Monica also said that if I ever did another movie with Bette, she was going to leave the country the day Bette arrived and not come back until I put her on the plane back to America. Not to worry, I told her. No way on God's green earth will I ever put myself through that again.

As a complete change of scene, I worked for Bob Baker and Monty Berman again when they bought the TV rights for *The Saint*. I wrote Episode One, to be told eventually by the American story consultant they brought over from Los Angeles that it was a piece of shit. It was no epic, and it might not have been what he was looking for, but neither was it a piece of shit. But he was right in one respect. It wasn't American TV fare. My only TV work in England had been the two serials I mentioned earlier and a couple of plays for a very prestigious program called *Armchair Theatre*. It wasn't until I became an American TV story consultant myself that I came to understand the many differences between stuff written for the silver screen and stuff written for the box. But that was much later. Long before that Hammer made me an offer I couldn't refuse. Bette Davis again.

Tony Hinds asked me to go to the theatre to see a play called *The Anniversary*, written by Bill MacIlwraith. It was a good play with a wonderfully over-the-top central character played by Mona Washbourne. Tony asked me to write the movie, which I did. Then he told me Bette Davis had been hired to star and would I produce it. No way, says I. Please, says Tony. Not for all the money in the world, says I. How much money is that, asked Tony. I told him, he agreed, and Monica packed her bags and went to our house in the South of France as she had threatened, leaving the same day Bette arrived.

But before that day arrived we had to go through the whole "auditioning the director" bit again. I had tried to get Seth Holt, who would have been ideal for the movie, but he was off in cloud cuckoo land making a movie with Zero Mostell. Two fat crazies together. Word was that when the money people saw what was happening on screen, they pulled the plug. Unfortunately they didn't pull it soon enough for me and we had to find somebody else.

Alvin Rakoff was a very good TV director, part of the group who worked for Sidney Newman who created *Armchair Theatre*. He came highly recommended and he

Tony asked me to write the movie [*The Anniversary*], which I did. Then he told me Bette Davis had been hired to star and would I produce it.

and I duly got ourselves onto an aeroplane to Los Angeles. Bette had moved, she was now living in an apartment off Wilshire Boulevard in Beverly Hills, right behind the Regent Beverly Wilshire hotel, made famous then, because Warren Beatty lived there, and now, because that's where they shot *Pretty Woman*.

We met her for dinner the night we arrived and the following day Bette and I had a meeting. She asked a few questions and finally said she was happy to go ahead with Alvin. She's have preferred Seth, but *c'est la vie*. I wanted to get straight back on an

During the shooting of *The Anniversary*, Bette hated everyone and everyone hated her.

aeroplane home but she insisted that I stay and have dinner with her that night. She was living with her daughter BD at the time and she wanted to give us both a home cooked meal. But this was purely social so I wasn't to bring Alvin, which suited him down to the ground because he had a whole bunch of friends he wanted to hang out with. I should have known I was in for trouble because as I arrived the chauffeur was just taking BD off to the movies. We were to have a dinner *a deux*. And a very nice dinner it was too. She was a very good cook. It wasn't until coffee time that she started chasing me around the sofa. I mean actually chasing me around the sofa like some dreadful scene from an old Chaplin movie. In the end I had to pretend to be a whole lot drunker than I was and pass out. I knew if I could keep my trousers on until 10:30 p.m. BD would be home and my virtue would remain intact. This I did and I have great respect for Bette that she never held it against me. I think she hoped I'd forgotten the whole incident.

I spent one more night in Los Angeles on that trip. Actor Donald Pleasance, an old friend of Alvin's, was in town so let's go party! We finished up at a club called The Daisy with Vanessa Redgrave and Richard Harris, who were shooting *Camelot* at the time. This was the night that Vanessa kept on and on at me about my politics, even while we were dancing. In fact, I think this was the only reason she wanted to dance with me. I'm a terrible dancer.

Back in England, we finished the preproduction work which included the construction of a set representing the house where Mrs. Taggart (Bette) lived. It was a huge set on three levels, beautifully designed by art director Reece Pemberton. One of its features was a wide staircase leading straight down to the main living room. At the top of the

staircase was a landing with a couple of bedrooms leading off and another set of stairs leading up to the third level. I only mention all this because of what happened later.

We cast Jack Hedley, Sheila Hancock, and James Cossins, all of whom had been in the play, together with Elaine Taylor and Christian Roberts. A good, solid cast, and finally, Bette Davis arrived and shooting commenced. I wrote at the beginning of this book that I was sure some of the bad memories would come creeping back once I got into my stride, that, "somewhere back there during the last fifty years there must have been a couple of bad days but, for the life of me, I can't recall them right now."

Okay! Cancel that. I recall them in all their gory detail.

Discount for a moment all the guff that Sheila Hancock came out with about Davis' "great entourage." As on the last picture, she didn't have one. She didn't even bring her son this time, just one middle-aged, gently gay ex-hairdresser. Sheila also said, "I was a working class actor and had no interest in the so-called star system."

That's really a very simplistic point of view. Without the "star system" the movie wouldn't have been made. Perhaps she's not interested in the "star system" because she's never going to be part of it. Make no mistake, Sheila Hancock is a first class actress and, I believe, a very good director. But she should understand, there is always another point of view which, whether she likes it or not, has to be dealt with. It's a tough world and we can't all have our own way.

But the problem on *The Anniversary* had nothing to do with Sheila Hancock. It was with Alvin Rakoff. Two days into shooting and we were a day behind schedule and slipping fast. By the end of the first week we were three days behind and all was doom and gloom. Bette hated everyone and everyone hated her. Most of all she hated Alvin.

After five days she summoned me to her dressing room one evening after shooting. I knew what her opening line would be before she opened her mouth. "I've starred in sixty-three movies..." (she'd obviously started including *The Nanny* in her CV) "...and this is the first time I've ever had to work for the camera. The camera *always* works for me."

What she was getting at was Alvin's *modus operandi*. He was a TV director, accustomed to blocking out the actor's movements on the set before running the scene. He'd worked very hard doing his homework and knew in his head exactly how he wanted the scene to play. Bette Davis enters on this line, crosses the room as she

From Hammer Films to Hollywood! A Life in the Movies

99

THERE IS NO NAME FOR THEIR KIND OF EVIL!

One offered sex...One killed with sex... One played the other sex—And one watched through a glass eye as they destroyed each other!

20th CENTURY-FOX presents

BETTE DAVIS
IN THE ANNIVERSARY

Also Starring SHEILA HANCOCK · JACK HEDLEY · CHRISTIAN ROBERTS · JAMES COSSINS
ELAINE TAYLOR · Produced by JIMMY SANGSTER · Directed by ROY BAKER · Screenplay by JIMMY SANGSTER
Color by DeLuxe · A Seven Arts-Hammer Production

The New Vaudeville Band ("Winchester Cathedral") sings "The Anniversary Song"

speaks that line, hits those marks we've put down there where she lights a cigarette, then she crosses the room to those other marks where she stubs it out as she says so and so. For television, in those days, this was how they worked. But not in movies. Bette Davis' argument was maybe I don't want to light my cigarette there, how do I know until we've played the scene a couple of times. Then she'd quote her William Wyler story. "Mr. Wyler would call all the actors onto the set and say this is the scene, play it. We'd play it while he watched. He'd make a couple of suggestions and we'd play it again. A couple more suggestions, then a couple more. Finally, when we were playing the scene we all felt comfortable with, he would turn to his cinematographer and say 'that's the scene, photograph it.'"

How true this was I never knew, but it sounded very reasonable to me.

"I'll tell Alvin," I said, wondering how the hell I was going to do that. But I didn't have to worry. Bette Davis hadn't finished.

"I can't work with him any more," she said. "He'll have to go."

I called Tony Hinds at head office. He was the executive producer on this one. At least he didn't jump into his car and drive off. We called the money people in Los Angeles. "Bette Davis wants to fire the director."

So what's your problem, they wanted to know. Then, just so we'd be sure where we stood they went on to say that *The Anniversary* wasn't an Alvin Rakoff film, neither was it an Anthony Hinds or Jimmy Sangster film and, if push came to shove, it wasn't even a Hammer film. It was a Bette Davis film. End of discussion.

Poor Alvin, who I'm sure had no idea the shit was going to hit the fan at all, let alone with such force, packed his briefcase and quietly left. I'm sure this did his career no good at all, and, to this day, I feel sorry for what happened. But... the show must go on. We had to find another director and we had to do it fast. Bette Davis asked me to take over. Fortunately I had the good sense to say no. Roy Ward Baker had just finished directing a movie for Hammer and was an old friend of Bette's from his Hollywood days. Yes, he was prepared to take over and yes, Bette Davis was willing for him to so do. Saved by the gong, I thought. But Roy is nobody's fool. He knew we'd already shot a week and he didn't want any of Alvin's material going into the final cut. Who knows, there could have been a credit dispute. So he told us he didn't like the way the staircase came down into the centre of the main room, he'd prefer it come down at an angle. Result, we had to rebuild the set and everything shot to date had to be thrown out.

It would be nice to be able to say that from then on everything was sweetness and light. It wasn't. The other members of the cast had been very fond of Alvin and they took his leaving very badly. They were all professional enough not to let it show in their performance, but the atmosphere on the set was wicked. Added to this, with the exception of cinematographer Harry Waxman, who was worried about the Six Day War in Israel, the camera crew was made up of untalented prima donnas. The focus puller quit because he said Roy Baker was rude to him, the operator who'd nearly quit when he heard Roy was taking over the movie never stopped telling me "I told you so," referring to the fact that he'd said at the time there would be trouble with Roy. The only trouble with Roy was he did the job as best he could but managed to get up everybody's nose in the process.

But all things come to an end. Bette Davis left. My wife returned from France. We put the picture together and, unfortunately, it wasn't nearly as good as it could have been. We really needed Seth Holt on that movie. As Bette had said, he was a "mountain of evil" and would have made a great job of bringing Mrs. Taggart to life. And that was the last job I did for Hammer for a couple of years.

Ralph Bates and I hanging around the set of *Fear in the Night*.

Do You Want It Good or Tuesday?

ENTRY FROM THE REFERENCE BOOK **FILM MAKERS**

Sangster has a bleak, near apocalyptic vision...

He makes even the most improbable plot developments quite credible giving a dream like sense of decay and inevitable disaster...

The characters in his screenplays drink and smoke far too much, take drugs, indulge in meaninglessly self destructive pastimes, and otherwise demonstrate that they are bored, vicious, and infantile...

EXTRACT FROM THE REFERENCE BOOK **SCREENWRITERS**

In many of his later works Sangster has been accused of drawing on his own personal characteristics to flesh out his fictional characters.

Act One. Scene Seven.
"At least I changed the names..."

I became a novelist. That is, I wrote my first novel. It happened, like so many things in my professional life, completely by accident. I had been hired by Sidney Box to write a script based on a novel he was hoping to buy. It was a pretty dire piece about an American escaping from the Viet Cong by floating down the Mekong river disguised as a log of wood. There was a temporary hold up in clearing the rights so Sidney, who had just formed a publishing company, told me to go off and try writing a novel. If he liked it, he'd publish it. The whole thing was reminiscent of my first writing job for Hammer... We like it, you'll get paid. We don't, tough! So I wrote it, he liked it, and agreed to publish it. As for getting paid, we won't even mention that. I mean, I did get paid, but hardly enough to bother with at the time. I've had eight novels published altogether. I've written eleven but three still languish on my agent's desk in New York. This tells you something about my novel writing or something about my New York agent. Or a bit about both perhaps. Maybe by the time I finish this book, one of them might be sold, but I'm not holding my breath.

The first, *Private I* (That's "eye," not "one." The book's written in the first person.) was published hardback in America and in England. It was also translated and published in five other languages. French, German, Italian, Swedish, and Japanese; and I still didn't make much money. Only later when I made TV movies of my first two novels did they show any real profit.

Let me tell you about novel writing. For me it's the most satisfying form of writing there is. In movies and television there are a dozen people between you and your audience. Producers, director, actors, they all put their mark on the material. I'm not complaining about this. In fact it brings up something I was going to write about anyway. A word in the ear of prospective screenwriters. The producer or production company has bought your script. They now own it and, hopefully, you've got the money in the bank to prove it. If you haven't, get yourself a new agent. At this point, in my opinion,

From Hammer Films to Hollywood! A Life in the Movies

103

the owners are entitled to do whatever they like with the material including dropping it in the trash can, which, I understand, a lot of them do these days. You may not agree with what they're doing, you may yell and scream that they're ruining your concept, desecrating your artistic integrity, even raping your child. But take my word, it ain't going to do any good. I found that out very early on. If you're lucky enough to write a stage play then your words are sacrosanct. Nobody will alter a comma without first checking with you. But for the screen, large or small, forget it! Everyone and his mother is going to make changes. Worrying or fuming about it is going to get you nothing but ulcers. If you're really offended, take your name off the credits. But remember, the credit list determines who gets paid residuals.

With novel writing, as I said, nobody messes with your material. I know your publisher will assign you an editor who may or may not gently suggest a couple of changes, but these will only be carried out if you agree. I'm not talking here about "vanity" novels which are, more often than not, written by the editor from page one, but your ordinary run of the mill novel which is never going to be nominated for any of the literary prizes but will give those kind enough to buy it, a good read. What I call an airport book. Your words, ideas, visions, whatever, reach your audience exactly as you want them. The whole operation is a very personal thing.

Another reason I like novel writing is that you set your own deadline. There's nobody calling you three times a week wondering where the pages are. You can write a thousand words a day or five thousand, you can take four weeks or twenty-four, work two hours or twenty-two. Who cares! In fact I'm reasonably disciplined. When I'm on a project I work set hours every day. But that's just me. Also the number of hours have grown less as the number of years have grown more. Whereas I used to put in a good eight hours at the typewriter, I now do three at the word processor.

A word about word processors. They're a wonderful tool once you get past the "gee whiz" stage, but I'm not sure that they're conducive to good writing. In the old days I would write in longhand using a pencil. I would read what I had written, make my changes, then type it up. Once more, further down the line, I'd make more changes and type it for the second time. I would read what I had just typed and maybe think this could be changed or that could be better. But the hell with typing it yet again! So the material would have a touch of spontaneity still left. On a word processor stuff gets changed, then changed again, changed once more, copied, cut and pasted, spellchecked, underlined, italicized, left and right centred. By the time you finish, you wonder whether or not you should give a shared credit to Bill Gates. Needless to say, I'm devoted to my word processor.

So, novel number one, *Private I*, safely into print, followed by novel number two, based on the same character. This I entitled *Foreign Exchange*. While I was writing it, Sidney Box sold his publishing business to a quite dreadful man named de Roth. The Roth of God, Sidney used to describe him. He decided he wanted to be a "hands on" type publisher and suggested a couple of plot deviations to me when I delivered the manuscript. They weren't particularly dramatic and only needed a couple of days' work. I mention this here because it had repercussions later. But right now, *Foreign Exchange* hit the bookstores with as much impact as *Private I*, namely very little. It did go to a second printing, but I suspect this was because they were so chintzy about the first.

foreign exchange

A NOVEL OF ESPIONAGE

JIMMY SANGSTER
author of private i

NORTON

Meanwhile, I looked around for my next assignment. A Hollywood ex-agent turned producer named Harold Cohen had bought the movie rights to a novel by an English writer, Victor Canning, and through my agent at the time, a flamboyant guy named Dick Blodgett, he hired me to write the script. I flew to Los Angeles and checked into an apartment-type hotel on Wilshire Boulevard in Westwood where I duly went to work.

He was a nice guy, Harold Cohen. He had run his own agency in New York, sold out to one of the big guys, and come to Hollywood to head up their literary department. Eventually he'd slid into producing. He and his wife Phylis lived in an enormous house in Beverly Hills, later bought by George Segal. It was one of the most over-the-top, uncomfortable places I've ever been in.

From Hammer Films to Hollywood! A Life in the Movies

105

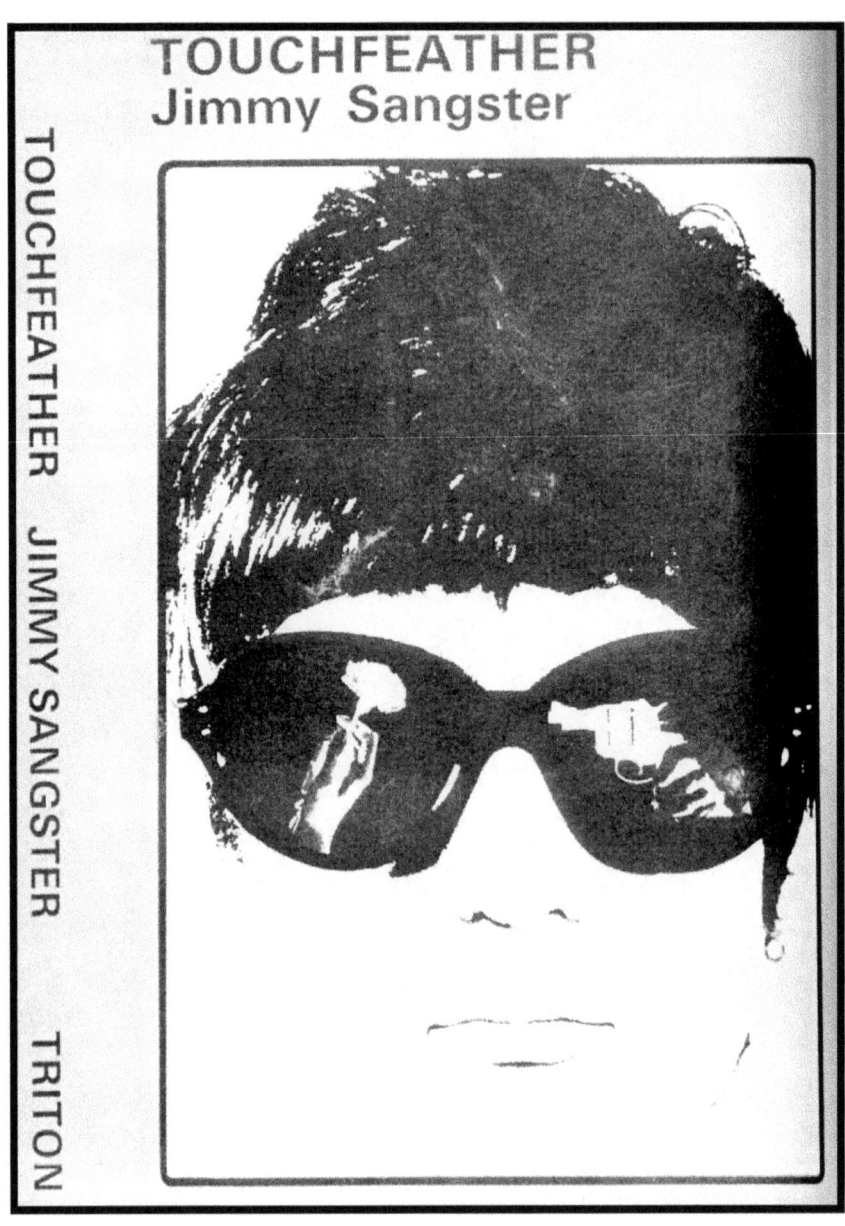

I'd hardly started on the script of the Canning book when Harold told me he'd far rather be making either or both of my novels. I was suitably flattered. I didn't think anybody had even read them. But maybe we could discuss that later, after I'd completed the current assignment.

During that assignment Monica and my son James came to Los Angeles for a short holiday. It was while they were here that Harold and Phylis Cohen decided that they would throw a real Hollywood-style party. Invite everybody who's anybody and hope enough of them say yes to ensure a write up in the trade papers the next day. It was a hell of a party. Valet parking, Harold and Phylis in a receiving line, tuxedos, dozens of

Do You Want It Good or Tuesday?

Sir Ralph Richardson and Shelley Winters appear in *Who Slew Auntie Roo?*

waiters passing round champagne and caviar goodies, marquees in the garden where there was a sit down dinner for over a hundred guests. The only fly in the ointment was that Martin Luther King had been assassinated the day before. Harold and Phylis had discussed canceling the party altogether but eventually decided against it. Instead they'd ask one of the guests to say a few words. The guest they chose was James Baldwin, the black writer who was such an important spokesman for blacks and the civil rights movement. While he didn't actually accuse anybody at the party of pulling the trigger, he did manage to say that we were all responsible for King's murder. I've never seen a party wrap up so quickly. By the time Baldwin had finished speaking, the only guests left were Monica and I and family.

I finished the script for Harold (it never got made) and went back to London where, with nothing else to do, I wrote a screenplay of my first novel and handed it to my agent who promptly turned round and set it up as a movie with a company called Gulf and Western, provided I could attract a reasonable star. We scouted around and finally came up with Rod Steiger who said he was interested. Back to Gulf and Western who told us we'd got a deal. I did a budget, putting in thumping great fees for myself as writer and producer, made out a shooting schedule, and set the start date. Then we get word from Hollywood, Rod Steiger is having second thoughts. His marriage with Claire Bloom was sliding onto the rocks and he wanted his next project to be something he could do with her. If she had been a bit player it would have been easy. In fact there was a small part, later played by Jill St. John, but Claire Bloom was a star. There was no way I could rewrite the script to accommodate her. I suppose I could have started all over again and written a completely different story, but then I would have been back to square one.

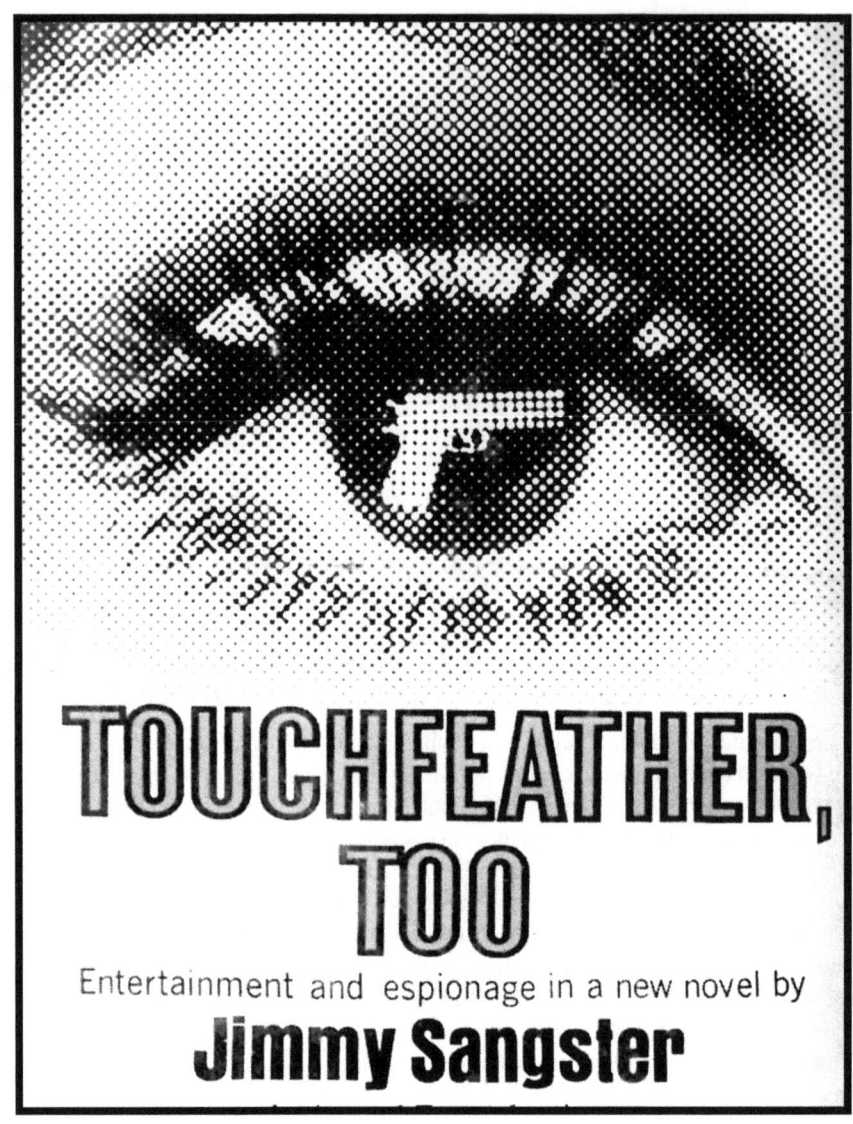

So I said the hell with it and wrote another novel, *Touchfeather*, about an English female Bond type person whose cover was as an air hostess. I wrote in the first person singular and had a lot of fun. It was reasonably successful because I was asked to follow it up with *Touchfeather, Too*. The only other novel I wrote during this period, bringing it up to five, was called *Your Friendly Neighbourhood Death Pedlar*. It was my favorite, but it was even less successful than the others. So, end of novel writing for the next fifteen years.

'Round about here my domestic life got screwed up. Monica and I divorced, quite amicably, after eighteen years and I started flitting back and forth to Los Angeles. I co-wrote a script for American International Pictures with an American writer named Stanley Ralph Ross called *The Zodiac Killers*, which didn't get made. I wrote another for AIP called *Who Slew Auntie Roo?* which did, starring Shelley Winters. And finally,

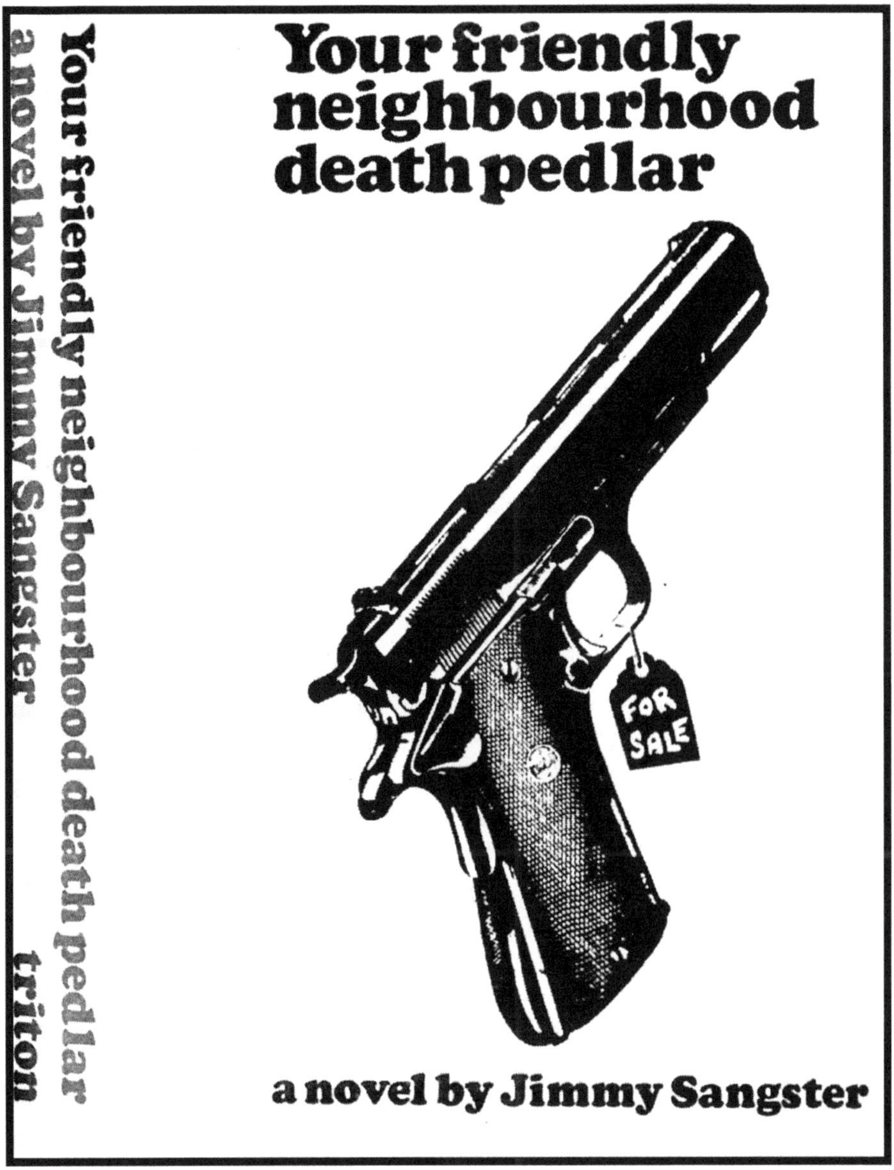
Your friendly neighbourhood death pedlar
FOR SALE
a novel by Jimmy Sangster
Your friendly neighbourhood death pedlar
a novel by Jimmy Sangster
triton

Harold Cohen got in touch with me again to ask if I would be interested in making TV movies of my two novels.

Movies for TV were a new concept. Dreamed up by Leonard Goldberg who was head of programming for the ABC network at the time, he wanted to make a series to be called *Movie of the Week*. He liked the script of *Private I* and he liked the novel *Foreign Exchange* (I hadn't yet scripted it). We went to see him and his assistant at the time, Barry Diller (*the* Barry Diller) and we made a deal. They wanted both movies to be available as 90 minute TV subjects, but also as 100 minute theatrical motion pictures. This meant two versions of each movie. And for both movies, they'd finance us to a maximum total of $800,000. $400,000 per movie to include overheads, contingencies,

Sebastian Cabot and myself on the set of *Foreign Exchange*.

completion guarantees, finance costs, and producer's fees. Harold Cohen threw up his hands in horror but I figured that if we shot in England we could just manage it. We were going to have to because there was no question of any back end financing. What we saw was what we got.

Back in England, I scripted *Foreign Exchange* and set about casting. Trevor Howard for the lead part, a slightly down-at-heel private investigator. For the head of the secret service, the man who double crosses the Trevor Howard character, I sent the script to Laurence Olivier. All his scenes for both movies were on one set, his office. That, and one day's location, five days' work tops, so I could afford his money. I got word back within a week. He was looking to do something on American TV and this seemed like a good opportunity. I hired Roy Baker as director, booked space at Pinewood Studios, scheduled both movies to be shot together. And by that I didn't mean back to back. Scenes in the lead's shabby office for both movies to be shot in sequence, same with the scenes in his apartment, same with the scenes in Olivier's office. The two scripts were printed on different color paper and the clapper boy had to check with the continuity girl before each shot to make sure he was using the right clapper board. No good marking a shot for *Private I* if it was meant to be for *Foreign Exchange*.

Then I got word from Hollywood. ABC, in their infinite wisdom, decided that Trevor Howard and Laurence Olivier weren't good enough TV names. They wanted to recast. They sent me Robert Horton (star of *The Green Slime*) for the Howard part and Sebastian Cabot for Olivier's. Horton had played second fiddle in a western soap, followed by first fiddle in another western which had fallen flat on its ass. Cabot, who long ago had worked for Hammer and been in the auto accident in which Don Stannard (*Dick Barton Strikes Back*) had died, had achieved celebrity status in an American sitcom playing an English butler (*Family Affair*). They also wanted to send me Jill St. John as the romantic interest. This didn't worry me because the part was too small to bother with, but I screamed blue bloody murder about the other two. It didn't do any good. Harold Cohen, my partner, was going through a crisis of his own and was absolutely no help whatsoever. So with nobody to plead my case in Los Angeles, I had to go with what they wanted to give me. I'd probably have had to anyway, but at least it would have been worth an argument. Horton arrived with his wife. They were a delightful couple but he had completely the wrong idea of the character. I'd written seedy, he was going to play suave. And he bought his wardrobe with him to reinforce the fact. I suppose I could have dug my heels in and told him to ditch his wardrobe and go to the nearest charity shop to buy another, but you could have put him in a sack and he still wouldn't have looked seedy. So I settled for suave. Even that didn't work. A couple of years later, when the whole affair was long over, I bumped into Len Goldberg at a Hollywood party. He had the grace to admit that he'd made a mistake and that we should have been left to go with Olivier and Howard.

We shot the two pictures on schedule and within the budget and duly delivered both versions, theatrical and TV. They never released them theatrically and they slid out on TV very quietly where they sank without a trace. I picked up a video of one of them a few months ago. It had been cut to ribbons.

One last word about *Foreign Exchange*. De Roth, the publisher who'd asked me to make certain changes in the novel, now demanded a share in the film rights. I told him to go take a flying jump and he threatened to sue. Apparently he was one of those guys, like the late Robert Maxwell, who threatened to sue everyone at the drop of a hat. I met with lawyers of my own who said they didn't think he had a leg to stand on but, win or lose, the case was going to cost me money. So I gritted my teeth and paid. I don't know what happened to de Roth. I just hope it was nothing good.

Me, I went back to Los Angeles to write a TV movie for Aaron Spelling. *Taste of Evil* I called it, which was a bit stupid of me because it was practically a word for word rewrite of *Taste of Fear* (the British title of *Scream of Fear*). I figured enough time had gone by and who the hell had seen the movie anyway. I'd used the storyline before and I'd use it again. It was based on Clouzot's *Les Diaboliques*, just like twenty-seven other movies before and since. It was as if Clouzot had made us all a template. The prime example was *Fatal Attraction* with Michael Douglas and Glenn Close. At least I didn't go so far as to play the finale in a bathtub.

I delivered the script, made a couple of changes for John Moxey, the director, and that was it as far as I was concerned. Then, a week before they were due to start shooting, my agent calls me. Apparently *Scream of Fear* had been last night's TV late night movie. Aaron Spelling, unable to sleep for whatever reason, had stayed up to watch it.

"He says there are similarities between it and the script you've just sold him," said my agent.

"I *did* change the names," said I.

HORROR OF FRANKENSTEIN

starring RALPH BATES KATE O'MARA
VERONICA CARLSON and DENNIS PRICE

Screenplay by JEREMY BURNHAM and JIMMY SANGSTER   Based on the characters
created by MARY SHELLEY

Produced and directed by JIMMY SANGSTER   TECHNICOLOR (R)

A Hammer Production for Anglo EMI   Distributed by Continental Films

Aaron went on to shoot the picture. It was pretty good. Barbara Stanwyck in the role that Ann Todd had played and the whole thing situated in America as opposed to the South of France. And he never held it against me because I worked for him often over the next few years.

I was enjoying myself in Los Angeles when I got a call from Hammer. They were going to do yet another Frankenstein movie. They'd had a script written by a man named Jeremy Burnham but it needed some work done on it, would I be interested in doing the rewrite? I told them I wasn't. What if they let me produce it? Still not interested. Then

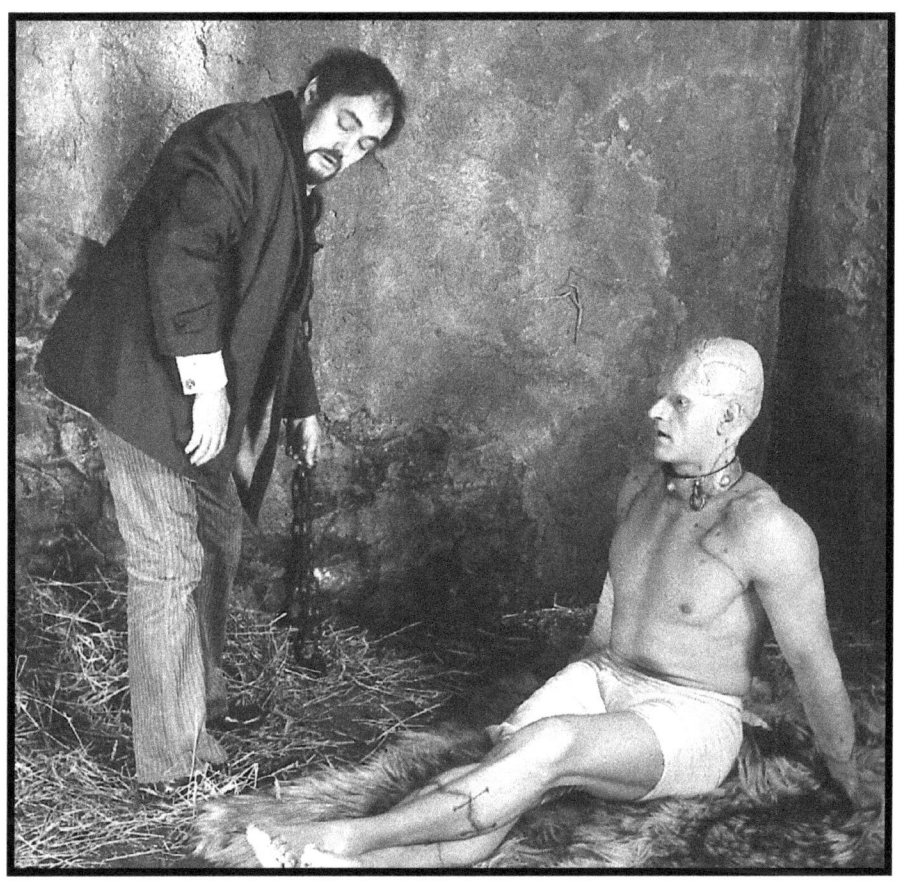

With David Prowse on the set of *Horror of Frankenstein.*

I had an idea. I'd rewrite their script and produce it—providing they let me direct as well. Short pause over the phone. They'd call me back. This they did about an hour later. Deal! The script's in the mail.

Three days later the script arrived. I read it and my heart sank. It was virtually identical to the script I'd written for Hammer umpty years ago, the first Frankenstein movie they made. As far as I could see they needn't have bothered paying a writer to come up with something they as good as owned already. All of a sudden I didn't want to do it any more.

But a deal is a deal is a deal and I duly started to work on the script, trying to bring something different to it. I packed my bags, moved out of my apartment, and went back to London where I eventually delivered my rewrites. They were pronounced acceptable to Hammer. I honestly don't think anybody read the final script. Tony Hinds had quit Hammer, content in the future to just write for them, and Michael Carreras was off doing his own thing. The company was being run by James Carreras, with the help of his long-time assistant, Brian Lawrence, who had been with the company since day one. Neither of them knew anything about production. As far as they were concerned, Sangster was making a *Frankenstein* movie. Let him get on with it.

With Veronica Carlson on the set of *Horror of Frankenstein*.

I had an apartment in the Carlton Tower Hotel at that time which I used as an office. It was there that I did my casting. Everything went fine except for the two major parts, Baron Frankenstein and the Monster. There was no question of using Peter Cushing again because I'd written the part much younger. James Carreras wanted me to cast the actor they'd just used in *Taste the Blood of Dracula*, Ralph Bates. I didn't think he was right and told him so. At least meet the man, said Sir James, who was grooming Ralph to take over the Peter Cushing parts in any number of upcoming movies. Not, I hasten to say, because they wanted to break with Peter, it was just that he was getting a little old to carry off the sex symbol image that Hammer was into selling by now. So I duly met Ralph, was suitably impressed, and he got the part. A couple of days later I cast David Prowse as the monster and we were off and running.

I have to admit here that I have never had such an enjoyable time as I did during the six weeks we were shooting *Horror of Frankenstein*. I loved every minute of it. Ralph Bates became a very good friend and later asked me to be godfather to his son William. The crew were wonderful. We kept to schedule and budget and we never stopped laughing. I read someplace that Veronica Carlson, whom both Ralph and I

David Prowse goes over the script with me on the set of *Horror of Frankenstein*.

lusted after (in an entirely innocent manner as far as I was concerned), said, "Neither Jimmy nor Ralph took the shooting seriously. They had a jolly good laugh."

Indeed we had a good laugh, but we also took the shooting very seriously. At least, I did. I'm pretty sure Ralph did too. Because we enjoyed ourselves it didn't mean we were turning out bad work. Some directors believe that unless the set is rife with fear and tension the end result won't be any good. Reduce the cast to a state of helpless terror so the director can better force his own will on them. Personally, I think that's a load of bullshit. But to each his own. Nevertheless, happy set or not, I am forced to admit that I didn't make a very good movie. I meant it to be lighthearted. It was so lighthearted its feet never touched the ground.

In spite of that, some of the critics seemed to like it. At least they understood what I was trying to get at.

"...tongue in cheek horror."

"...the first hour is not only painless but fun."

And from *Variety*, who really got the point. "Lighthearted."

I think one of the reasons it wasn't as good a movie as it should have been was that there was nobody to keep me in check. I was the writer/producer/director, the closest you can get to being God. Nobody was around to say "you can't do this" or "that doesn't work." James Carreras never saw the dailies and never visited the studio. Maybe I

Filming _Horror of Frankenstein_, Ralph Bates and I became good friends. Top: Dennis Price and Ralph Bates. Below: Ralph Bates and Graham James.

Do You Want It Good or Tuesday?

On the set of *Horror of Frankensten*.

would have spotted all this in the cutting room after we finished shooting, and maybe I could have done something about it. But we'll never know because three days after I finished shooting I went straight onto another movie.

Lust for a Vampire. The title alone should have warned me off. Earlier on in this book I said one of the worst things that can happen to a director is that he be hired when the movie has been cast, the sets built, and they've dotted the i's and crossed the t's in the script. Terry Fisher had been hired to do the picture, but he took sick and really wasn't up to it. Peter Cushing had been cast in the part of Giles Barton, but his wife

DEVILS IN FEMALE BODIES
...whose embrace is the kiss of death for man or woman!

GHOULISH! GHASTLY! GORY!

LUST FOR A VAMPIRE

Starring
RALPH BATES BARBARA JEFFORD SUZANNA LEIGH MICHAEL JOHNSON and YUTTE STENSGAARD [R]
Screenplay by Tudor Gates Based on characters created by J. Sheridan Le Fanu Produced by Harry Fine and Michael Style
Directed by Jimmy Sangster · Technicolor® A Hammer Production for Anglo EMI Distributed by American Continental Films, Inc.

Helen became very ill just about then and he begged off. So Harry Fine and Michael Styles, the producers, checked with James Carreras who gave them the go-ahead to hire me to take Terry's place and Ralph Bates to take Peter's. I wish they hadn't. Not I hasten to say because of Ralph Bates. He might have been wrong for the part but he was the only relief from gloom on the whole picture.

Example. First day's shooting. Interior set at Elstree Studios. The coach drawn by four horses is driven into the school yard where it pulls up.

"Cut," says I. "Print it. Next set up!"

"We can do better than that," came a voice from the back.

It was Michael Styles trying to behave the way he thought a producer should. "You can do better than that then *you* shoot the fucking picture," says I heading for

Ralph Bates and Yutte Stensgaard in Hammer's *Lust for a Vampire*.

the   nearest exit.

End of that particular incident. End also of any rapport between me and the producers.

A producer is perfectly entitled to criticize the director. After all, he hired him and is responsible for paying his salary. But you don't do it in front of the entire crew on the first day of shooting. Also it helps if he knows what he's talking about, which Michael Styles didn't. I don't think Harry Fine did either, but at least he stayed off the set.

I shot a sequence later of a bunch of sexy girls in diaphanous gowns dancing on the lawn outside the house which was supposed to be a finishing school for young ladies.

On the set of *Lust For a Vampire*.

Do You Want It Good or Tuesday?

Lust for a Vampire "is one of the few Hammer horrors to have nothing to recommend it."

The producers said I wasn't moving the camera enough. So I shot it again, moving the camera so much nobody knew where the hell they were. End result, we used the original version, which was what I intended.

I read someplace in an article by somebody called Nicolas Barbano that the reason our star Yutte Stensgaard wasn't a huge success in *Lust for a Vampire* was because it was a weak script, badly directed. I grant you, the script was weak and the direction wasn't all that it could have been, but Mr. Barbano fails to mention the main reason Yutte wasn't a success was because she wasn't a very good actress. A very pretty girl who shouldn't have been in the picture. But then neither should Ralph Bates or, for that matter, Jimmy Sangster.

Johnson and Del Vecchio got it right in their book when they said: "*Lust for a Vampire* is one of the few Hammer horrors to have nothing to recommend it. The film was a low point for the company and is embarrassing—or should be—for all concerned, including the audience."

Forget the audience, guys. They couldn't have felt as embarrassed as I did. As soon as I finished shooting I was hurried off the picture so I had no part in the cutting or scoring. I eventually went to see it at a local cinema, hearing for the first time the dreadful song on the sound track which served to compound the unpleasantness I felt over the whole sorry affair.

Next came *Fear in the Night*. This was a script I had written earlier under a different title. Hammer had bought it but never got around to making it. I reread it and decided

(Top): Judy Geeson, myself, Peter Cushing; (Bottom): with wardrobe mistress Rosemary Burrows on the set of *Fear in the Night.*

My birthday party during *Fear in the Night*. Pictured are Judy Geeson, myself, Roy Skeggs, and Michael Carreras.

the reason they hadn't made it was because it wasn't good enough. I gave it to a writer friend of mine, Michael Syson, to see if maybe he could inject some juice into it, and he came up with the idea of situating it in a boys' boarding school. It was all that was needed. He did a quick rewrite and I gave it back to Michael Carreras who decided that it was worth making. He was back at Hammer now, full time. And very grateful we all were to see him. It wasn't until much later that I discovered he was having serious problems hanging onto the company that his father, Sir James, had tried to sell from right under his nose. For a blow by blow description of what went on backstage, Denis Meikle's book, *A History of Horrors* is an absolute must. There was more horror going on backstage than in front of the cameras.

One of the reasons Michael decided to go ahead with the movie was because he wanted to make a double bill. One of the pictures was called *Straight on 'Till Morning*, to be directed by Peter Collinson, so let's call the other *Fear in the Night*. It was a nice idea and deserved to do better than it eventually did. He also asked me to produce and direct it. Why he did that after the last fiasco, I don't know. Maybe he too realized *Lust for a Vampire* wasn't entirely my fault.

We cast pretty strongly with Ralph Bates in the lead. We persuaded Peter Cushing to come back to work. A sad man now, who never fully recovered from the death of his wife. Not that it affected his performance in any way. He was still gentle and considerate and as sharp as a razor when he needed to be. As the female lead we cast Judy Geeson who had starred in *10 Rillington Place* and, as the heavy, Joan Collins. This was her pre-soap days, and she hadn't worked for some time. This was just as well because we'd never have gotten her for the money we were able to offer. She made a great villainess. Unfortunately she wasn't an easy lady on the set. That could have

Anglo EMI Film Distributors Ltd. present
A HAMMER PRODUCTION

"FEAR IN THE NIGHT"

starring **Judy Geeson · Joan Collins
Ralph Bates** and **Peter Cushing**

as the Headmaster

Screenplay by **JIMMY SANGSTER & MICHAEL SYSON**
Produced and Directed by **JIMMY SANGSTER**
TECHNICOLOR® Distributed by Anglo EMI Film Distributors Ltd.

been because she was pregnant at the time, a fact she'd omitted to mention when we were casting. The first time we knew about it was when the wardrobe mistress came to me and said that none of the clothes she'd bought for Joan a couple of weeks before production fitted her any longer, and, please, would I tell her to stop eating so much. I mentioned it to Joan who told me she was pregnant and what the hell was I going to do about it. As with her general behaviour throughout the shooting, she managed to give the impression she was doing us all a big favor being in our picture. I suppose, in retrospect, she was.

I read in a book on Peter Cushing by Del Vecchio and Johnson that the only real crime in *Fear in the Night* was the casting of Peter Cushing. It then goes on to say that he was the only character to elicit audience sympathy. That seems like espousing two complete opposites. It was wrong to cast him but he's the only good thing in the movie. Make up your mind, guys! The book also goes on to talk about, "this lacklustre script

It's a wrap! End of shooting of *Fear in the Night*.

and Sangster's dull direction merely adds to the ennui."

Talking of ennui, you should trying reading their book. Still, they couldn't have thought all that badly of me. They asked me to write an introduction to their next book, the *Hammer Films*, without which, as I may have already mentioned, I wouldn't even have been able to start this one.

The shooting was pretty straightforward. As usual Ralph Bates and I had a lot of fun which, in retrospect as I said earlier, probably wasn't good for the picture. There are directors who deliberately create tension on a set because they feel that by getting people worked up they will give a better performance. All I know is that on *Lust for a Vampire* there was so much tension I dreaded coming to work every day. If it had produced good performances, it would have been okay, but it didn't. But then on *Fear in the Night*, which was fun, the performances weren't very good either. I think I'm writing myself into a trap here. Fun or not, happy set or miserable, Sangster-directed movies aren't very good. And having dug the trap I guess there's nothing I can do to avoid dropping into it. Sangster-directed movies weren't very good. Not any of them.

But having said that, *Fear in the Night* was an okay movie. Some people liked it a lot. As it happens, I'm not one of them. But that's not because I think it was a bad script badly shot. I think it's because I became disenchanted with this type of subject. As I just said, I didn't like any of the movies I directed. *Horror of Frankenstein* and *Fear in the Night* just missed, *Lust for a Vampire* was a mile off. All, I feel, would have been better had they been directed by Terry Fisher. The only memorable thing about *Fear in the Night* was that it was the last time I worked for Hammer. It was more than 25 years ago.

Darren McGavin as Carl Kolchak from *Kolchak, The Night Stalker*.

Do You Want It Good or Tuesday?

EARTHQUAKES :

Like a great many things in Los Angeles, the expectation is often far greater than the reality. I have been fortunate in that the earthquakes I've experienced have been pretty low on the Richter scale. I missed the big ones. Mine were over almost before I was aware they'd started. Five in the morning, I wake up suddenly to a rumbling sound and a picture falls off the wall.

"Jesus Christ, it's an earthquake."

By the time I've stumbled out of bed and run round the room twice, it's over. Something that has been lurking in the back of my mind, something I've been anticipating for a long time, over in what seems like a second, and I hardly knew it happened. Not unlike my Hollywood career.

Act Two. Scene One.
"What does a story consultant do...?"

I mentioned right at the beginning of this book that there was a life after Hammer. This is where it started. So if you are only interested in my Hammer movies, I guess you can quit reading now. If you're curious about what happened next, read on.

Because I moved to America I missed the decline and fall of the House of Horror. I kept in touch with Michael Carreras. He and his wife Jo spent time with us in Beverly Hills. But I was never really aware of what bad times he was going through, and it is unlikely I would have been able to do anything about it even if I had. But I would have liked to have tried.

All in all, I spent twelve years in Hollywood. I still live in California for the requisite six months a year. It's where my money comes from, where I pay my taxes. I spend more time in London nowadays for a number of reasons. First I like it, second I am married to a lady who likes it as much as I do, and third, there is no longer a need for me to have access to the studios and/or networks. But during the seventies and early eighties Los Angeles was my home base. I became a resident alien, the possessor of a green card, a large house in Beverly Hills, a Rolls Royce and a Mercedes (at the same time), a dog, a condominium at Mammoth Mountain, a Gucci charge account, and an American wife, not necessarily in that order of importance. I worked at all the studios at one time or another, those legendary places I'd dreamed about since I was twelve years old. I became a member of the Writer's Guild, the Director's Guild, the Beverly Hills Health and Fitness Center, the Marina City Club, and the Academy of Motion Picture Arts and Sciences which entitles me to vote for the Oscars each year. It also gets me into a lot of screenings for free both in Los Angeles and London. I'm also a member of the Cinema Veterans Society in England, which also gets me into the movies free. These days, if I have to pay to go to a movie, I don't see it.

Wild horses wouldn't get me to live in Los Angeles again. The place is truly as awful as people say it is. No matter where you live, nothing is closer than twenty minutes' drive away. There are isolated communities which are not quite as awful as the rest, like Beverly Hills, where most of the houses look as though they'd been designed by a cake shop, where each front yard carries a sign threatening trespassers with "armed response," and where the wives of the rich, as opposed to the super rich, drive down to Sunset Boulevard every morning to pick up the cleaning lady from the bus stop outside the Beverly Hills Hotel. But, like Bel Air or Brentwood, these places are little more than plush ghettos. I know because I lived in all of them at different times. I also lived in West Hollywood, which wasn't much fun, and at Marina del Rey, which was. But I'm talking about just Los Angeles. Southern California as a whole is great. How can anybody not like it! The climate, the food, the ocean, the mountains, the desert, it's all there multiplied by ten.

It all started with a job offer. I was in Los Angeles for no other reason than I was dating this lady. Her name was Sandy and she was an ex-air hostess, or sky goddess as they sometimes like to be called, recently divorced from her first husband. She was very pretty, sexy, and a lot of laughs. A blind date where I'd gotten lucky for a change. At least, I thought so at the time.

On this particular trip I'd been in America for around four weeks just enjoying myself. We went to Houston, Texas, to see a friend of Sandy's in a play. We went to New York to stay with another friend. We took a trip to Hawaii just for the hell of it and we went to Las Vegas where Sandy's parents lived. I was staying at Sandy's apartment which she shared with another stewardess who was rarely home because her airline was busy flying American servicemen back and forth to Vietnam. It was a very pleasant apartment, later rented by the unfortunate Peter Lawford. In the apartment below lived Michele Marvin, the common-law wife of Lee Marvin. In fact, right then she was the common-law ex-wife, still desperately trying to get alimony from her ex. Her attorney, F. Lee Bailey, finally got it for her, establishing in law the Rights of Palimony. A victory for law, but not much help to Michele who was awarded around a hundred bucks. One of her complaints against Lee Marvin was he and his buddies drank too much. They lived on the beach and Marvin's kids by a previous marriage would come stay with them. When they complained to him they were bored, he'd tell them to shut up and "go watch the fish fuck."

I had just decided that it was time to pack my bags and go back to London and get a job when I got a call from Tony Hinds in London saying that Screen Gems, the TV branch of Columbia, were calling from LA trying to locate me. I called Mark Lichtman, my LA agent, and told him to check it out. He called back to tell me that Screen Gems had just sold a series to a network entitled *Ghost Story* and they were looking for me to see if I would like to come aboard as story consultant,

Apart from the couple of plays and serials I'd done for UK TV years ago, I'd never worked in television. Never particularly wanted to. Shit, man! I was a movie writer with more than thirty screen credits. I didn't even know what a story consultant did. My agent assured me it was an important job, one step down from series producer and that the money was good.

"But what does he *do*?" I asked, having ascertained just how good the money was. "Don't worry about it. They're lucky to get you. I had to do a big selling job."

"I thought they called me."

"It was still a hard sell."

Do You Want It Good or Tuesday?

Agents! I've had close to a dozen during my career. To hear them tell it, it was solely because of their hard grafting that I ever worked at all.

"Why? I mean why *me*?" I wanted to know.

It seems they were after me for three reasons. One, the executive producer of the series was William Castle, the old time schlock horror moviemaker, who'd once shot a movie called the *Old Dark House* for Hammer and who had later gone on to bigger and better things with *Rosemary's Baby*. He knew me from way back. Two, the head production man for Screen Gems was Seymour Friedman, who'd once misdirected a movie for Hammer on which I was his first assistant. And third, I had the reputation of being able to write scary stuff.

"So you want to take a meeting?" my agent wanted to know.

I took a meeting where I met all the aforementioned, together with the man who was going to be the line producer, the guy who did all the work. His name was Joel Rogosin and he didn't know me from a hole in the ground. Quite understandably, he was a little hesitant to take me on. What did I know about American TV! How many local writers was I on speaking terms with! And who wants a foreigner anyway! But under pressure from the others he finally agreed, providing he could hire a second story consultant to work with me, somebody he knew and trusted.

I wasn't sure I wanted the job. First, I still hadn't found out what a story consultant actually did. I mean, who did he consult with, and about what! Secondly, I knew there would be movie work for me back in England. But, in those days, I liked it in Los Angeles and the idea of staying for a spell was quite exciting. Besides, I'd be doing work that I'd never done before. Who wanted to write another *Dracula* movie or a boring old *Psycho*-type drama! I'd done that. From today's point of view the arrogance of it was astounding. Anyway, the initial contract was only to be for thirteen weeks. There was an option after that, exercisable by either party, to renew for the balance of the year or to call it quits. So I took the job on condition they let me direct at least two of the scheduled twenty-two episodes. They didn't like the idea too much, but eventually they agreed.

After a great deal of trial and error I eventually worked out what the job was about. For the benefit of the uninitiated, let me describe the functions on a TV drama series of the story consultant, also known as story editor. At least, let me describe what they were in America in the seventies. It might have changed by now. I read a great deal these days about staff writers doing most of the work, but even so, there's probably still a head honcho who calls everybody into line and carries the title of story consultant. But in my day, there was usually just the one guy who would take meetings with writers who he thought would turn out a good script for the series. These were usually writers he knew, guys he'd worked with before. Unfortunately I was new in town and didn't know anybody. My agent took care of that. The day I started, there was a note from him listing half a dozen names.

I called him.

"Who are these people?"

"They're writers. You need writers, now you've got writers."

"How do I know they can write?"

"They're clients of mine. Trust me. They can write. And a couple of them could do with the money."

From Hammer Films to Hollywood! A Life in the Movies

129

So, stage one in being a story consultant is you call the writer, tell him roughly what the series is about, invite him to a screening of the pilot, and then you ask him to take a meeting. Hopefully at the first meeting he can come up with a story idea which will fit the series' concept. If he does, the story consultant runs it past the producer who either buys the idea or not. If he buys it then the writer is commissioned and sent off to write a treatment. Subsequently, if everything goes well, he goes on to do the script. If on the other hand, at the first meeting the writer can't come up with an acceptable story idea, the story consultant might give him one that he and the producer have worked out, simply because they want this particular writer to work on the series. And why this writer? Because you know he's going to keep his shooting script within the parameters laid down by the series' concept. If the series stars a character who's only got one leg, it's no good the writer creating a sequence where he runs in the marathon. An extravagant example I admit, but you'd be surprised how far out some of the writers I employed wanted to go.

Having agreed upon the storyline, they would duly deliver a treatment which I, as story consultant, would meet with them on. Maybe I'd ask for a couple of changes, maybe not. I'd suggest a direction for the script, not too much of this, a little more of that, this scene doesn't work, and that one would be better someplace else. Armed with the notes they'd go off and write the first draft. This done, there would be another meeting during which changes for the final draft would be suggested. Three weeks later, hopefully, the final script would land on my desk. The writer would be paid and that, as far as he was concerned, was that. End of job.

If I'd chosen the right man, if he'd followed the notes I'd given him, then it was the end of the job. Dot a couple of i's, cross a few t's and on to Episode Six or Seven or whatever. If, on the other hand, the writer was not the right man, then I was in for some hard work putting the script into the shape we needed. Not necessarily because the script was bad, but because it just didn't fit the guidelines of the series. It could be something silly like a scene turning on the fact that our hero has a couple too many drinks when the character we've established throughout the series never touches a drop. Another version of the one-legged guy in the marathon. So, when you found a writer who you knew would stick to the rules, you were inclined to employ him again. The more he stuck to the rules, the less work the story consultant had to do.

But having explained all that, the first series I worked on didn't have those type of restrictions. *Ghost Story* was an episodic show. Each story was self-contained. There was no running character except for the guy who introduced the show on air each week. The bookends, they were called. I wrote all his stuff. Coincidentally it was Sebastian Cabot, the actor who'd played in my two *Movies of the Week*, and also in the very first Hammer film I ever worked on, *Dick Barton Strikes Back,* nearly twenty-five years earlier.

I remember well my first day at work. Columbia were still using the old studio on Gower Street, the place that Harry Cohn had ruled for so many of the golden years of Hollywood. My office was a grubby little room at the back of the suite of offices assigned to the show. But I didn't care how grubby it was because sitting at my desk I could look out through the window and see the HOLLYWOOD sign. Okay, so I'd been to this town a dozen times already, written a few scripts, but always on a freelance basis. Now here I was, part of the system, and outside my window was the sign to prove it.

I bought myself a Cadillac Eldorado convertible. Red, with white upholstery. Talk about flash! Sandy and I rented Richard Chamberlain's beautiful little house high in the Beverly Hills and we flew to Las Vegas to get married. I keep telling myself that we were going to get married anyway but we decided to do it then and there because suddenly I needed a green card. Get an American wife, fill in the right forms and, for reasons I never quite figured out, have a chest x-ray and a blood test, and the green card followed.

We landed at Las Vegas around 10:00 p.m. on Friday evening and went straight to City Hall to join the all night queue to get ourselves a marriage license. The following day we lined up outside the Little Chapel on the Prairie, built in the parking lot of the Frontier Hotel, where we were duly escorted inside by a girl in a short buckskin skirt and tasseled top designed to show off her tits. There we were pronounced man and wife by a preacher wearing western boots and a string tie. After cracking a bottle of champagne with my new in-laws, who lived permanently in Las Vegas, and my brother and sister-in-law, who'd flown in from Houston, we flew back to Los Angeles where we checked into the Beverly Hills Hotel for a one-night honeymoon. Monday morning I was back at work, and Sandy went house hunting.

Columbia spent a lot of money trying to make *Ghost Story* a good series. The casting director, Rene Valente, got permission to pay well over what was then considered "top of the show" money for actors. This pissed off the other TV production companies, but it got us some great people in our shows. Helen Hayes, Melvyn Douglas, Gena Rowlands, Janet Leigh, Patricia Neal, a whole bunch of actors and actresses who'd never done TV before. The scripts were pretty good and Screen Gems decided to renew my contract for the balance of the year. At the same time the other consultant quit for a better job which left me on my own. They also told me that I'd better pick the two episodes that I wanted to direct. I thought about it and finally I chickened out. They shot everything so damn fast. A one-hour show (around 54 minutes' screen time) in six days. They were so bloody efficient it was scary. And here I was, doing well in the story consultant/writer department. Did I want to screw it all up by directing an episode and taking eight or nine days to shoot it? So I said "no thank you," releasing them from that section of their contract.

What I did do was to direct the bookends. Each episode was introduced by Sebastian Cabot and then wrapped by him at the end. We did half a dozen on location at the Hotel Del Coronado in San Diego and the rest on a set we built at the studio. I also wrote one of the episodes that starred Patricia Neal, which Screen Gems insisted on putting up for an Emmy nomination. It didn't make it. I was also called on to write a pilot script for Screen Gems based on the old radio show entitled *The Shadow*. Why me, I don't know. I'd never even heard of The Shadow. But they paid me the going rate, and as far as I was concerned, it was just like doing another episode of *Ghost Story*.

It was while we were shooting the interiors at Gower Street that Columbia moved to the Warner's lot in Burbank. We left our offices in Gower Street on a Friday night and came to work in Burbank on Monday morning to find our parking places marked out, and our new offices furnished with our old stuff in the cupboards and drawers we'd left it in right down to the half-full file tray on my desk. Would that the series had been as successful as the move.

Traditionally, episodic series don't work in America. The viewer likes a character he can get used to, an old friend he can welcome back into his home each week. This applies to England as well as America, but it's not so obvious in England because shows are never booked for more than six at a time. Then, if they're popular, they'll do another six next year. On *Ghost Story* we were contracted to deliver 22 one-hour shows in the first season. If there had been a second season it would have been for the same number. Sitcoms were bought in batches of 30. Maybe they still are. Anyway, *Ghost Story* didn't work. They took it off the air for a couple of weeks in mid-season and then brought it back without the bookends and with a new title, *Circle of Fear*. Whatever they hoped to achieve by doing this, they didn't succeed. The series limped to a close and, after forty weeks steady work, I was out of a job. It deserved a better fate. It was a good show with good people involved. Everybody, including Screen Gems, spent a great deal of time, money, and effort trying to bring it off. As for me, it was my first nine to five job in Hollywood and I had a ball.

The only break during those forty weeks was an unhappy personal one. I received a call in my office one day from Jo Carreras, Michael's wife, that Monica, my ex-wife, had been diagnosed as having leukemia and was dying. Seeing as my son James, aged 15 at the time, was living with her and the guy she'd married, I had to do something about it. I told Joel Rogosin that I was going to have to take a week off to go to London to sort out a family problem. After throwing a minor fit, Joel accepted the inevitable. I flew to London, hung around uselessly for a week, finally giving James the option of returning with me to Los Angeles or staying in London until his mother died and then coming out to join me. He chose to come right away. It was pretty harrowing visiting with his mother in hospital when most of the time she didn't even know who he was. So we flew back together. A couple of weeks later we got the call from London. Monica had died. James moved in with Sandy and me on a permanent basis. He was 15, she was around 30 going on 12. It was a complete disaster ending a couple of years later in an "either he goes or I go" type ultimatum. James was the one who went, with a vast sigh of relief. Considering what happened later maybe I'd have been better off if I'd let Sandy go.

But, during all this, we finished shooting *Ghost Story*. As I said earlier, it had been fun, and I'd learned a hell of a lot. Joel had been great to work with in spite of his inability to read a script without a pencil in his hand. That may sound like an exaggeration, but I would put a script on his desk and he'd reach for a pencil before putting on his glasses. And he never stopped bitching about my "limey writing and spelling." It's color, not colour. It's check book, not cheque book. Center not centre. And "what the hell does that word mean?"

I'd written in a script about this couple driving along the highway having a row. He isn't looking where he's driving. Suddenly she shouts for him to "look out!" He looks up to see a huge pantechnicon bearing down on them.

I dropped the script on Joel's desk and went back to my own office next-door. A short time later I hear this howl of anguish followed by a request to get my ass in here.

"What the hell is an elephant doing in the middle of the highway?" he wanted to know. It took me fifteen minutes to convince him that pantechnicon was a large removal truck and not a malaprop or typing error of pachyderm.

Then there was Bill Castle, the overall boss who, as far as I could tell, did nothing except be excessively nice to us all. He'd made a name for himself in the old days making very cheap exploitation horror movies. They even made a movie loosely based on him starring John Goodman (*Matinee,* 1993). Then he produced *Rosemary's Baby* and all of a sudden he was big time. I don't think he ever recovered from the surprise. I got on with him extremely well in spite of the fact he did the dirt on me once. He was planning to make a feature movie from the Robert Ludlum novel *The Osterman Weekend.* He'd had a script written and he asked me, as a favor, to read it and make comments. This I did. Bit long here. Could do without that scene. Maybe this character doesn't work. Okay, says Bill Castle, would I mind meeting with the writer and telling him where he's gone wrong. There was no writer's name on the title page, but I said yes anyway. Bill set up the meeting at his house, and two minutes before the writer arrives, he tells me his name. Dalton Trumbo. A long time hero of mine, twice winning an Academy Award (in 1953 under the pseudonym Ian Mclellan Hunter for *Roman Holiday* and in 1956 under the pseudonym Robert Rich for *The Brave One*), the first time he was nominated was in 1940 for *Kitty Foyle.* Writer of more top movies than practically anybody else in town. He would have been right at the top if he hadn't fallen foul of the McCarthy mob and been sent to jail for sticking up for his principles. This man was arriving in two minutes and I was supposed to tell him what was wrong with his script. He duly arrived and I was introduced as a script editor from London who had some suggestions to make in reference to his first draft screenplay. I stuttered and stammered for a few minutes, during which time he listened politely. Then he told Bill Castle that, for the first draft, he had followed Bill's preliminary notes faithfully, even if he hadn't agreed with a lot of them. Now, if Bill insisted, he'd incorporate my notes and write a second draft. But eventually he was going to write his own version and the sooner Bill let him do it, the sooner the script would be ready for shooting. Bill, rather sheepishly I thought, agreed, I asked for Mr. Trumbo's autograph and the meeting came to an end.

Another member of the *Ghost Story* staff was a guy named Rick Blum who is now head of the film school at the University of Central Florida and the author of a book about television and screenwriting which I'd recommend to anyone who thinks they can learn writing from a book. Unfortunately, I don't.

The option of my going back to London didn't apply any more. During my time with Screen Gems we had bought a house. As usual, I bought far beyond my means. This wasn't a difficult thing to do married to a lady like Sandy. The house was in Beverly Hills, high above Coldwater Canyon, built on two city lots with a view all the way to the ocean. There was a 40 foot pool, and a guest house with a bar and a restaurant-sized kitchen. There was room to seat fifty people for dinner. (Which we did on one occasion.) The financial obligation to support the house and the lifestyle that went with it was sufficient to keep me in LA. The immediate neighbors were George Peppard, Richard Basehart, Anthony Newley when he was married to Joan Collins, Vincent Price, Rock Hudson, and Esther Williams. What you might call a plush "retirement community." Apart from Peppard, I think I was the only person in anything like regular employment.

Fortunately, as soon as *Ghost Story* shut down, I found plenty of work. I was now a member of the TV writing fraternity. Some of the guys who had written for me on *Ghost Story* were now story consultants on their own shows and were only too happy to have me do a script for them. Also word had got around that I was one of those writers so beloved by makers of TV drama series, namely reliable, and not likely to rock the boat. If they said they wanted a script where the lead actor breaks his leg and is confined for the whole episode to a hospital bed, so be it, that's what I'd give them. I wouldn't have him climb out of the window or hijack a wheelchair or capture a run-

away gurney. I'd give them exactly what I asked of my writers, no surprises. Sometimes I would come up with the basic story idea, sometimes they would give it to me. And if all this sounds unimaginative, maybe it was, but it was a living. A very good one. And every time you got paid, the company who paid you also paid into your Writer's Guild pension plan and your health insurance.

Then, out of the blue, the Writer's Guild called us all out on strike. I suppose it couldn't have been out of the blue. We must have had meetings and discussions, votes must have been taken. But all I remember is coming home one night after a WGA general meeting and telling Sandy that we were on strike and consequently, up shit creek.

I think the strike went on for around 10 weeks. I may be wrong and I am sure there are people who will correct me if I am. It seemed like 10 months. Every day we had to walk picket outside one or other of the studios or networks. Four or five writers carrying signs outside every entrance. We were there, ostensibly, to stop WGA members crossing the line and going to work. I wouldn't have known another WGA member if he'd bitten me. Apart from that, the vast majority of writers work from home. But there we were, every day, blocking the sidewalk for three-or four-hour shifts. We'd get our assignment from the WGA office over the phone and at 8:30 each morning we'd arrive at the studio we were going to picket that day, ask permission to use their parking lot, park our Cadillacs and Mercedes, collect our UNFAIR TO WRITERS signs, and plod up and down for the next two or three hours. I got to meet a lot of fellow writers during that period. I also got to discover how important the writer is to Joe Public.

Walking the beat outside Paramount Studios one morning, a delivery truck pulls up and a young guy gets out with a delivery for the studio. Polite, obviously a union inclined man, he asks if we mind him crossing our picket line. No problem. In he goes to make his delivery. Ten minutes later, he's out again. He watches us for a moment, pacing up and down with our WGA signs. Then he comes over to me.

"You guys are on strike. Right?

"Right," I say.

"What do you do?"

"We're writers."

"Like book writers?"

"We write TV shows," says I.

He thinks on this for a moment. "Okay. So what are you striking for?"

"Lots of things," says I. "But mostly for more money."

Another pause. Finally, "You mean you get paid for doin' that shit!"

There was another WGA strike I was involved with years later. They chose a different tactic for this one. Instead of having a couple of dozen members outside each studio, they called out the full membership, around three or four thousand, to picket a different studio every day. This was much more enjoyable. We kept getting moved on by the police for obstructing the traffic, the Guild served coffee and donuts, and it was a big social occasion where you got to bump into every writer and producer in town by the end of each day.

The television series *Columbo*, starring Peter Falk, was a top show.

People have asked me, how effective can a writer's strike be? In Los Angeles, it can close down the industry, both movie and TV. The guilds wield a lot of power in this town, none more so than the writers. The Director's Guild could close down shooting if it wanted to, so too could the Screen Actors Guild. But neither of them ever have. The WGA, on the other hand, at least while I was in Los Angeles, were ready to strike at the drop of a hat. A more militant bunch I've yet to come across. Admittedly a writer's strike doesn't close down anything that is shooting at that moment (unless it requires rewrites). What it does is give the studios no material to work with. A theatrical movie can be postponed or delayed, but if a studio has committed to delivering a TV series, it's got to do just that. No scripts, no show.

The new TV season starts around September. By the time the first episode goes on the air the network likes to have about four or five complete episodes in the can. To be sure of this the producer has to start shooting in early May. And to start shooting in early May he needs to have at least four or five scripts ready. Seeing as he doesn't get his order for the show until late March, having four scripts ready in what amounts to around five weeks is quite a job, particularly if the writers go on strike at the same time.

Eventually the strike was settled. The minimum fee was raised by a few dollars. The producers agreed to pay a larger contribution toward the WGA pension and health

I scripted several *Wonder Woman* episodes starring Lynda Carter.

plans. Everybody breathed vast sighs of relief and the writers delivered the scripts they'd been working on quietly over the past few weeks. And I went back to work.

I've always been a quick writer, and word of this had got around. So with everybody desperate for scripts I was in demand.

"Do you want it good or Tuesday?" I'd ask the prospective buyer.

They always wanted it Tuesday. I tried to give it to them good as well. Or at least adequate. Truth be told, the work was pretty easy. As I've already mentioned, the lead

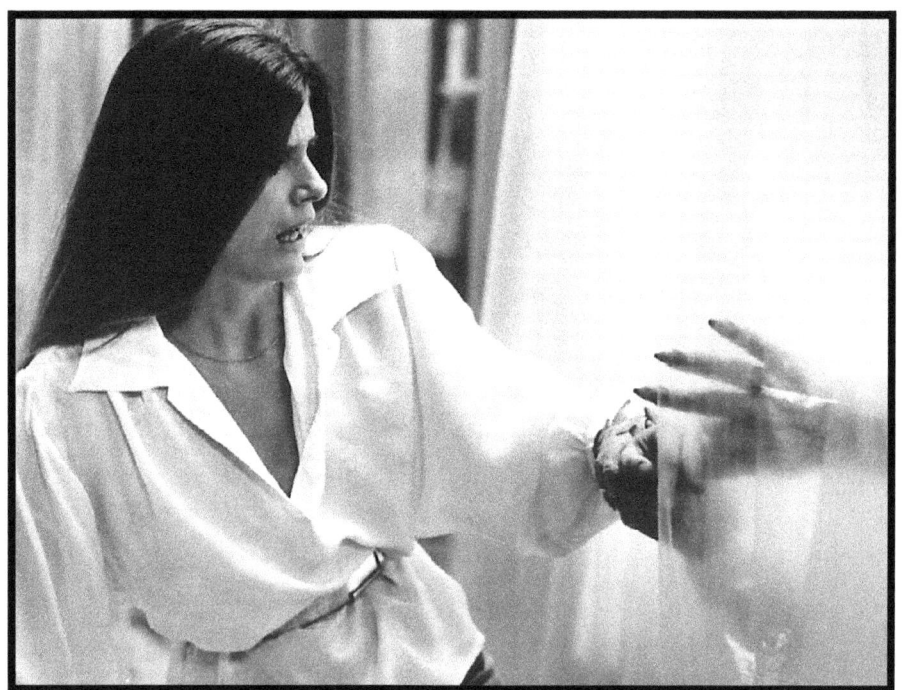

The Legacy, **starring Katharine Ross, was critically not well received.**

characters were well established and the producer and/or story consultant would give you a rough idea of what the story requirements were. I found myself writing for two or three shows at the same time, none of which ever proved a problem.

I wrote just over one hundred hours of prime time television in total. Some of the shows I liked, some I couldn't have cared less about. *The Night Stalker* with Darren McGavin was a cut above most. *Columbo,* of course, was a top show. Then there was *Six Million Dollar Man.* I was reading an interview with Steve Bochco recently in which he said he had spent his formative years writing for *Columbo* and *Six Million Dollar Man.* We all did. We also wrote for *Wonder Woman* and *Banacek* and *McCloud.* I wrote two or three episodes of all those shows. When Joel Rogosin, who'd been my boss on *Ghost Story,* took over *Ironside,* I worked for a short time as script consultant on that, also writing a couple of episodes. I wrote for *Cannon* and *B. J. and the Bear* and *The Magician* and *S.W.A.T.* In fact, looking back from here, I figure if it was on the air I probably wrote an episode sometime or other.

And someplace in there I found time to do a couple of movies for TV. Bette Davis came back into my life peripherally in a movie of the week I wrote called *Scream Pretty Peggy.* Then I did one called *The Billion Dollar Threat* for a producer named David Gerber. He must have been satisfied with it because he asked me to do another called *Once Upon a Spy.* This was designed as a pilot and starred Ted Danson with Christopher Lee playing the villain.

I also found time to write another couple of theatrical movies. One was called *The Legacy* starring Katherine Ross and Sam Elliot with Roger Daltrey playing a small part. The executive producer was Arnold Kopelson who, according to *Variety,* is "one of

The studio's graphic design promotion for *The Legacy*.

the preeminent film producers of the '90s." Even I have to admit he's got some pretty heavyweight credits including *Platoon*, *The Fugitive,* and *Seven*, good movies all of them. But he still owes me from way back then. The line producers he hired to do *The Legacy* wanted some rewrites which they weren't prepared to pay me for. I made a deal with Kopelson himself that I would do them in exchange for two first-class return airplane tickets LA/London. I did the rewrites and heard nothing. Then, one night in Chasens restaurant I spot Kopelson and I send him a note via a waiter reminding him he owes me the two tickets. He sends a note back. He didn't like the rewrites and, as far as he's concerned, he owes me zilch. Eventually he got the rewrites he wanted because he hired another couple of writers. I still think the basic script of mine was

***The Legacy* was originally scripted as set in Detroit, not England.**

a good one, but somewhere down the line, when the other guys were brought in, and Richard Marquand was taken on as director, the whole thing became a mess. I looked the picture up in one of the film guides and, at the risk of infringing on somebody's copyright, let me quote you the potted review it was given by a gentleman named Paul Taylor. "A typical loony English-country-house horror from the pen of Jimmy Sangster, which dumps its statutory American leads into a hardly stirred plot of diabolic conspiracy—and slowly congeals..."

Unfortunately I don't disagree with Mr. Taylor one little bit. In the original script I wrote all the action took place in a rundown hospital in downtown Detroit. God only knows where the English country house appeared from. I'd given up on them years before.

I also wrote a movie that John Huston directed and, I'm sure, wished he hadn't. It was called *Phobia*. Again, I believe my original concept was better than the end result. It certainly couldn't have been worse. I see by a credit list that I am sharing credit with two other writers. Invariably when there are three or more writers on a script the end result is a mess. *Phobia* was no exception.

I also sold a project to Disney. Years before I'd written an original script for Hammer entitled *The Fairytale Man*. It was specifically designed for Vincent Price to star in, a truly delightful man both on and off the screen. To this day I believe it was one of the best scripts I ever wrote. But, for whatever reason, Hammer was never able to get it off the ground. Now I fished it out of my bottom drawer and had my agent send it to Disney who immediately made an offer. I called Michael Carreras in London and asked if I could buy the script back. He agreed and I duly sold it to Disney. They, for whatever

Paul Michael Glaser in John Houston's *Phobia*.

Assistant devil Barney Satin (Bill Cosby) reveals his true colors in *The Devil and Max Devlin*.

A new high
in being low down

The Devil
and
Max Devlin

their main goal is swiping soul

WALT DISNEY PRODUCTIONS PRESENTS THE DEVIL AND MAX DEVLIN
Starring ELLIOTT GOULD, BILL COSBY, SUSAN ANSPACH, ADAM RICH
Introducing JULIE BUDD Co-Starring SONNY SHROYER, DAVID KNELL
Story by MARY RODGERS and JIMMY SANGSTER Screenplay by MARY RODGERS Music for Songs by MARVIN HAMLISCH
Roses and Rainbows Lyrics by CAROLE BAYER SAGER "Any Fool Could See" Lyrics by ALLEE WILLIS
Produced by JEROME COURTLAND Executive Producer RON MILLER Directed by STEVEN HILLIARD STERN TECHNICOLOR®

reason, had it completely rewritten. They retitled it *The Devil and Max Devlin* and cast Bill Cosby in the part originally designed for Vincent Price. I never saw the movie so I can't say if it was good, bad, or indifferent. What I can say is that it couldn't have been as much fun as my original script. And it's not often I say something like that.

Then Joel Rogosin called me and said he'd taken the job as producer on a new series and would I like to join him as script consultant. He'd guarantee that I could write at least three of the episodes, which was a recognized way of subsidizing one's weekly salary. Not that I ever complained about my weekly salary. I always thought it was very generous.

I wrote the "Mary Ellen" 1979 episode of *B.J. and the Bear* starring Greg Evigan (right in case you couldn't guess) and Bear.

The series was called *Most Wanted*. It was another cop show to be made by a producer named Quinn Martin, who was very successful at the time having at least two series running on different networks. The show was to star Robert Stack as the head man of a team of special cops who ran down the most wanted criminals of the day. Let's face it, there wasn't an original idea in the entire concept. Joel and I wrestled with ideas. I wrote an episode, and we had a couple more in the pipeline when Joel upped and quit. At least, he told me he quit. I believe he was fired. In Hollywood parlance he either ankled (walked off the job) or was axed. In either case he probably collected a handsome cut-off payment. I was busy packing up my stuff when Quinn Martin asked me to stay on. Apparently the new producer didn't have his own script editor and quite liked the work I was doing.

I was still trying to make up my mind whether to stay or not when I received a call from an old friend, Leigh Vance, asking if I'd like to go to England and write a pilot based around Formula One Grand Prix racing. Apparently he'd been asked, but for whatever reason, he didn't want to do it. I told Leigh I'd call him back. Then I told Quinn Martin that I wanted to quit. I'd come aboard with Joel Rogosin and I honestly didn't feel I could stay on now that he had left. Quinn was sorry, but he said he understood. He offered to give me two weeks' money as a settlement of my contract. Much to the annoyance of my agent, I turned it down. To this day I'm not sure why. It must have been guilt at abandoning a sinking ship, because the *Most Wanted* ship most certainly did sink eventually. I read a review of the series much later. "What starts as a serious police drama becomes totally conventional and eventually hilariously inept."

Maybe if they'd kept Joel as the producer it would have turned out OK. Who knows!

As soon as I'd cleared my desk, I called Leigh back and told him I was ready to make a deal. Leigh was an Englishman I'd known way back who had come to Hollywood a couple of years before I did. In fact, I could have come at the same time. A top American TV producer named Bruce Geller had come to London looking for writers. He'd interviewed a number of people including Leigh Vance and my agent had made an appointment for me to see him. I remember arriving at his office and being asked to wait. At fifteen minutes past my appointment time I started to bitch. After half an hour, I bitched a little more and left. Leigh was obviously seen on time because he and a couple of others got the jobs and went to Hollywood. I worked for Bruce Geller much later as script consultant on a cop show starring Jack Palance. Geller was a nice man and extremely good at his job. He was killed in an airplane accident a few years later.

I made the deal with the people in London and off I went, with Sandy in tow. I attached myself to the Formula One team run by Max Mosely, The March Team. I went to their works and to their practice runs and finally to Silverstone for the British Grand Prix. It was all immense fun and I came up with a couple of pretty good story ideas.

The concept was, and still is, a good one. The series was to follow this fictional Grand Prix team around the circuit from country to country. The same central characters, with good guest shots in each episode. The whole Grand Prix set up is little more than a circus. The team performs, wraps up its stuff, travels to the next venue where it performs again. It's not unlike the tennis circuit, the same guys and girls playing the same opponents in a different country every other week.

But good concept or not, the series never made it off the ground. I delivered, and was paid for two scripts and a couple of story outlines, but nothing ever came of them. The one memory that sticks with me about the whole venture happened at Silverstone on the big day. Halfway through the race Sandy, who was extremely bored by then, asked me who was winning.

"Lauda," I told her. Nikki Lauda was world champion driver at the time.

"WHO'S WINNING?" she yelled at me.

Since that day I've heard that story attributed to a number of people. The ultimate urban myth. But take my word for it, this was the first.

We came back to Los Angeles and I started trolling for work once more. I wrote for half a dozen, all eminently forgettable series, and I got myself the ultimate Hollywood status symbol, a business manager. This is a guy who takes five percent of what you earn and is supposed to make your money work for you. Mine took the five percent and kind of made my money work for me inasmuch as he set up a good pension plan for which, right now, I am extremely grateful. Unfortunately he also invested a large amount of my spare cash in Las Vegas property before the boom. Take it from me, there's more than one way to lose your money in Las Vegas. The real bonus that came from this association was that I got to meet his assistant, Ruth Alley, the lovely lady who eventually took over the running of my affairs and whom, to this day, I would trust with my life as well as my money.

I get a call from my agent—would I go see a guy who was producing a series about a couple of truck drivers down South. He'd heard about me from Joel Rogosin and perhaps I'd like to meet with him to see if we hit it off and, if so, whether or not I'd be interested in coming aboard as his story consultant.

I remember bitching to Sandy. Who wants to get tied up with a series about a couple of truck drivers! I want to write something important, something meaningful.

"Like another episode of *Wonder Woman*?" said Sandy, who could be pretty sarcastic when she put her mind to it.

So, as I wasn't doing anything else right at that moment, I went to see the man. And that took care of the next three or four years of my professional life.

My big scene (it ended on the cutting room floor) in *Young Dan'l Boone*.

Do You Want It Good or Tuesday?

I'm the producer. I get a call very late one night from the hotel manager where the unit is staying. Seems the restaurant staff wanted to empty the night's garbage into the garbage tip out back but they couldn't because there was a girl's body in the tip and the manager thought I'd like to know in case I wanted to do anything about it before he called the police. I dragged the production manager out of bed, figuring he was the guy who ran the unit and if any bodies had to be identified, he'd be the one to do it. In our robes we joined the two night cleaners who were still waiting to dump their garbage, not at all put out by the sight of two female legs sticking up vertically from the depth of the tip. I persuaded the production manager, under pains of losing his job if he didn't, to climb into the skip and see if, God forbid, this was anything to do with us. It was. She was the local girlfriend of one of the crew and fortunately she wasn't dead, she was just slightly bruised. She was also stoned out of her head, having been dumped in the skip by the crew member she'd been partying with whose wife had suddenly arrived on a surprise visit from LA.

Act Two. Scene Two.
"No surprises please..."

Ernie Frankel was the man I went to see. He'd been hired by a company called Dantoni Weitz to produce the second year of a series called *Movin' On*. Apparently the first-year producer had screwed up and they were looking for somebody new to take over. Ernie had been at a party a couple of evenings before where he had bumped into Joel Rogosin. He was wondering where the hell he was going to find a reliable script consultant and Joel, bless him, had suggested me.

"An Englishman! On a series about two American truckers down South! You're crazy!" said Ernie.

"Are you looking for somebody who knows about scripts or somebody who knows about trucking down South?" Joel wanted to know.

Ernie admitted to the former and called my agent.

Ernie Frankel is a Southern gentleman. He's also Jewish, so when Ernie says, "Y'all have a nice day, you hear!" he means it. He'd joined the US Marines at an early age, fought in WWII, worked his way up through the ranks to Colonel. It seems I was fated to work with ex-colonels, first Jim Carreras, now Ernie Frankel. He'd been recalled for Korea and again briefly for Vietnam. When he retired from the military, he'd written two novels and then gone into the TV business as a scriptwriter and consultant. He wrote for every show in town, finally becoming a producer on the highly rated show *I Spy*, unfortunately just before it was taken off the air. This, incidentally, is a natural progression in American TV. Ninety-five percent of series producers have come up through writing. I did it myself later. Unfortunately I didn't have Ernie's military background. When I started producing for American TV, it would have been a welcome asset dealing with some of the people I had to.

Ernie had been taken on by Phil D'Antoni, the movie producer who'd made *The French Connection*, and Barry Weitz, his partner in TV. His brief was to produce 16 one-hour shows, all to be shot on location, starting in West Virginia then going to Baltimore,

Washington D.C., North and South Carolina, and a dozen more places, and finishing up somewhere around New Orleans.

The show had been on the air the previous season and had pretty good ratings, good enough to get the renewal. Problem was the costs had started to run away with themselves, and unless the budget was brought under control, then D'Antoni and Weitz would be in deep shit. The network paid a fixed license fee for each episode, the balance of the money had to be found by the production company, pre-selling second and third runs, and syndication rights. So, as a clean sweeping new broom, Ernie Frankel had been brought aboard. The original idea was for Ernie to control the show from the MGM studios in Culver City while another guy went on the road with the unit as a "line producer."

But all this I found out later. Whatever Joel Rogosin had told him about me, Ernie wasn't going to commit himself until he was quite sure. So at the first meeting he discussed the series in general, gave me a rough story idea, and commissioned me to write a script. Before I could even ask whether he wanted it "good or Tuesday," he told me Tuesday. I did it Tuesday, and obviously I did it good enough to convince Ernie that I knew what I was doing. He wanted me to start work the following day as script consultant with a series contract and, if I could find the time, I could earn a few extra dollars writing a couple of episodes myself.

So I duly moved into the offices at MGM studios and Ernie and I started to interview writers. We saw half a dozen guys, all of whom we knew from old, and not one of them came up with a decent story idea. So we took a couple of days off from meetings, and Ernie and I blocked out the bare bones of twenty stories. Our budget allowed us to get twenty scripts written although we were only going to shoot sixteen. This was standard practice in the industry to allow for the odd lemon which could turn up however hard you worked. Then we called the writers back in, gave them a story idea, and sent them off to write the treatment. In a few cases it was fine. The treatment was okay and they went on to write the first draft screenplay which I'd go over with them, make a few small changes, and they'd go off and write their final draft. But, as I just said, this was in a few cases only. Mostly the scenario would run something like this.

We'd give a storyline to the writer. A week later he would return with the treatment which had absolutely no bearing on the storyline we'd given him. With *Movin' On* this was particularly disastrous. We'd give the writers a storyline that we were scheduling to shoot in, for instance, Hendersonville, North Carolina and they'd write a sequence where the guys run out of gas in the middle of the desert. A slight exaggeration perhaps, but it amounted to the same thing, unworkable treatments. So, I'd go over the treatment with them, dragging them back to where we wanted them and finally, after two or three hours, they'd go off and start on the first draft script. Same problem. Somehow the desert had crept back in. Or maybe now it was Yosemite National Park. Or one of our two heroes had developed a drinking problem. I'd spend as long as a day meeting with them over their first draft, trying to pull it back so that it fitted into the series concept. Then I'd send them on their way to do the final. They would eventually deliver, collect their check, and, as far as they were concerned, that was that. Then I'd rewrite the bloody thing from page one.

I must say here that there were three or four guys who turned out first class work. Any of you out there reading this will know who I'm talking about. And to you lot, many thanks, you made my life a lot easier. But the rest! Forget it.

A couple of weeks after the cast and crew disappeared to Washington D.C. to start shooting Episode One, Ernie had to fly out to take care of a couple of things. They were already hopelessly over schedule and budget. He fired the road producer, the transportation captain, the prop man, and the assistant director. When he couldn't find anyone in Los Angeles to take over a show that was going to be on the road for six months, he was stuck with having to take over himself. This meant I was left on my own to take care of providing him with scripts while the post-production work had to be handled by the editor Art Seid, a tough old guy who had worked with Ernie for years and who knew more about the business than practically anybody. As for the two executive producers, I never even met Phil D'Antoni, who lived and worked in New York. The other, Barry Weitz, was the "on the spot" guy. I don't know why he bothered.

Eventually I got tired of rewriting the scripts from page one then typing the title page "Episode Nine by Charlie Farnsbarnes." So I cut out Charlie and all the other Farnsbarnes and wrote the bloody things myself, which I was doing anyway. Only now, I stuck my own name on them. I think out of the sixteen shows we shot, I wrote around ten of them. What I do remember is that I made a hell of a lot of money that year and Ernie was perfectly happy with the scripts I was sending him. While basically an episodic show, in that our two heroes were in each episode, at least the locale was different every week. They would drive into town in their eighteen wheeler, get involved in some local dispute, sort it out, and drive off into the sunset for the fade out. Good, clean family entertainment.

On a couple of occasions I flew out to join the crew for a few days to catch up with some on the spot rewrites. That way I got to see New Orleans and a whole bunch of places that I only thought existed in movies like *Deliverance*. There was one evening when the local cop who had been assigned to the crew drove Ernie and me into the boondocks where he was going to pick up his monthly supply of moonshine. We seemed to drive uphill into the forest forever. He stopped the car after about twenty minutes and we sat there in total darkness until somebody flashed a light at us from further up the track. The cop told us that if he hadn't got the signal we wouldn't have gone any further for fear of getting ourselves shot by the guy whose moonshine still we were bound for. We drove for another ten minutes until we arrived at this old shack where we sat on the verandah drinking moonshine, which is pretty foul, and swatting at fireflies. Meanwhile our host, who had a beard down to his navel, sat in his rocker strumming on his banjo while his son, a twelve-year-old mentally retarded boy wearing nothing but soiled diapers, stomped out the rhythm.

After the first four weeks on air, the show was getting the kind of ratings that these days would have got it instant renewal. The two leads, Claude Akins (nice guy) and Frank Converse (pain in the ass), played well together and the audience loved them. At least, the middle American audience loved them. East Coast or West Coast, forget it. They weren't into shit kickin' unless Burt Reynolds was doing the kicking.

Then, as usual, the rush started. We had three shows ready for airing when we first transmitted. By the time those three had aired, we had two more ready. That's when the problems start. The network aired one show a week. It takes, on average, five weeks to complete an episode. After about seven weeks on the air there's a good chance you're going to run out of shows. That's when you start to pray that the president might be assassinated or war declared, anything, just so long as the timeslot for your show is pre-empted that week and you get a breathing space.

But we made our schedule, the show ran its sixteen episodes and the network, in their infinite wisdom, decided not to pick it up for the following season. I said a temporary goodbye to Ernie Frankel and went to work at Fox.

Bruce Geller was executive producer on a show produced by Leigh Vance. They were well into their season, but were having script trouble. Would I come help out. The show was called *Bronk*. It was a cop show starring Jack Palance. I wrote a couple of episodes, edited a few more and left. I didn't even get to meet Jack Palance. That came much later.

Ernie Frankel called me. He had moved to Fox just after me. The studio had just sold a series to CBS entitled *Young Dan'l Boone*. Would I like to join him as producer of the show. He would be the executive producer while I took the crew off to hell and gone to shoot the series. It sounded like it might be fun, which only goes to show how easy it is to con yourself.

The head of Fox TV at the time was a man named Sy Salkowitz, an ex-writer/producer, now trying to make a name for himself as big wheel executive. To the best of my knowledge, he never made it. Certainly he didn't make it at Fox. His assistant, whose name I've conveniently forgotten, was a man with maximum aggression and minimum talent. The only thing I really remember about him was that he was enamored with the history of the Navaho Indians and, I firmly believe, was definitely pissed off that Fox was going to make a period, open-air drama about Daniel Boone and not about the Indians. On reflection, maybe they'd have been better off to go with the Indians.

We started work, as always, with high hopes. Ernie had already shot a presentation reel, a glorified trailer, based on which the network had ordered the series. So by the time I came aboard, the lead cast was already set. Young Dan'l Boone was to be played by a guy I'd never heard of named Rick Moses. His girlfriend was played by a pretty little girl named Devon Ericson and, just so we'd be politically correct, there was a character played by a very tall black guy. He played a trapper who kept bumping into Dan'l Boone way out there back of beyond. Umpty million square miles of unexplored, uninhabited territory and they were forever tripping over each other.

We had a script editor, David Harmon, whom both Ernie and I had worked with before and we made the mistake of employing his daughter as local casting director. Hang in there and I'll tell you why it was a mistake later on.

While the first four scripts were being put together and the crew being hired, Ernie and I went to Knoxville, Tennessee where we intended to shoot the whole series. We were heavily wooed by next-door Kentucky, which wanted our business. They sent a helicopter for us and gave us a quick one day tour of the state, including a flight below the rim of the Cumberland Falls. Very impressive. Frightening too.

Ernie and I scouted the general locations around Knoxville. They were magnificent. The Great Smoky Mountains, acres of forest, hills, lakes. An hour's drive out of town could be like driving back two hundred years. We checked in with the local police and were assured of full cooperation while we were shooting. We checked out the accommodations, bearing in mind that if the series went the whole way, the crew were going to be down here for six months, and finally we drove to the nearest Indian Reservation to check out the availability of locals we could use as extras. We'd already been warned by Fox's labor relations people that Indians should only be played by Indians. And seeing that Daniel Boone was forever getting mixed up with or fighting with or partying with one tribe or another, we were going to need a lot of Indians on the set.

The local community leaders at the reservation assured us there would be no problem getting as many Indians as we needed.

We flew back to Los Angeles to complete the final pre-production work and a couple of weeks later I flew out with the main part of the crew and set up shop in the local Howard Johnson Motel, where we took over an entire wing and where we started getting down to the serious business of getting ready to shoot.

The first episode was a story about a slaver, a trapper who'd decided there was more money in trapping Indians and selling them as slaves than there was in beaver skins. Whether or not anything like this ever happened way back

Stars of *Movin'On*: **Claude Akins (nice guy) and Frank Converse (pain in the ass).**

then, I don't know, but it was an okay story to kick off with. For it we needed around twenty-five reasonably healthy Indians whom we were prepared to pick up from the reservation, put up in our hotel for a week, feed them, pay them good money, and return them home at the end of shooting. So on July 4th weekend the Harmon girl and I drove over to the reservation having put an ad in their local newspaper a few days before. We arrived at the appointed rendezvous on time. After half an hour we figured we'd come to the wrong place. I checked the address in the ad. Right place, but no Indians. Finally, almost an hour late, four overweight guys turned up. They were very polite. They told us they didn't think anybody else would be coming along because, quite honestly, everybody on the reservation was too busy making a great deal of money off the tourists. The only reason this quartet had turned up was they were keen film fans and they didn't mind slumming it for a few days if there was the faintest chance they might get themselves a one-way ticket to Los Angeles and a life in showbiz.

And that was it. Four fat Indians. I called the labor relations people at Fox and told them what had happened and that I was going to have to go elsewhere. We went to the University of Tennessee in Knoxville and got us twenty good looking young guys who were only too happy to be made up as Indian braves. On screen they made far better looking Indians than the Indians. And, believe it or not, the day we started shooting the Equal Rights for Indians people, or whatever they called themselves, descended on us like a ton of bricks. How dare we employ white men and make them up as Indians when the place is teeming with the real thing. I told them to get twenty to teem in my direction and I'd use them. Needless to say, nothing happened.

The balance of the crew checked in and suddenly it was first day of production. To celebrate the occasion the head guys from Fox flew in. They even got out of bed early enough on the first day to be on location as the opening shot was set up. A long shot of a file of manacled Indians being led by the slaver and his men across the side of a mountain; they go out of sight, and into big foreground suddenly steps Dan'l Boone. He reads a couple of tracks and he's off after them. At least, he was supposed to read a couple of tracks. Rick Moses, the young actor whose first starring part this was, looked at the tracks, wondered a while whether they were in fact tracks, if so were they Indian tracks, and that being the case, were they the tracks of the Indians he was supposed to be tracking. By the time he'd read the tracks and taken off after the Indians, they could have been in New York. Ernie Frankel gave me a nudge and told me to go have a word with the director. I dragged the director aside and asked him to shoot it again and tell Rick to give it a shade more urgency. But this is the first day's shooting, everybody's nervous, "so be gentle with the kid," I said. "Hey Moses!" yelled the director, loud enough to be heard in Nashville. "The producer wants you to get a fucking move on for Christ's sake!"

A couple of episodes later I get a call from Ernie in LA.

"The kid's terrible. He's got to go."

The "kid" in question was Rick Moses. Young Dan'l Boone himself. The star, for God's sake!

I had to agree with Ernie. The kid was pretty terrible. I hadn't realized just how terrible because way out there in Knoxville we never got to see any dailies. Not a foot of film had we seen, whereas in LA, Ernie and the Fox honchos had been exposed to the stuff every day.

This was a huge decision to make. It would mean reshooting everything we had done to date. But, urged on by Ernie, they'd bitten the bullet. I was told to go tell poor Rick Moses he'd been fired. This I did and within a couple of hours he and his wife were on the plane back to LA. The crew got two days off before Ernie arrived with three young actors to test. One of them was the son of Paul Newman and Joanne Woodward who later died of a drug overdose.

The tests were shot. Ernie and the actors flew back to LA and a couple of days later Ernie called me with the name of the new star of the series. Rick Moses. The network had dug their heels in and insisted we reinstate him. He flew back into Knoxville like a conquering hero, and remained as series lead until the show was eventually canceled, something that he was largely responsible for.

Another memory I have is when we were shooting Episode Four or Five, I get a call from the location, around ninety minutes' drive away. "Better get over here. Somebody's been shot!"

Maybe it's one of the lead actors, I thought hopefully. That way the series will be canceled, the insurance will pay up, and we can all go home. Which was a pretty good indication of what a shitty time I was having by then.

I arrive on the location to discover that it wasn't one of the cast. Not even one of the crew. One of the prop men had recently cleaned one of the rifles we were using and the ramrod had broken off in the barrel. He'd put the gun aside to deal with later. But there had been a panic on the set and the assistant prop guy had been sent scrambling for a couple of rifles and grabbed up this one by mistake. In shot Rick Moses had fired it towards the camera, narrowly missing the director, and hitting a spectator who was standing behind the barrier we'd erected to keep out the public. The twelve inches of ramrod had whacked into him like an arrow, fortunately missing his heart, but doing a lot of damage everywhere else. When I arrived they'd already carried him off to hospital where the doctors were even now trying to get the ramrod out of his chest. I called Fox in LA who sent down a team of lawyers and that was the last I ever heard of the situation.

One of the directors talked me into playing the part of a British redcoat officer in one of the episodes. I flatly refused at first, but he kept at me, on and on. A nice guy and a good director so, mainly to keep him happy, I finally agreed. I was fitted with my white wig and red coat, I learned my lines, and I eventually played one scene with Jeremy Brett who was the guest star in that particular episode and another with Rick Moses, who had started speaking to me again by then. I thought I was quite good, but the episode ran five minutes too long when it was cut together so I wound up on the cutting room floor. The next time I had actors complain to me about their scenes being cut I was able to tell them that in this business nothing was sacred. It had happened to me and I was the bloody producer.

The series turned out to be a real ball-buster to make. One of the problems was that I would get directives from the studio, over Ernie's head.

"How come you didn't finish the river location yesterday?"

"Why did you rewrite the penultimate scene without checking with us?"

We didn't finish the river location because it got dark and I rewrote the penultimate scene because it didn't work on the location the director wanted to use. No problem. Things like that happen every day on location. But how the hell did the studio know about it before I'd even had time to talk to Ernie, who was based at the studio in an office a hundred yards away from the executive block. We finally worked it out. The Harmon girl called her father in Los Angeles every night to tell him about the events of the day. David Harmon was our script editor based at the studio. He was also a personal friend of Sy Salkowitz, the overall boss man, and David would pass on the information.

Another problem was that every location seemed to be around two hours' drive from the motel. The crew would climb into their bus around six-thirty every morning and stumble out around eight-thirty that evening. Working as hard as they did, their time off was extremely important and they made full use of it. The hotel bar had to hire extra staff and a whole bunch of local groupies attached themselves to various members of the crew. This could lead to problems when family members decided to fly in from LA to spend a few days with their beloved.

Ernie took over the local chores for a couple of weeks to give me a spot of time back home where I went to the studios every day and worked on the upcoming scripts. When I returned to Knoxville it was to find that Ernie had moved the whole crew to a motel on the other side of town on the basis that we seemed to be doing most of our locations in that direction and it saved us getting caught in the rush hour every day. It didn't make any difference. It still took us up to two hours a day to get to the locations, and the new motel wasn't as comfortable as the original one. The morale of the crew, not particularly high at the best of times, sank even further and there were mumblings of wanting to quit. I knew just how they felt. But, in the end, nobody needed to worry. We were just into shooting Episode Eight, when the show opened on air. The first week it kept its head above water, the second it was wallowing, and by the third it had sunk without trace. The network pulled the plug. The studio told us to finish up the current episode and call it a day. We paid everybody off, packed our bags, and all went home. I'd like to say I left a lot of pleasant memories behind me, but I can't.

Mary Peach

WANTED: SCREENWRITING TUTOR.

Recently I saw an ad placed by the University of Bournemouth in England for a teacher of screenwriting. It was a six-month contract, so it wouldn't affect my American/British residential status. I applied, sending them my CV. They asked me down for an interview. They also asked five other people, guys and girls, who were half my age. They stuck me at the end of the list of interviewees which meant I had to hang around for three or four hours. I took a walk around the campus. A grim looking concrete place. I decided, after fifteen minutes, that I didn't like the place, that screenwriting can't really be taught or, if it can, I'm not the person to do it. And, although I hate to admit it, I figured the reason they'd placed me at the end of the interview queue was because they thought I was too old for the job. So I went home and wrote this book instead.

Act Two. Scene Three.
"On the road again..."

My marriage with Sandy started to go wrong. It didn't so much "start to go wrong" as collapse around my ears. An attorney who lived a couple of houses up the hill from our place called one night and told me if I didn't know what was going on between him and my wife, I was an ignorant asshole and a liar to boot. I admit to the ignorance. Seems they'd met while jogging and one thing had led to another. Sandy admitted to the affair. I've learned since that time that she positively thrives on drama. If there isn't any laying around she'll whip it up herself. Anyway, she moved into an apartment, one of a small block of six we'd bought as an investment, while I stayed in the house. Later, when we had started talking again, albeit a trifle warily, we swapped over. I got the apartment, she got the house which was what she was really after in the first place.

I only bring all this up as an excuse for lapses of memory that may occur during this section of the book. I find trouble in putting jobs in their correct sequence. Did I make *Concrete Cowboys* before or after *Ebony, Ivory and Jade* and where did *Murder in Music City* slot in, was it before or after *Good Against Evil*? So rather than grope around trying to organize the time frame, I'll just deal with the movie in question and the hell with which came first.

Ernie was to make a pilot, *Murder in Music City* starring Sonny Bono. He had already pitched the idea to the network and he now invited me aboard to co-write the script and line produce the show. We moved into offices at the old Gower Street Studio, where I'd originally started on *Ghost Story*.

Sonny Bono's girl friend Suzy was hired as the co-star. She was both beautiful and extremely pleasant. And it's no good looking for her name in the credit list, because she isn't there. A couple of weeks before we were to start shooting, Leo Penn, father of Sean, who was our director, came to us and said that there was no way she could handle the part. Bottom line, she just couldn't act. Immediate panic! What are we going to tell Sonny. Not so much what, as how. He was a partner in the project and we were going to have to tell him his girlfriend was out. Eventually Ernie told him. Sonny took it like a man. If she's not good enough, screw her! Get somebody else! A true pro in every sense of the word. We got a young lady named Lee Purcell. But before we were able to settle on Lee, Ernie, as executive producer and co-owner of the show, had a battle royal with the network. They wanted "stunt" casting, and as Sonny's live-in girlfriend, Suzy had fitted the bill. When she was dropped the network suggested she be replaced by a lady who, it was rumoured, had slept with the Kennedys. They gave up on her when we objected and gave us a long list of girls who had slept with other famous people. Finally they zeroed in on a young lady named Barbi Benton. While all this was going on we were only days away from sending director and crew to Nashville to look for locations. The network kept up the pressure by threatening to pull the plug and not reimburse Ernie for around a hundred grand he'd already spent. Finally he went to an early morning meeting with the network who presented him with the ultimatum. Barbi Benton or no show. Ernie politely declined and walked out. He made it as far as the door before they realized he wasn't bluffing. They let us go ahead with Lee Purcell.

There was a love song needed in the final picture and Sonny wrote one which he presented to Ernie. Ernie, who's got a tin ear, didn't even look at it. He sent it straight on to our music man Earle Hagen for his opinion. Earle called and said we must be nuts. The song was truly dreadful. It began "We knew that they'd come far from the dead bugs on their car."

This presented a small problem to Ernie. Sonny had been decent when we fired his girlfriend and he'd stood by Ernie in his fight with the network over casting. Ernie didn't want to hurt his feelings so he asked Earle to call him and find some gentle excuse for not using his song. We didn't find out until much later what Earle had told him, "Sonny, I can fart a better song that that."

When the network first screened the show for their top people, they congratulated us on getting some of the top country music stars to perform cameo roles. Among them was a young girl, on her way up. The network didn't like "the blonde girl who sings that dreadful song." They suggested that we reshoot it with somebody else and they'd pick up the cost. Ernie, as was his wont, dug his heels in, insisting the girl was going to make it and the song was going to get in the charts. The network backed down and the girl stayed in, as shot. It was Barbara Mandrell, and the song was "Sleeping Single in a Double Bed." Maybe that won't mean much to non-followers of country music, but the aficionados will understand.

At the same time as we were making the pilot, NBC ordered four one-hour episodic scripts as part of the package. I wrote two and Ernie wrote two. All I can remember is that mine were called *Murder in Las Vegas* and *Murder in Monte Carlo*. The latter was based around the Monte Carlo Grand Prix. Never being a person who threw anything out, I recycled one of the ideas I'd had for the earlier Grand Prix series. Waste not, want not. I needn't have bothered. We made the pilot but that was as far as it went.

We shot the whole thing in Nashville, one of the many times I worked in music city. It aired eventually and quietly slid into obscurity while Sonny Bono went on to become Mayor of Palm Springs, then Congressman Bono in Washington. Who knows, he might make president one day! He wouldn't be the first bad actor to make it to the White House.

Meanwhile my marriage had slid even further downhill. The lawyers were already at work racking up their bills and we also had the shrinks. At one time there were three, all going at it at the same time, hers, mine, and ours. I'd spend an afternoon a week bitching to some disinterested guy who kept telling me I was very angry. I didn't need to be paying $50 per hour to know that. Meanwhile Sandy was doing the same to a lady shrink except she didn't have to worry about the $50 per hour because I was paying it and one day a week we pitched up *a deux* in front of yet another mindbender. I realized that I was paying one group of professionals, the lawyers, to organize the break up of the marriage at the same time as I was paying another group, the shrinks, who were working to piece it back together. Crazy! But what the hell, this was Beverly Hills.

To provide a change of scenery, I rented myself an apartment at the Marina City Club at Marina del Rey. It was rumoured that they wouldn't let you into the place unless you had jogging shoes, roller skates, a tennis racquet, and a broken marriage. I had the latter and I quickly acquired the rest and started to enjoy myself. I mean, how could you not! The place was like a rabbit warren, crammed with single guys and girls all looking for a good time. I learned to play tennis, I jogged a bit, I learned to disco dance, and all in all, I behaved like a complete twit. But it was a lot of fun.

My agent, Mark Lichtman, called me. Two years earlier I had written a spec script which I was rather fond of. *Leave it to Harry*, it was called. Mark had put it on the market in the usual way but it hadn't lit any fires. Finally, an independent producer who shall be nameless for the moment, took a one-year option on the piece. It wasn't what I wanted, but what the hell, I was working on all kinds of other stuff at the time. I accepted the option money and got on with my life. Exactly one year later the guy asked for another year's option. I'd practically forgotten about the script. I let him have the second option for the same amount of money. Dissolve to right now, end of the second year. Mark calls me. The guy wants to take the option again. This time I said no. If he couldn't get the project off the ground in two years he was flogging a dead horse. I told Mark to turn him down and put the script on the open market again. Mark talked me out of it. I pocketed the third option payment and went on about my business. Two weeks later I get another call from Mark. Seems that a bunch of Italian money men in New York were putting up some money to make a movie. They'd got a script and they wanted to know from Mark whether Joe Sargent, a director he represented, would be interested. Mark told them he'd check it out, but first he'd have to read the script. They had their LA office deliver him a copy. After all this it doesn't take three guesses to come up with the title of the script that landed on his desk. *Leave it to Harry*.

Mark calls me, fit to bust, accusing me, among other things, of making deals behind his back. Me, I'm lily-white innocent, and I tell him so. He gets back to the Italians. How come they're planning to make a movie from a script they don't own? Sure we own it, we bought it six months ago. Paid a lot of money for it. We bought it from the guy Jimmy Sangster sold it to.

Seems what had happened was that my guy, the one who'd taken the options, needed some ready cash to invest in a studio project down south so he'd sold my script to the Italians, forging my name on contracts assigning him all the rights. Mark calls him. You want to pay Jimmy Sangster his full contract fee or you want to go to jail? The guy didn't want to go to jail, but he didn't have the necessary amount of money to buy me out. Seems the studio project down south had gone belly up. I finally accepted around two-thirds of my original fee and a lien on a hot dog stall he'd just opened in Beverly Hills to cover the balance. Bad move. Two weeks later the hot dog stall went under. They're not big on hot dogs in Beverly Hills.

There's an extra sting in the tail to that story which didn't turn up until many years later. I was in London at the time when Mark called me from Los Angeles. Did I want to send the guy to jail, because he'd just done the whole scam again. He's telling everyone it's the first time, terrible error of judgment, all that shit. It just needs me to blow the whistle. I couldn't be bothered. So, all you aspiring writers out there. If a guy in LA offers to take an option on your spec script, be very careful. Check him out. As a last resort, call me, and I'll tell you if it's the same guy.

While all this was going on, I wrote a *Movie of the Week* for Ernie called *Good Against Evil*. Part of the deal he'd made included the services of a co-producer, a formidable lady named Lin Bolen, so there was no room for me on the production side. No big deal! The money was good, the script was no problem to write, especially as Lin Bolen had it rewritten after I'd delivered it. I can't even remember who got the final credit. Maybe we shared.

A lot of people say what does it matter about the final screen credit? Especially if the picture was a non-event anyway. But it is only by getting an onscreen credit that you get residuals. And in LA, residuals are really something else. Providing you have sole credit on a reasonably successful show you can expect to double or treble your initial fee. The residuals are proportioned according to the number of writers up there on the screen. This used to lead to a lot of shouting and screaming until the WGA came up with their arbitration rules. Any time there is a dispute about screen credit, the whole thing gets turned over to the Guild who set up groups of four or five writers to pass the final judgment. I was called on to arbitrate a number of times; every member of the guild is. You get sent every word that has been put to paper during the writing of the script. The original story idea, the first treatment, the second treatment, the first, second, third, and God knows how many other screenplays and, of course the final shooting script. None of these have any names attached. The writers are identified as A, B, C, etc. You get a list that tells you writer A did the original treatment, A and B worked on the first draft screenplay, C came in to do the rewrites on the second draft, and D worked with A on polishing the final. A wants a shared screenplay and separate story credit, B wants at least a half screenplay credit, and C thinks he deserves the whole enchilada. Now, in your considered opinion, how should the onscreen credits read? The main problem I found in working on arbitrations was having to read five or six versions of the same script while wondering how the picture had ever got past first base originally.

The next work I did was also for Ernie. I did a script rewrite and came aboard as producer. It was called *Ebony, Ivory and Jade*. Straightforward, simple, well tried characters. A couple of girl entertainers, one white, one black, are employed by this secret service guy, Nick Jade, to do undercover work. The girls were played by Martha Smith, who tried incredibly hard but who had very little talent, and Debbie Allen, who didn't have to try at all because she positively oozed talent. Typically, the network loved Martha but couldn't stand Debbie, who later went on to become a big-time dancer and a Tony award winner in New York. Martha, bless her, sank without trace. The male lead was played by Bert Convy, a reasonably big TV name, and we had entertainers like Frankie Valli doing guest shots. John Moxey was hired to direct. We shot on location around Los Angeles and then we went to Las Vegas for a week.

Any problems I'd had with the crew in Knoxville, Tennessee were nothing compared with Las Vegas. We were there a couple of weeks, working in the Aladdin Hotel and out in the desert. The people at the Aladdin were cooperative providing we didn't interfere with their main business, namely fleecing the tourists. Trouble was, everywhere we tried to shoot we collected our own group of rubberneckers who, as long as they were watching us, weren't gambling. So everybody lost. The casino because they weren't gambling and us, because they were getting in our way. I fired the lighting cameraman for being drunk on a night shoot on the roof of the hotel where we were trying to land a helicopter in a high wind. He insisted on being accompanied by a little hooker he'd picked up. The hotel told us that, because of insurance regulations, only crew were allowed on the roof and either she went or we all went. The cameraman refused to be parted from his new love, so he went. Fortunately the camera operator was able to take over. I fired the production manager for not managing the production. I got lucky there too. Ernie hot-footed it down from LA to take over. I then found myself in the position of having to check which hat he was wearing at any given moment. If he was wearing his production manager hat, I could yell at him and give him orders. If he was wearing his executive producer's hat, I'd be the one *getting* the orders.

Next on the agenda was a two-hour movie for CBS called *Concrete Cowboys*. It starred Tom Selleck and Jerry Reed playing a couple of drifters in the urban South. It was shot in and around Nashville. Jerry Reed, who'd played virtually the same part in dozens of movies, was big in Nashville. Through him the production was able to grab a whole bunch of country western stars to do guest shots. We also shot a sequence at the Grand Ol' Opry.

We delivered the final print to the network who professed to like it a lot. That's it, we thought, we're going to get a series order. We started to get some scripts together. Then the network came back to us. Sure, we like the piece, we love Jerry Reed, but we don't like the big guy with the mustache, he slows the thing down. Get rid of him. We argued back and forth and finally Ernie said screw you and he took the show to another network. They liked it too, but get rid of the big guy. By the time all the to and froing had finished, our option on Tom Selleck had expired. Immediately, the first network announced that he was going to star in their new series *Magnum P.I.* As a sweetener for us they gave us an order for a few shows with Jerry Reed and some other guy to replace Tom Selleck. I can't even remember who he was. We shot the four episodes and another potential series bit the dust. To this day, the network denies this took place. But I was there.

Ernie went on to shoot another pilot down South, a cop show starring Claude Akins called *Nashville 99*, which went to four episodes. I wasn't involved in this one because I was busy elsewhere.

Mark called me. "A guy named Ron Lyon wants to see you. Says he knows you."

I didn't know Ron Lyon from a hole in the ground. As for what he wanted to see me about, he'd just got an order from ABC for a series based on Ripley's *Believe It or Not*. Would I be interested in writing some of the pieces and then taking the first unit out on the road with the star, Jack Palance, and directing the segments I'd written. I'd never done any documentary type work in my life. Why me, I wanted to know? I've been good friends with Ron now for more than 15 years, and to this day the only answer I've got was that my agent, Mark, did a good job of selling me. If he did, it was the only time then or since.

Me (center) and Jack Palance (right) on location in Cremona, Italy filming *Believe It or Not*.

But at the time, it sounded like it could be a lot of fun. This time, "on the road" didn't mean North and South Carolina, it meant London, Paris, Vienna, Venice, Amsterdam, Madrid, Lisbon, Copenhagen. I was busy falling in love at the time with a lady who lived in London so, apart from anything else, this job would put me 6,000 miles closer.

As you know by now, the new lady in my life (she still is) was an actress named Mary Peach. She'd starred in a good few English movies in the late sixties and seventies, she'd done a great deal of television work in England and she'd starred (above the title) with Rock Hudson in the Hollywood movie *A Gathering of Eagles*. She has fascinating stories to tell about Hollywood. Her husband was a business partner of Douglas Fairbanks, Jr. and through him when she came to LA she was introduced to Peter Lawford. These were the days when he was pimping for the Kennedys. I hasten to say he didn't try fixing Mary up with a date, but he did invite her to a party for Bobby Kennedy, where Nat King Cole was playing the piano. At dinner she sat at a table with Jack Lemmon who told everybody at the table to laugh when he gave them the cue, that way the rest of the party would think they were having a wonderful time. Later, Kirk Douglas made a play for her but gave up after ten minutes saying there was nothing he disliked more than an intelligent broad. Mary sat most of the evening out on the

Jack Palance, host of *Believe It or Not*.

stairs talking to Marilyn Monroe. She decided that Marilyn was a very sad young lady. She was right. It was a week later Marilyn killed herself. When I first met Mary, all that was a long way back in her life. Right now, she was going through an unhappy divorce. She had two children, a daughter Joanna who was 14 and a son Andrew, aged 16. Two of the most delightful people I've ever met. Just like their mother. Not long after we met, Mary came on a trip to Los Angeles. She took one look at the set-up I had going for me at the Marina City Club and announced that if our relationship was going to blossom, we were going to have to find someplace else to live. So we bought a condominium in Bel Air. And we're still living happily ever after.

From Hammer Films to Hollywood! A Life in the Movies

159

Me (left) and Jack Palance (behind pig) in Burgundy, France.

I checked into the *Believe It or Not* offices just off La Cienega and met a couple of the other executives, Jack Haley, Jr. whose main claim to fame was that he was the son of the man who co-starred as a tin man or scarecrow in *Wizard of Oz*. Either would have been a recognizable parent for Jack Junior. He had been briefly married to Liza Minnelli and he'd put together a couple of archive-type movies about Hollywood. The other man I met was Mel Stuart, who was hired to supervise the post-production work. I'd been briefly involved with Stuart earlier when I'd rewritten a *Movie for Television* for a producer named Chuck Fries. Mel had been hired to direct it. The movie was never made, which wasn't all that surprising because the whole thing took place in Venice. Venice, California it might have stood a chance, but Venice, Italy, forget it! Mel and Jack Haley had been taken aboard to oversee the Hollywood side of the series, while Ron Lyon took up residence in Paris complete with wife Linda, two sons, three dogs, and their Los Angeles maid. From there he was to act as executive producer and supervise the production units.

I wrote a couple of pieces and ran them past everybody I could find before presenting them to the powers that be. I'd never written anything like this before and I had no idea how good, bad, or indifferent they were. It seems they were good enough. I got a pat on the head and sent off to write another twenty-five. Meanwhile others were writing pieces for the second unit which was going on the road with a lady host and yet another for a third unit who were responsible for dramatic reconstructions.

I met Jack Palance one day at the office. A formidable man if ever there was one. Just as menacing as he appears on screen and twice the size. He scared the life out of me. How was I to know he was going to be such a pussy cat?

A week before we were all due to meet up in Paris, I took off for London to spend a few days with Mary. Then we both flew to Paris to meet up with everybody else. My crew were all Dutch, under the command of lighting cameraman Andre Gunn. They were a good bunch of people, which was just as well as we were going to be living in each other's pockets in 12 different countries over the next 14 weeks. Or maybe it was 14 countries in 12 weeks. It became very confusing. The only American on the unit apart from Jack Palance and his girlfriend was a lady called Joan Kahn. Formerly a secretary to Alfred Hitchcock, she had some wonderful stories to tell about the old guy. But right now, she was with us as script girl, cash dispenser, and "make sure you get to the airport on time" person.

We had three days of meetings in Paris before flying to Copenhagen and then on to Arhus in Denmark to shoot a piece about mummified bodies. From there to Rotterdam where we shot a piece about Van Meegeren, the famous art forger, to Luxembourg to shoot the hopping festival of St. Vitus, followed by a day at the Maginot line, and finally to Amsterdam where we had a day off. That was week one.

It went on like that for the next 12 weeks. Things that stand out in one's memory are the mundane. Following Jack Palance down endless airport corridors. The night he told us the story of how he was starring in a movie opposite Charlton Heston. Jack played a rogue red Indian and Heston the hero. During the shooting Jack had become very friendly with the real Indians who had been cast as members of his tribe. Apparently they adored him. Big climatic scene, a fight between Jack and Heston which Heston is supposed to win. But Jack couldn't lose face in front of his new fans who kept cheering him on. The only way they were finally able to get Heston to win that fight was in the cutting room. Another memory, in Venice, Jack poling a gondola with me and the camera crew trying to keep our balance in the same gondola while he spouted the lines I'd written about how Venice was drowning. The Italians on the numerous water buses recognized him as they swept past yelling "Ola, Jacko!" and each time he felt honor bound to wave back at them. The only thing that came near to drowning that day was us.

I also remember having quite a few rows over the phone with the rather unpleasant, not particularly talented, highly dictatorial Mel Stuart in Hollywood. Sometimes it was because he didn't like the stuff I was shooting but mostly it was to bitch about Ron Lyon. These two guys positively loathed each other, and it is because of this and the fact that Ron contractually wasn't allowed to leave Paris for LA to sort things out, that he eventually lost the show, even though it went on shooting for another four years. Mel Stuart and Jack Haley got rich, Ron Lyon didn't. On reflection, it was probably just as well Ron wasn't able to confront Mel Stuart personally. He'd probably have killed him.

As for me, after twelve weeks, I said enough of the directing, but I'd be happy to stay on as a writer if they were interested. They stayed interested for about ten weeks, during which time I lived in a suite at the Hotel Raphael in Paris and flew to London each weekend. I always knew this was going to be a job with great fringe benefits. But all things come to an end and eventually I ankled or was axed, I'm not sure which. On second thought, I am sure. It was too good a set-up for me to ankle, so I must have been axed.

At Hotel Del Coronado, San Diego, California

Do You Want It Good or Tuesday?

Dear Jimmy,

Here, at last, are four copies of the contract covering Russian language publication of your novels Snowball *and* Hardball.

I can't tell you how pleased I am by this sale. It's not much money but it's a new frontier.

EXTRACTS FROM A LETTER FROM MY AGENT (May '94)

Dear Jimmy,

You are, of course, entitled to an explanation regarding the non-payment of   Russian monies.

Here's what I know: the Russian publisher who acquired your books has been murdered.

I understand that the mob has... a strong foothold in Russia...

...so I don't think we should threaten to cancel the contract.

Act Two. Scene Four.
"Man-eating fish..."

Just after I returned from Europe, Irwin Allen, the producer who'd made blockbusters like *The Poseidon Adventure* and *Towering Inferno,* decided he wanted to dabble in TV. I was summoned to his presence at Burbank Studios. Would I be interested in developing this idea he had for a *Movie of the Week*? As with everything he put his hand to, it was to be big and spectacular, probably the most expensive movie made for TV ever contemplated. I said I thought I would be very interested, please tell me the idea.

"Man-eating coelacanths attack San Francisco," he said.

I didn't want to appear completely stupid so I felt my way very carefully.

"And I always thought a coelacanth was a prehistoric fish," I said. I didn't add "silly me," but it was self-evident in the tone of my voice.

"It is," he said. "Thought extinct for two hundred and fifty million years. Now suddenly they come marching out of San Francisco Bay, eating everything that gets in their way."

"Fish?" says I.

"Man-eating fish," says Irwin.

"Sounds good," says I.

I wish I'd kept a copy of the script I wrote, I truly do. I can't even begin to remember what happened, who they ate, who or what saved San Francisco and finally sent them back to extinction. All I can remember is that I was very well paid by Columbia, who was financing Allen, and that the film was never made. Be thankful for small mercies.

That remark "wish I'd kept a copy of the script" crops up more and more these days. For a time I kept copies of the old movies I wrote, the *Dracula*s and *Frankenstein*s, but eventually I dumped even those. I've been told that an original copy of the script of the first *Dracula* movie I wrote, complete with my penciled corrections, would be worth a lot of dollars right now. Somebody who's supposed to know about these things gave me a figure. It was five times what I was paid for writing the script in the first place. But I didn't keep any of them, just like I didn't keep a copy of Irwin Allen's fish saga.

My only other memory of Irwin Allen was to do with my place of work. I took the initial meetings with Irwin and we thrashed out a treatment which was acceptable to him and to Columbia. They told me to go ahead with the first draft screenplay. I immediately packed my overnight bag and caught a plane to London where I'd rented a small *pied a terre*. Then, just to be polite, I dropped a note to Irwin telling him where I was and that I would deliver the first draft in three weeks, give him one week to make his notes, and be on his office doorstep at Burbank Studios exactly four weeks from today. The moment he got the note he calls me. He tells me he's employed all the top writers in Hollywood and always they were available to be at his office within an hour of his calling, and if I didn't get my ass back to LA pretty damn quick, fifteen different brands of shit were going to hit the fan. To add weight, he had Columbia business affairs people on the phone at the same time. So I repacked and went back to LA, where, as promised, I wrote the first draft in three weeks, delivered it, and, one week later, presented myself on his office doorstep. Not once did he call me in the interim. In spite of that, Irwin was a nice guy.

There had been a hugely successful TV series in the sixties, *Route 66*. Now, the guy who'd made it, Bert Leonard, got one of the studios interested in doing a remake. His idea was to use the two original actors, whose names I've forgotten, but who were now very middle-aged gentlemen. I worked long and hard over that one. Bert was definitely a hands on producer, one of those guys who makes you wonder why they bother to employ a writer in the first place. The one thing he had going for him was he loved a game of tennis. Every time I went to a script meeting at his house, I took my tennis racquet. He wasn't very good, but then neither was I. Between sets I finished the script, everybody announced they were extremely happy with it, and that was the last I ever heard of the project.

Looking back on what I've written so far in this book, it reads like I wrote a hell of a lot of stuff that never got made. I've learned that around eighty percent of scripts are never made. I'm not talking about the spec scripts that everybody and his brother is writing. The percentage there is around ninety-nine point nine. I'm talking about scripts that are commissioned by reputable, viable production companies and are paid for. I wasn't aware of this until I came to Los Angeles. I remember once, when I was still writing for Hammer, I was in Los Angeles at a party and I mentioned that I'd written around twenty-five movie scripts.

My host, who was a writer himself, wagged a finger at me (they do a lot of that in LA). "But how many of them were actually made into movies?"

I didn't know what he was talking about. All of them were made into movies. That's how it was in those days. A producer would come to me and ask if I'd like to write this, that, or the other script. I'd write the script, they'd pay me, and they'd go make the movie. What was the point of writing a movie that nobody was going to make? At least, that's how it was with me. I was so shocked when my first bought and paid for script in Los Angeles just didn't get made, I nearly gave them their money back. Now I was used to it. And with subjects like man-eating coelacanths and middle aged roadies, I'm grateful too.

Do You Want It Good or Tuesday?

Around here I wrote a couple of TV moves that were made. *No Place to Hide* was a rehash of a couple of my old Hammer subjects. I don't remember much about it except that it was directed rather badly by John Moxey and the other was for a company which was run by Peter Guber and John Peters. They wanted to do a movie starring Mr. T., the monolithic, gold-draped guy from *The A-Team*. We came up with a story where he runs a downtown gym for deprived kids etc., etc. and is persuaded to enter a competition to find *The Toughest Man in the World*. I wrote it. The director didn't like what I wrote and had it rewritten and it was shot. I don't often say this but they would have been far better off going with my script. At least they would have saved the money they had to pay the second writer. I read a potted review years later. "A comedy drama designed purely as a vehicle for a star who can't act and isn't required to do so."

I believe he's since become quite a star in English pantomime where acting isn't a prime requirement.

Just to keep the balance straight, the same people who employed me on *Toughest Man* which was made, also commissioned me to write a political satire which wasn't. The movie *Trading Places* had done very well at the box office and they wanted to use a similar idea where the black cleaner in the senator's office gets the job of Senator by mistake and confounds everybody by doing it well. They also wanted him to move into the Senator's house, and maybe, just perhaps, they'd be able to get Denholm Elliott to play the butler. I have to admit that, over the years, I have borrowed ideas from other people, but at least I've had the good manners to be as subtle about it as possible. These days a writer come up with an original idea and the executives will shake their heads.

"Don't think we should make that. Hasn't been done before. How about we re-make so and so?"

But I wrote their script for them and, thankfully, it was filed away and forgotten.

Meanwhile, I wrote a novel. It had been around fifteen years since I had written my last and I thought it was about time I tried again. I called it *Snowball*. I came up with this English guy, James Reed, an ex-cop who lives in a house on Malibu beach given to him as a divorce settlement by his super-rich film star wife. I found him a fun character to write and eventually, when the novel was published by Henry Holt in New York, so did a lot of other people. *The New York Times Book Review* said: "...this is a very nice job, smooth, sharp, believable, well written." Another critic said it was: "...crammed full of sex, drugs, and Hollywood. A bright evocation of La La Land. Welcome Mr. Reed, come back soon."

Who could resist such an invitation? Over the next couple of years I wrote a follow-up called *Blackball* and a third called *Hardball*. Same character, different situations. I thought, still do, they were very entertaining books of their genre. Trouble is, very few people agreed with me. Let me rephrase that, trouble is my publishers didn't agree with me. In the first instance books aren't bought, they have to be sold. The publisher's rep has got to get his act together and the publisher has got to be prepared to put a little muscle into the sales campaign. If he doesn't, the book shop just ain't gonna buy the product, and if the book shop doesn't buy, the reader won't even know the book exists. Same problem as I had with my first group of novels.

In fact, I wrote a fourth book in the series which I called *Fireball*. This time I decided the best way to make the publisher get behind the finished product was to get him to pay such a large advance that he'd simply have no choice. Either the book sells or he loses his shirt. Maybe it would have worked for Elmore Leonard or Ed

McBain, but not for Jimmy Sangster. They refused to increase my advance, my New York agent told them to take a jump, she'd sell it elsewhere. That was four years ago. As far as I know, my manuscript is propping open her office door. The three that were published went into half a dozen different languages. Two of them even sold to Russia. But I'm not pressing them for the money.

The nearest I came to making any proper money with the James Reed books was when a TV company bought an option to make a series based on the James Reed character. It seems that Pierce Brosnan just might be interested in taking the part. He was just coming off a very successful TV series of his own (*Remington Steele*) and this company thought he could possibly be persuaded to dive head first into another. Wrong! He didn't, their option lapsed, and that was that. Mr. Brosnan went on to become James

Bond number whatever, while my books are still available. All rights have reverted to me, but it's not going to do me any good because they're all out of print now and I'm not lending my copy to anybody.

I wrote (or rewrote) a script for Ernie Frankel about this time called *Northbeach and Rawhide*. The Northbeach of the title referred to that lowlife section of San Francisco where the winos, druggies, and tourists hang out, and the Rawhide was the name of a fictional bootcamp for young offenders run by an ex-cowboy, played by an ex-spaceman, William Shatner. One of the kids was played by Christopher Penn, Sean's brother. He's a good actor. Maybe not quite as good as his brother, but then very few people are. As TV movies go, it didn't break any records. But at least it was made.

I was wondering what to do next when I got a call from London. Brian Hutton, the American who had directed *High Road to China* and *Where Eagles Dare*, among

HARDBALL

A RINEHART SUSPENSE NOVEL

Jimmy Sangster

By the author of SNOWBALL and BLACKBALL

many others, had been signed to direct a movie based on a book by Jack Fishman called *And the Walls Came Tumbling Down*. The story was a true one. During WWII a precision bombing raid had been mounted on Amiens prison in France where the Germans were holding, along with all the petty criminals, a number of French resistance fighters, spies, and saboteurs. The raid was designed to bring down the outside walls of the prison allowing these people to escape, without killing any of the occupants in the process. A script had been written which wasn't very good and they wanted a major rewrite. It would have to be done in London, and it would have to be done quickly. Also they wanted two versions. A two-hour version for the theatres and a four-hour version for TV.

Do You Want It Good or Tuesday?

I came to London, met with Hutton who almost immediately left to scout locations in Romania. This was before the downfall of Ceaucescu, so why they wanted to go there God only knows. I started work on the script. The problem with a project like this is whether to write the four-hour version and then abstract the two, or write the two-hour version and then build it to four. Which is more important, the movie or the TV? I wrote the movie version first, on white paper, then added another two hours using blue paper. The finished script looked like a Christmas streamer. I wish I'd kept a copy. It was an interesting exercise. I say "exercise" because that's all it turned out to be. It was never made.

Before I could escape back home to Los Angeles, two things happened. I met a Norwegian producer named Stein Monn Iversen who wanted to do a TV series about Vikings. Was I interested in developing a storyline for him spreading over 13 one-hour episodes. If I was, would I please come to Oslo and we'd talk about it. I went to Oslo, we talked, we visited a number of Viking sites, I bought some books on Vikings, made a deal, and came home. At the same time Mary was cast in a play on Broadway so we moved to New York. I rented a typewriter, we borrowed an apartment on the West side close to the Lincoln Center, Mary started rehearsals with Peter O'Toole, and I started typing.

We had a good time in New York. We'd play tennis in the morning, lunch out, then Mary would catch the bus to the theatre and I'd hammer at the typewriter. The only hiccup I recall was on our first weekend there. We hadn't yet organized the apartment and were staying at the Gramercy Park Hotel. It was Easter. We'd watched the parade on Fifth Avenue, had some lunch, and Mary had gone to the theatre to rehearsals. I walked back to the hotel, around twenty blocks. I was almost there, ambling along 23rd Street, watching the kids with their balloons when this well dressed, tidy looking black guy comes up behind me while I was waiting for a crossing light and tells me he's gonna blow my motherfuckin' head off. Not "gimmee your money or I'll blow etc., etc." No option, he's just gonna do it. For some reason I can't explain I became very English all of a sudden. "I'm terribly sorry, you can't do that. I turn off here."

And I turned off down Lexington to walk the last two blocks to the hotel. The bastard followed me. He followed me right into the lobby of the hotel where he watched me collect my key and disappear into the elevator. To this day I don't know why I didn't tell the hotel clerk as I collected my key that the guy standing at the entrance behind me is "gonna blow my motherfuckin' head off." But I didn't, and he didn't, and that was my main New York adventure.

Mary's play opened. There was a big opening night party at Sardi's, where the food was terrible. But we hung in nevertheless waiting for the early morning papers. They arrived and almost immediately the big wheels like O'Toole and Duncan Weldon (the producer) left. I've never seen a party come to such a sudden end. Frank Rich, then of *The New York Times*, didn't like the play. That was equivalent to the kiss of death and we immediately canceled any long term plans for staying in New York.

But I was there long enough to finish the job for the Norwegians. I mailed it off to Oslo and forgot about it. Anybody asked me I'd tell them that, in my opinion, any TV series that opens each week with forty Vikings in a longboat off to yet another foreign shore just ain't going to get made. Nobody's got that much money. It seems I was right. The series never got made.

Mary on Broadway in *Pygmalion* with Peter O'Toole.

Mary's play, which turned out to be an even bigger disaster than predicted, limped on for a few more weeks. One of the stars, either Peter O'Toole or Amanda Plummer, were off more than they were on, especially O'Toole who, once he'd read the notices, lost all interest in the play and just wanted it to close as quickly as possible.

James Jr. and his wife Joan on their wedding day, Catalina Island, California.

Apart from my "gunman" interlude in New York, two other memories of that trip remain. One is I flew back to Los Angeles and on to Catalina Island to attend my son's wedding, the other is the night Mary and I were locked in the theatre. Douglas Fairbanks, Jr. and his wife had been to see the show and then come 'round to say hello to Mary. They'd chatted about old times for a while and then left. Mary changed out of her wardrobe and we started to leave the theatre. Everybody had gone. The stage door keeper, an unreliable man at the best of times, had locked up and gone home. And he'd really locked up. We couldn't get out of the stage door and we couldn't get out

In my office, 1997.

through the front of the house. While we were trying to get out front, some enthusiastic member of the public spotted us and called the police, reporting that there were suspicious looking people in the Plymouth Theatre on West 45th Street. Mary and I were still wondering how we were going to get out when we were confronted by half a dozen armed policemen as they crashed into the theatre front and back.

While we were in New York, Mary and I quit smoking. She'd quit successfully once before and only started again when she met me. On the other hand, I'd been a regular smoker since I was around twelve, anything between 20 and 30 a day. I used to say that it was impossible to work without a full ashtray sitting on the desk. Anyway, we quit, and seven weeks later I had a heart attack. To this day I think it was brought on by the shock my system suffered when I quit smoking. We were in London at the time, playing tennis at Queen's Club. An ambulance was called and I was carted off to the Charing Cross Hospital where my heart quit beating completely for a short time. I've got to tell you, dying is a much overrated experience. There were no lights at the end of any tunnel, no heavenly music, just the shock of being electrocuted back to life. During all this, Mary, still in her tennis clothes, was kept in a small room being fed endless cups of tea, waiting for news. She had a far worse time than I did. Eventually they moved me to Guys Hospital where I had an angioplasty, and a couple of weeks later I was back at my typewriter wondering what I might do next.

The name Monn Iversen suddenly reappeared in my life. Not Stein this time, but his sister Bitte. She worked for the Norwegian Broadcasting Corporation and they were having some trouble with a four-part series they were going to shoot and it needed some rewrites. Was I interested. I told them perhaps, but I'd have to read the script first. A

Do You Want It Good or Tuesday?

week later it thuds through my mailbox. Four episodes, all in Norwegian. I call them and apologize, but I don't read Norwegian. They too apologize. Another three weeks go by and finally the translation arrives. The piece was originally called *Here's to Your Health*, and it was, without doubt, one of the most unprofessional pieces of writing I'd ever come across. One episode ran to sixty pages, the next to twenty, the third to around twelve, and the last I didn't even bother to count. There was no story and the dialogue would have read better if they'd kept it in Norwegian. I called Oslo. How come they'd become involved with such a terrible piece of work. They told me that there had been a Scandinavian television scriptwriting competition. First prize, the script would be shot. This was it. And please, could I help?

What could I say. The money was good, I wasn't doing anything else at that moment. Bottom line, I agreed. It took me around four weeks and two trips to Norway. Everybody seemed happy and around six months later they send me the video tapes of the show. To this day I haven't seen how well or badly they treated my script because I still don't speak Norwegian.

'Round about then I had another heart attack. This one was on the tennis court too. Poor Mary had to drive me to the hospital again. And for the second time, she was sent to a small room and fed cups of tea, while she waited to know whether I was alive or dead.

I finally got out of hospital, vowing to put my feet up and take it easy from now on. I was just getting into the swing of it when my agent came to me with a proposition. This was my New York agent, as opposed to my Los Angeles or London ditto. Having three agents may sound very flashy. As far as I can see it just makes you three times more likely to be out of work. Anyway, my New York agent who goes by the name of Fifi calls me to tell me about William Shatner and his new career as a science fiction novelist. Seems that Mr. Shatner hadn't (at that time) put pen to paper. Somebody else had written the book, he'd put his name on the title page as author, claimed most of the take, and then done the publicity tour telling all the talk show hosts that writing a novel was almost as easy as falling off a log. In his case, it was a lot easier.

Interesting story, I say to Fifi, but what's it got to do with me? Would I like to ghost a novel for Robert Stack, a private eye type novel. He's got himself a well recognized name on TV and we might all make a bit of money. It seems she'd already sent him a copy of *Snowball* and he liked my style of writing sufficiently to meet with me. I say okay, a meeting is set up, and I duly arrive at his house in Bel Air.

Robert Stack is old Hollywood. The walls of his study are lined with photographs of him playing polo with Spencer Tracy, or big-game hunting with Clark Gable. Stack himself is a world-renowned marksman, a one-time Academy Award nominee, the star of the TV series *The Untouchables* which ran, it seemed, forever, the star of the Quinn Martin series that I dallied with briefly, *Most Wanted,* and currently (when I visited him) the presenter of a well-rated weekly TV documentary (*Unsolved Mysteries*). He is also a perfect gentleman and a very pleasant person. As for this novel business, he wasn't altogether sure that he wanted to go along with it. Fair enough, I thought. We had a glass of wine, he introduced me to his wife, who was equally charming, and I went on my way.

Fifi called me a couple of weeks later. Seems that Robert was now willing to get his feet wet. I could start work on the novel. Block the story and write the first couple

Enjoying lunch with Michael Carreras and Hugh Harlow four weeks before the death of Carreras.

of chapters. This I did without much enthusiasm and they were duly sent to Robert for his approval. Yes, he liked what I was doing, carry on. I carried on for a couple more chapters and was just beginning to enjoy myself when I get another call from Fifi. Robert Stack has changed his mind. Basically he can't see himself going on talk shows or to book signings claiming to be something he isn't, namely the author of the novel with his name on it. Might be all right for somebody like William Shatner, but as far as Robert was concerned, it just wouldn't be honest.

I was angry at the time I had wasted, angry at Fifi for getting me into it in the first place, and angry with myself for ever getting involved. The only person I wasn't angry with was Robert Stack. At least he'd stuck up for his principles. My only complaint with him was he didn't do so at the start and I'd not have wasted all that time.

Fifi was in a placatory mood. Finish the novel and publish it under your own name she said. I reminded her that she already had the manuscript of *Fireball* which she hadn't been able to get published, not to mention my favourite novel of them all, which I'd called *Best Riches* and, if memory serves me, yet a third entitled *To Name But a Few*. I certainly wasn't going to provide her with another doorstop.

On reflection, that last paragraph is quite depressing. I know I'm inclined to make light of my writing. But even enjoying it like I do, it is hard work, and to think of the amount of time and effort that went into writing those three unpublished novels is intimidating, to say the least. I say "unpublished" as opposed to "yet to be published" because I honestly don't think they ever will be now. Fifi's office has lost interest and I haven't the energy to wield a sharp stick. The same applies to a couple of screenplays I wrote that have been sitting on one or another of my agents' desks these past couple of years. They've both attracted options. One of them, *Not in Front of the Children,* has been optioned twice, the other, *One More Time*, three times. Admittedly, that means money, at least it does for me. I've heard tell recently of production companies in London saying to writers that they'd like to run with their script or their idea so take it off the market, but we're not going to pay you any money until or unless we get it going. They'd be locked up if they tried to behave like that in Los Angeles. As for my two subjects, I'm happy to get the option money, but I'd rather they got made which, unfortunately, I'm convinced now that neither of them ever will be. I think middle-of-the-road writers, like myself, definitely have a sell-by date, and I've reached it.

I'm reminded of an incident that took place around six or seven years ago. Mark Lichtman's office called me to say that Disney had just signed with ABC to deliver fifteen *Movies for Television* and they had made an appointment for me with one of their executives, Steve Fazekas, to discuss doing one or two. I wasn't over enthusiastic about the idea but I went along anyway. I arrive for my appointment and am shown into the office of a guy who's younger than my son. No big deal, there's a lot of young talent in town. In fact, the only talent working these days is the young talent. But this particular young talent hadn't done his homework or maybe it was my agent's fault. Anyway, the first thing he said to me when I sat down was: "Tell me about yourself."

I was writing successful movies before he was born and now here I was auditioning for a job I didn't even particularly want. Still, the same thing happened to Fred Zinneman, so I'm in good company. Maybe Steve Fazekas is a big wheel by now. If he is, I hope he's learned some manners. Incidentally, he didn't give me a job.

After the Robert Stack fiasco I worked again for the guy who'd made *Believe It Or Not.* Ron Lyon had put his own show together calling it *Beyond Belief.* By now he had remarried a very bright, very pretty, very tough lady, whom he had met in Mary's house in London, Jenny Paschall. If she'd been Mrs. Lyon when *Believe It Or Not* was being made, Ron would have wound up owning the show. She would have made mincemeat out of the Hollywood bunch. Also under Ron's auspices I wrote a treatment for a cop show in Paris, I did a rewrite of a script by Bruce Dickinson, lead singer with the heavy metal group Iron Maiden, and I had another heart attack and a triple bypass operation. I wrote a spec script called *Fifty Fifty* which is being handled by my Los Angeles agent and remains, to date, like the others, unsold. Come to think of it, this one hasn't even been optioned. And that about covers it. I'm sorry if the last few chapters bored you, but you were warned that there was a long life after Hammer.

And what of Hammer? The people who shaped the foundations of my career. Those responsible for my becoming a cult figure. The corporation is owned and run nowadays by Roy Skeggs, who started with the company as a production accountant. I'm sure he's very good at what he does. Trouble is, he doesn't seem to do all that much. Every now and then announcements are made. Hammer is going back into production. Hammer is going to partner the big Hollywood investors in a new program of horror blockbusters. Hammer is going to be reborn. Trouble is, Hammer is just a name now. It isn't Michael Carreras or Tony Hinds. It isn't Terry Fisher or Bernard Robinson or James Bernard. It isn't Peter Cushing or Christopher Lee. It isn't even Jimmy Sangster. And, when one comes to the bottom line, wasn't that what Hammer was really all about?

Mary and me in Paris, September, 1996.

As for my life right now, I suppose a lot of people might call it boring. I love it. I pick away at my word processor, I play some gentle tennis, we travel a great deal both to visit our children in London, California, and Paris and just for the joy of traveling. On the downside, I miss some old friends a great deal. Michael Carreras particularly. But at my age one is forced to get used to the idea of friends and associates dropping from the trees like coconuts. What makes the whole thing worthwhile is that I love Mary very much and she loves me. Who could ask for more!

Actually, let's not be modest, I could ask for more. I'd like not to have to live outside England for more than six months a year. I'd like to have won an Oscar or at least have been nominated. I'd like my lottery numbers to come up, California or Camelot, either will do. I'd like to be under fifty years old again with all that time ahead. I'd like not to have had a couple of heart attacks and finally, when my time comes I'd like a...

...QUICK FADE TO BLACK...

No hanging around please, and nobody messing with my coffin. Unlike Dracula, when I'm dead I'm going to stay that way.

By way of an epilogue, a few years back, I get a call from Sandy, by then my longtime "ex" wife. It seems that her dog, Raisin, whom I'd become so attached to

James Jr. and Sr. in Ojai, California.

Three generations: father, son, and granddaughter.

My daughter-in-law Joan and Claire.

Joanna Clyde, Mary's daughter, my stepdaughter.

Do You Want It Good or Tuesday?

while we were married that we'd nearly had a custody battle, had developed cancer and was going to be put down in the near future. Would I please call my son, who was a sometime carpenter sometime sea urchin fisherman living on his boat in Santa Barbara, and ask him to make a suitable coffin for burying in the back garden. I duly contact James Jr. and he makes the coffin and a couple of days later he delivers it. I call Sandy and tell her it's ready. She asks me to bring it up to the house ASAP and, if possible, bring James Jr. with me to help dig the hole it's eventually destined to be buried in. He bitches all the way up to the house about how this is the best piece of cabinet making he's ever done and she's going to bury it three feet underground. But we deliver it, dig the hole, give the poor sick dog a pat on the head, and go back to our separate lives. Phone call a couple of days later. Please will I come to the funeral. I tell her I'll be over and I'm sorry Raisin died.

"She's not dead yet," said Sandy.

It wasn't exactly *Dead Man Walking*, but it came a pretty close second. There were half a dozen of us, friends of Sandy, who stood around in the living room looking embarrassed while the vet gave the poor little dog her lethal shot. In the background there was music playing, a tune that Sandy had commissioned to be written and recorded especially for the dog. Afterwards a couple of us screwed down the coffin lid, lowered it into the grave, and filled it in. Then we all got drunk.

If I develop something fatal, that's how I want to go, surrounded by friends, music in the background, and a party afterwards.

THE END

Jimmy Sangster
Los Angeles (June 1997)

X—The Unknown

Do You Want It Good or Tuesday?

FILMOGRAPHY

Compiled by Tom Johnson, Gary J. Svehla & Svehla, Tom Weaver

A MAN ON THE BEACH (1955)

An Exclusive Release; A Hammer Films Production; Produced by Anthony Hinds; Directed by Joseph Losey; **Screenplay: Jimmy Sangster**; Based on the Story "Chance at the Wheel" by Victor Canning; Photography: Wilkie Cooper (Color); Editor: Henry Richardson; Art Director: Edward Marshall; Music: John Hotchkis; 29 minutes

Michael Medwin (*Max*), Donald Wolfit (*Dr. Carter*), Michael Ripper (*Chauffeur*), Edward Forsyth (*Clement*), Alex de Gallier (*Casino Manager*)

Short subject crime drama scripted by Sangster and directed by blacklisted Joseph Losey. Losey would go on to direct *Finger of Guilt* (1956) and *The Concrete Jungle* (1960).

"...absorbing and entertaining..." — *The Kinematograph Weekly*

X — THE UNKNOWN (1957)

Released in the U.S. by Warners; Released in England by Exclusive Films; A Hammer Film Production; Executive Producer: Michael Carreras; Produced by Anthony Hinds; Directed by Leslie Norman; **Story and Screenplay: Jimmy Sangster**; Photography: Gerald Gibbs; Editor: James Needs; Music Composed by James Bernard; Musical Director: John Hollingsworth; Production Design: Bernard Robinson; Special Effects: Bowie Margutti Ltd. and Jack Curtis; Makeup and Special Makeup Effects: Phil Leakey; **Production Manager: Jimmy Sangster**; Camera Operator: Len Harris; 78 minutes

Dean Jagger (*Dr. Adam Royston*), Edward Chapman (*Mr. Elliot*), Leo McKern (*Insp. McGill*), Anthony Newley (*Corp. "Spider" Webb*), Jameson Clark (*Jack Harding*), William Lucas (*Peter Elliot*), Peter Hammond (*Lt. Bannerman*), Marianne Brauns (*Zena*), Ian McNaughton (*Haggis*), Michael Ripper (*Sgt. Grimsdyke*), John Harvey (*Maj. Cartwright*), Edwin Richfield (*Old Soldier*), Jane Aird (*Vi Harding*), Norman Macowan (*Old Tom*), Neil Hallet (*Unwin*), Kenneth Cope (*Private Lansing*), Michael Brook (*Willie Harding*), Fraser Hines (*Ian Osborne*), Archie Duncan (*Sgt. Yeardye*), Neil Wilson (*Russell*), John Stone (*Gerry*), Brian Peck, Edward Judd (*Soldiers*), John Stirling (*Police Car Driver*), Shaw Taylor (*Police Radio Operator*), Frank Taylor (*P.C. Williams*), Brown Derby (*Vicar*), Max Brimmell (*Hospital Director*), Robert Bruce (*Dr. Kelly*), Stella Kemball (*Nurse*), Anthony Sager (*Gateman*), Phillip Levene (*Security Man*), Barry Steel (*Soldier in Trench*), Lawrence James (*Guard*), Stephenson Lang (*Reporter*)

The first full-length screenplay by Jimmy Sangster. *X — The Unknown* featured Sangster's terror from underground, a mud-like creature terrorizing the Scottish moors. An often over-looked Hammer gem that deserves closer inspection.

"...highly imaginative..."—*Variety*

"...the film suffers from an over-padded plot and poor effects work which make the monster look no more threatening than a giant helping of chocolate pudding."—*Hammer, House of Horror* (Howard Maxford, B.T. Batsford Ltd., 1996)

"*X—The Unknown* was an impressive start for the horror film genre's greatest writer."—*Hammer Films* (Tom Johnson and Deborah Del Vecchio, McFarland, 1996)

"...smartly directed and inventive science fiction picture about a living glob that feeds on radioactivity."—*The Motion Picture Guide*

"Not only is *X—The Unknown* an above-average SF entry of the mid-1950s, but it also has the historic distinction of being the first film to feature an ambulatory blob as its central—rather than peripheral—plot gimmick."—*Midnight Marquee* (Ed Bansak, #47)

THE CURSE OF FRANKENSTEIN (1957)

Warner Brothers; A Hammer Film Production; Associate Producer: Anthony Nelson-Keys; Executive Producer: Michael Carreras; Produced by Anthony Hinds; Directed by Terence Fisher; **Screenplay: Jimmy Sangster**; Photography: Jack Asher (Color); Editor: James Needs; Music Composed by James Bernard; Music Director: John Hollingsworth; Production Designer: Bernard Robinson; Art Director: Ted Marshall; Production Manager: Don Weeks; Camera Operator: Len Harris; Assistant Director: Robert Lynn; Casting: Dorothy Holloway; Hair Stylist: Henry Montsash; Makeup Supervisor: Phil Leakey; Makeup: Roy Ashton; Assistant Makeup: George Turner; Wardrobe: Molly Arbuthnot; Filmed at Bray Studios; 83 minutes

Peter Cushing (*Baron Victor Frankenstein*), Hazel Court (*Elizabeth*), Robert Urquhart (*Paul Krempe*), Christopher Lee (*The Creature*), Melvyn Hayes (*Young Victor*), Valerie Gaunt (*Justine*), Paul Hardtmuth (*Prof. Bernstein*), Noel Hood (*Aunt Sophia*), Fred Johnson (*Grandfather*), Claude Kingston (*Small Boy*), Alex Gallier (*A Priest*), Michael Mulcaster (*Warder*), Hugh Dempster (*Burgomaster*), Anne Blake (*Burgomeister's Wife*), Sally Walsh (*Young Elizabeth*), Raymond Ray (*Uncle*), Patrick Troughton (*Kurt*), Henry Caine (*Schoolmaster*), Joseph Behrman (*Fritz*), Raymond Rollett (*Father Felix*), Ernest Jay (*Undertaker*), J. Trevor Davis (*Uncle*), Bartlett Mullins (*A Tramp*), Eugene Leahy (*Second Priest*), Jock Easton (*Stunt Double for Christopher Lee*)

"I've always had a brilliant intellect!"—Baron Frankenstein in *The Curse of Frankenstein.*

Jimmy Sangster's script immediately establishes the emphasis in the Hammer series upon the character of monster-creator, Baron Victor Frankenstein, instead of focusing upon the Monsters, as Universal did 25 years earlier. The script cleverly tells its story in flashbacks, a priest coming to visit the Baron in prison before his execution for the murder of Justine the maid.

The color film thrust Peter Cushing, as Baron Frankenstein, into the horror spotlight where he would soon be followed by Christopher Lee (who in this film portrayed the tragic monster).

"A spine chilling story."—*The Kinematograph Weekly*

The Curse of Frankenstein

"The most significant British horror film ever."—*The Motion Picture Guide*

"Sangster's script moves at a commendable clip while Fisher's direction, if occasionally a little clumsy, makes the most of the situations at hand."—*Hammer, House of Horror*

"...the film had several advantages: it had the novelty appeal of being a fully-fledged British horror picture; it was filmed in colour; it took its subject seriously..."—*The House of Horror* (Edited by Allen Eyles, Robert Adkinson, and Nicholas Fry; Lorrimer Publishing Limited, 1973)

"...a routine horror picture"—*The New York Times* (Bosley Crowther)

"...one of the most intriguing variations on the classic man-made-monster theme."—*The Films of Christopher Lee* (Robert W. Pohle, Jr., and Douglas C. Hart, Scarecrow Press, 1983)

"The breakthrough movie, not only for Hammer but for the entire generation in the post-war era."—*The Encyclopedia of Horror Movies* (Edited by Phil Hardy, Harper & Row, 1986)

THE SNORKEL (1958)

Released in the U.S. by Columbia; A Hammer Film Production; Associate Producer: Anthony Nelson-Keys; Produced by Michael Carreras; Directed by Guy Green; **Screenplay: Jimmy Sangster** and Peter Myers; Story: Anthony Dawson; Photography: Jack

Asher; Editors: James Needs and William Lenny; Art Director: John Stoll; Music: Francis Chagrin; Conducted by John Hollingsworth; Makeup: Phil Leakey; Camera: Len Harris; 90 minutes (England), 74 minutes (US)

Peter Van Eyck (*Paul Decker*), Betta St. John (*Jean Edwards*), Mandy Miller (*Candy Brown*), Gregory Aslan (*The Inspector*), William Franklyn (*Wilson*), Henry Vidon (*Italian Gardener*), Marie Burke (*Gardener's Wife*), Flush (*"Toto"*), Irene Prador (*Frenchwoman*), Robert Rietty (*Station Sergeant*), Armand Guinie (*Waiter*), David Ritch (*Hotel Clerk*)

A wealthy woman is murdered by her scheming husband who almost manages to convince the authorities it was suicide. His plans are thwarted by the woman's young daughter Candy (Mandy Miller). In the original script the daughter was to leave the murderer trapped under floorboards to perish; however, Sangster was forced to change the script and have the girl report the murderer's whereabouts to the police.

"A clever film that works."—*The Motion Picture Guide*
"A tense murder thriller."—*The Kinematograph Weekly*
"...an underrated Hammer chiller that is inexplicably difficult to see, but worth the effort."—*Hammer Films*
"A tolerable potboiler which could have made more of its ingenious central plot gimmick."—*Hammer, House of Horror*

BLOOD OF THE VAMPIRE (1958)
Universal-International; Produced by Robert S. Baker and Monty Berman; Directed by Henry Cass; **Story and Screenplay: Jimmy Sangster**; Photography: Monty Berman (Color); Editor: Douglas Myers; Music Composed and Directed by Stanley Black; Art Director: John Elphick; Production Manager: Charles Permane; Camera Operator: Geoffrey Seaholme; Assistant Director: Lucky Sacripanti; Makeup: Jimmy Evans; Wardrobe: Muriel Dickson; Sound Recording: Bill Bulkley; 85 minutes

Donald Wolfit (*Dr. Callistratus*), Vincent Ball (*Dr. John Pierre*), Barbara Shelley (*Madeleine Duvall*), Victor Maddern (*Carl*), William Devlin (*Kurt Urach*), Andrew Faulds (*Wetzler*), John Le Mesurier (*Judge*), Bryan Coleman (*Monsieur Auron*), Cameron Hall (*Drunken Doctor*), George Murcell (*First Guard*), Julian Strange (*Second Guard*), Bruce Whiteman (*Third Guard*), Barbara Burke (*Housekeeper*), Yvonne Buckingham (*Serving Wench*), Bernard Bresslaw (*Tall Sneak Thief*), Hal Osmond (*Small Sneak Thief*), Henry Vidon (*Prof. Bernard Meinster*), John Stuart (*Madeleine's Uncle*), Colin Tapley (*Commissioner of Prisons*), Muriel Ali (*Gypsy Dancer*), Max Brimmell (*Warder*), Dennis Shaw (*Blacksmith*), Otto Diamant (*Gravedigger*), Milton Reid (*Executioner*), Richard Golding (*Official*), Theodore Wilhelm

"The most loathsome curse ever to afflict the earth was that of the vampire, which nourishes itself on warm living blood."—*Blood of the Vampire*
A Universal-International horror film filled with British comedians. A vampiric doctor (Wolfit) is raised from the dead and begins to acquire his much- needed blood

Blood of the Vampire

supply at an insane asylum. Wolfit would go on to appear in films such as *Lawrence of Arabia* (1962), *Becket* (1964), *Hands of Orlac* (1964), and the *The Charge of the Light Brigade* (1968), Also in the cast was Barbara Shelley, whose portrayal of characters in horror films always managed to stay interesting and intelligent.

"...written by Jimmy Sangster, an excellent writer in the genre, but he must have run afoul of director Cass and the producers because this one misses."—*The Motion Picture Guide*

"This was probably the routine Cass's best movie, but all prints of it appear to have been destroyed."—*The Encyclopedia of Horror Movies*

"Almost everything in *Blood of the Vampire*, from the raucous Victorian tavern scenes, and the Dickensian workhouse prison, to the menaced décolleté of Barbara Shelley, is typical of Jimmy Sangster's Victorian underworld, and exactly similar to the tone of his early Frankenstein movies for Hammer."—*The Vampire Cinema* (David Pirie, Crescent Books, 1977)

DRACULA (1958)

Released in England by Rank; Released in the U.S. by Universal-International as *Horror of Dracula*; A Hammer Film Production; Associate Producer: Anthony Nelson-Keys; Executive Producer: Michael Carreras; Produced by Anthony Hinds; Directed by Terence Fisher; **Screenplay: Jimmy Sangster**; Photography: Jack Asher (Color); Production Designer: Bernard Robinson; Music Composed by James Bernard; Music

From Hammer Films to Hollywood! A Life in the Movies

185

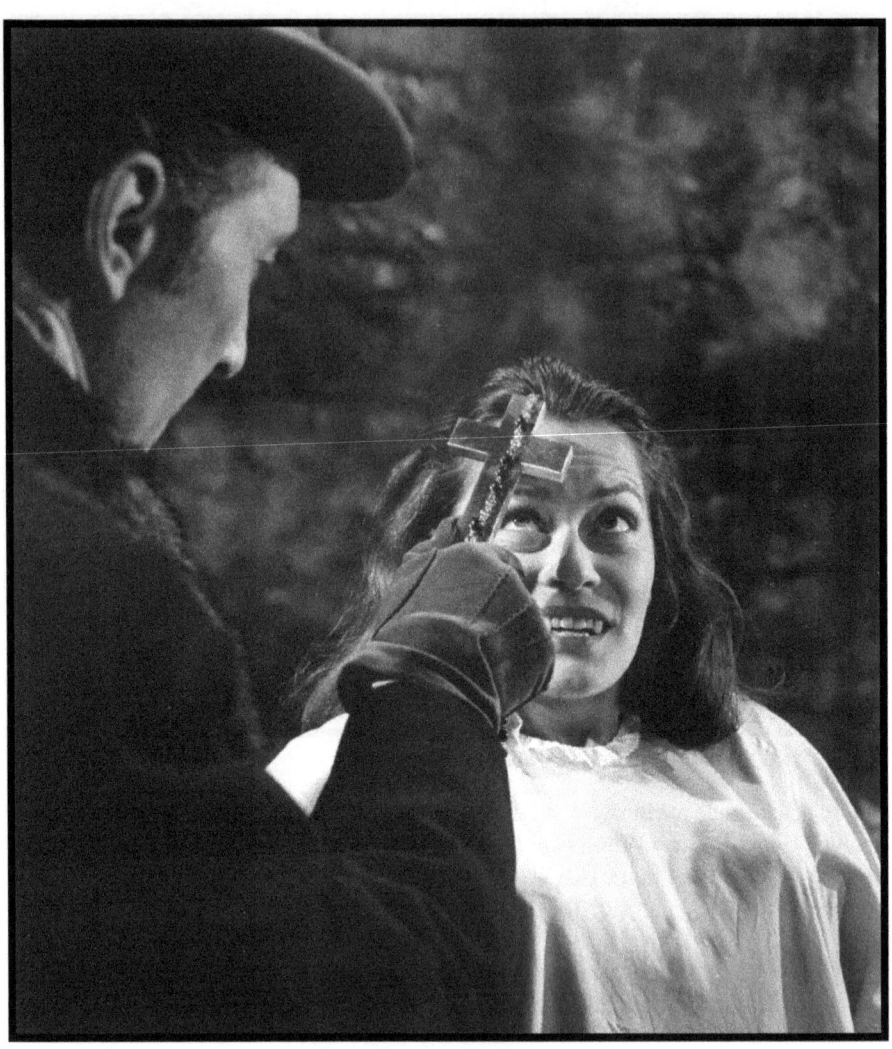

***Dracula** [**Horror of Dracula**, U.S.]*

Conducted by John Hollingsworth; Production Manager: Don Weeks; Special Effects: Syd Pearson; Assistant Director: Robert Lynn; Camera Operator: Len Harris; Supervising Editor: James Needs; Editor: Bill Lenny; Makeup: Phil Leakey and Roy Ashton; Filmed at Bray Studios; 82 minutes

Peter Cushing (*Dr. Van Helsing*), Christopher Lee (*Count Dracula*), Michael Gough (*Arthur Holmwood*), Melissa Stribling (*Mina Holmwood*), Carol Marsh (*Lucy Holmwood*), Olga Dickie (*Gerda*), John Van Eyssen (*Jonathan Harker*), Valerie Gaunt (*Vampire Woman*), Janine Faye (*Tania*), Barbara Archer (*Inga*), Charles Lloyd Pack (*Dr. Seward*), George Merritt (*Policeman*), George Woodbridge (*Landlord*), George Benson (*Frontier Official*), Miles Malleson (*J. Marx, the Undertaker*), Geoffrey Bayldon (*Porter*), Paul Cole (*Lad*), Guy Mills (*Coach Driver*), Dick Morgan (*Driver's Companion*), John Mossman (*Hearse Driver*)

Inarguably Hammer's best Gothic horror film, and often cited as the best film they ever made. The Dracula legend is spiffed up with glorious color and a decidedly more sexual/feral Count in the dominant presence of Christopher Lee. Peter Cushing appears as Dr. Van Helsing, turning in his usual stellar performance.

"Performance-wise, the film [*Horror of Dracula*] confirmed Peter Cushing and Christopher Lee as the genre's top stars, having inherited the crowns of Boris Karloff and Bela Lugosi."—*Hammer, House of Horror*

"He [Christopher Lee] was aided by Sangster's script which managed to juxtapose almost all the novel's highlights, without jeopardizing the story's continuity."—*The Vampire Cinema*

"The acting of the most famous horror duo in film history—Cushing and Lee— is impeccable... but it is Fisher's uncanny sense of atmosphere, rhythm and colour, his poetic ellipses—the swirling autumn leaves outside Lucy's window indicating Dracula's arrival and his knack of building sequences in parallel action... which makes this one of the most enthralling films made in Britain."—*The Encyclopedia of Horror Movies*

"Bloody well done. Hammer finally gave the Dracula legend the treatment it deserved... entrusting it to the brilliant director Terence Fisher, who injected glorious life into the familiar material."—*The Motion Picture Guide*

THE REVENGE OF FRANKENSTEIN (1958)

Columbia; A Hammer Film Production; Associate Producer: Anthony Nelson-Keys; Executive Producer: Michael Carreras; Produced by Anthony Hinds; Directed by Terence Fisher; **Screenplay: Jimmy Sangster**; Additional Dialogue: Hurford Janes; Photography: Jack Asher (Color); Music: Leonard Salzedo; Music Director: Muir Mathieson; Music Supervisor: John Hollingsworth; Production Designer: Bernard Robinson; Makeup: Phil Leakey; Supervising Editor: James
Needs; Editor: Alfred Cox; Sound Recording: Jock May; Hair Stylist: Henry Montsash; Production Manager: Don Weeks; Camera Operator: Len Harris; Continuity: Doreen Dearnaley; Wardrobe: Rosemary Burrows; Filmed at Bray Studios; 91 minutes

Peter Cushing (*Baron Frankenstein/Dr. Victor Stein/Dr. Franck*), Francis Matthews (*Dr. Hans Kleve*), Eunice Gayson (*Margaret Conrad*), Michael Gwynn (*Karl*), John Welsh (*Bergman*), Lionel Jeffries (*Fritz*), Oscar Quitak (*Dwarf*), Richard Wordsworth (*Up Patient*), Charles Lloyd Pack (*President*), John Stuart (*Inspector*), Arnold Diamond (*Dr. Molke*), Margery Gresley (*Countess Barscynska*), Anna Walmsley (*Vera Barscynska*), George Woodbridge (*Janitor*), Michael Ripper (*Kurt*), Ian Whittaker (*Boy*), Avril Leslie (*Gerda*), Michael Mulcaster (*Tattoo*)

After the success of *Curse of Frankenstein* and *Horror of Dracula*, sequels were inevitable. However, Hammer's sequel to *Curse* was superior in every way, simply because screenwriter Jimmy Sangster felt free of the Universal Pictures' formula and created his own version of the Frankenstein mythos. Also, the sequel was better able to embellish the character of the Baron, and actor Peter Cushing was, as always, enthusiastic to reveal far more of the subtleties inherent in the mad doctor's inner soul.

"Viewed today, the film has its points of interest, most notably Bernard Robinson's plush design work and Cushing's performance, now less maniacally driven. Taken as

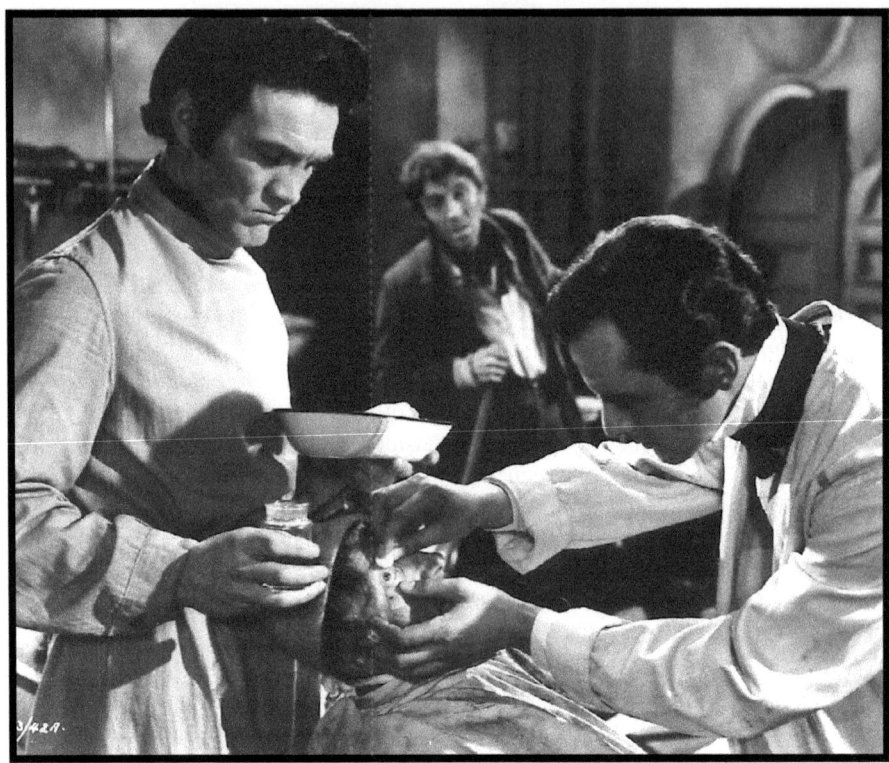

The Revenge of Frankenstein

a whole, however, the film, though quite entertaining on the surface, is not without its faults."—*Hammer, House of Horror*

"Sangster's screenplay is one of his best, and took the Hammer series in a completely different direction from its predecessor."—*Hammer Films*

"Sangster's wit is equally in evidence when he is glossing over the inherent grotesqueries of his own plot... Terence Fisher's direction is assured, if a touch perfunctory."—*A History of Horrors* (Denis Meikle, Scarecrow Press, Inc., 1996)

"[Jack] Asher's gloriously saturated Technicolor photography helps to make this one of the most complex and intelligent treatments of the story to date."—*The Encyclopedia of Horror Movies*

INTENT TO KILL (1958)

20th Century-Fox/A Zonic Production; Produced by Adrian D. Worker; Directed by Jack Cardiff; **Screenplay: Jimmy Sangster**; Based on the Novel by Michael Bryan; Photography: Desmond Dickinson (CinemaScope); Editor: Tom Simpson; Music: Kenneth V. Jones; Music Director: Muir Mathieson; Art Director: Allan Harris; 89 minutes

Richard Todd (*Dr. Bob McLaurin*), Betsy Drake (*Dr. Nancy Ferguson*), Herbert Lom (*Juan Menda*), Warren Stevens (*Finch*), Carlo Justini (*Francisco Flores*), Paul Carpenter (*O'Brien*), Alexander Knox (*Dr. McNeill*), Lisa Gastoni (*Carla Menda*), Peter Arne (*Kral*), Catherine Boyle (*Margaret McLaurin*), John Crawford (*Boyd*), Jackie Collins

(*Carol Freeman*), Kay Callard (*Carol's Friend*), John McLaren (*Anesthetist*), Maggie McGrath (*Night Nurse*)

An assassination plot foiled by a doctor (Richard Todd) and detective (Paul Carpenter).

"Once the thriller element is added, the excitement never stops."—*The Motion Picture Guide*

THE TROLLENBERG TERROR (1958)

DCA/A Tempean Production; American title, *The Crawling Eye*; Produced by Robert S. Baker and Monty Berman; Directed by Quentin Lawrence; **Screenplay: Jimmy Sangster**; From the BBC-TV Serial *The Trollenberg Terror* by Peter Key; Photography: Monty Berman; Editor: Henry Richardson; Music Composed by Stanley Black; Production Supervisor: Ronald C. Lisles; Art Director: Duncan Sutherland; Camera Operator: Desmond Davis; Production Manager: Charles Permane; Assistant Director: Norman Harrison; Makeup: Eleanor Jones; Special Effects: Anglo-Scottish Pictures Ltd.; Special Effects Supervisor: Les Bowie; Made at Alliance Film Studios, Ltd.; 84 minutes

Forrest Tucker (*Alan Brooks*), Laurence Payne (*Philip Truscott*), Jennifer Jayne (*Sarah Pilgrim*), Janet Munro (*Anne Pilgrim*), Warren Mitchell (*Prof. Crevett*), Frederick Schiller (*Mayor Klein*), Andrew Faulds (*Brett*), Stuart Saunders (*Dewhurst*), Colin Douglas (*Hans*), Derek Sydney (*Wilde*), Richard Golding (*First Villager*), George Herbert (*Second Villager*), Anne Sharp (*German Woman*), Leslie Heritage (*Carl*), Jeremy Longhurst (*First Student Climber*), Anthony Parker (*Second Student Climber*), Theodore Wilhelm (*Fritz*), Garard Green (*Pilot*), Caroline Glaser (*Little Girl*), Jack Taylor

Tentacled aliens terrorize a Swiss town, beheading anyone who gets in their way. Forrest Tucker starred in this quirky little horror film.

"If you were lucky enough to have seen *The Crawling Eye* [*The Trollenberg Terror*, U.K.] during

From Hammer Films to Hollywood! A Life in the Movies

189

Jack the Ripper

its premiere run in 1958 you probably still remember the vivid one-sheet illustration, with its depiction of a tentacled human eye tormenting a young maiden. No one passing theatre marquees in 1958 could have ignored this poster. What's so nifty about it is that the film it advertises actually lives up to the hype." — *Midnight Marquee* (Randy Palmer, #52)

"Both direction and screenplay create considerable tension, notably in Tucker's rescue of a young girl from the monster." — *The Encyclopedia of Science Fiction Movies* (Phil Hardy, Woodbury Press, 1984)

"Average acting, but particularly awful special effects." — *Videohound's Golden Movie Retriever* (Editors: Marion Connors and Julia Furtaw, Visible Ink, 1994)

JACK THE RIPPER (1959)
Embassy/Paramount; Mid-Century Film Productions; Photographed, Produced and Directed by Monty S. Berman and Robert S. Baker; **Screenplay: Jimmy Sangster**; Story: Peter Hammond and Colin Craig; Editor: Peter Benzencenet; Music Score (U.S. version): Jimmy McHugh and Pete Rugolo; Music Score (British version): Stanley Black; Makeup: Jimmy Evans; 85 minutes

Lee Patterson (*Sam Lowry*), Eddie Byrne (*Insp. Mike O'Neill*), Betty McDowall (*Anne Ford*), Ewen Solon (*Sir David Rogers*), John Le Mesurier (*Dr. Hillary Tranter*), Endre Muller (*Louis Benz*), George Rose (*Clarke*), Philip Leaver (*Music Hall Manager*),

The Man Who Could Cheat Death

Barbara Burke (*Kitty Knowles, alias Mary Clarke*), Anne Sharpe (*Helen Morris*), Denis Shaw (*Simes*), Esma Cannon (*Nelly*), George Woodbridge (*Blake*), Garard Green (*Dr. Urguhart*), Jack Allan (*Assistant Comm.*), Jane Taylor (*Hazel*), Dorinda Stevens (*Margaret*), Hal Osmonde (*Snakey*), George Street (*Station Sergeant*), Olwen Brooks (*Mrs. Boulton*), Helen Digby (*First Victim*), The Montparnasse Ballet (*Dancing Troupe*)

Mid-Century challenged Hammer on the gore front with this Jack the Ripper export. An American detective works with Scotland Yard to discover the grisly murderer of prostitutes.

"Though there are occasional atmospheric moments, this is largely a bloody, exploitative exercise in filmmaking."—*The Motion Picture Guide*

"...routine, somewhat stagebound thriller..."—*The Encyclopedia of Horror Movies*

"Jimmy Sangster's script exploits to the full the subconscious cruelty that may be inherent in any form of surgery."—*A Heritage of Horror* (David Pirie, Gordon Fraser, 1973)

"Rather dull retelling of the story of London's phantom killer."—*Horror and Science Fiction Films* (Donald C. Willis, Scarecrow Press, Inc., 1972)

THE MAN WHO COULD CHEAT DEATH (1959)

Paramount; A Hammer Film Production; Associate Producer: Anthony Nelson-Keys; Produced by Michael Carreras; Directed by Terence Fisher; **Screenplay: Jimmy Sangster**; From the Play *The Man in Half Moon Street* by Barre Lyndon; Photography: Jack Asher (Technicolor); Supervising Editor: James Needs; Editor: John Dunsford; Music Composed by Richard Bennet; Music Supervisor: John Hollingsworth; Production Designer: Bernard Robinson; Camera Operator: Len Harris; Assistant Director: John Peverall; Makeup: Roy Ashton; Filmed at Bray Studios; 83 minutes

Anton Diffring (*Dr. Georges Bonner*), Hazel Court (*Janine DuBois*), Christopher Lee (*Dr. Pierre Gerard*), Arnold Marle (*Dr. Ludwig Weiss*), Delphi Lawrence (*Margo Phillips*), Francis De Wolff (*Insp. Legris*), Gerda Larsen (*Street Girl*), Middleton Woods (*Little Man*), Michael Ripper (*Morgue Attendant*), Denis Shaw (*Tavern Customer*), Ian Hewitson (*Roger*), Frederick Rawlings (*Footman*), Marie Burke (*Woman*), Charles Lloyd Pack (*Man at Exhibit*), John Harrison (*Servant*), Lockwood West (*First Doctor*), Ronald Adams (*Second Doctor*), Barry Shawzin (*Third Doctor*)

A 104-year-old man keeps his youth through surgical transplants of his parathyroid gland.

"This Hammer horror film is as intelligent and well crafted as the rest of their productions."—*The Motion Picture Guide*

"Although its few horror elements were well-staged, *The Man Who Could Cheat Death* is more talk than action."—*Hammer Films*

"...rather awkward variation on the Dorian Gray motif..."—*The Encyclopedia of Horror Movies*

"...despite re-uniting Sangster, Fisher, and Asher, proved to be one of Hammer's weakest ever horror entries."—*Hammer, House of Horror*

THE MUMMY (1959)

Released in the U.S. by Universal-International; Released in England by Rank; A Hammer Film Production; Associate Producer: Anthony Nelson-Keys; Executive Producer: Michael Carreras; Produced by Anthony Hinds; Directed by

Terence Fisher; **Screenplay: Jimmy Sangster**; Photography: Jack Asher (Color); Art Director: Bernard Robinson; Makeup: Roy Ashton; Masks: Margaret Carter Robinson; Supervising Editor: James Needs; Editor: Alfred Cox; Music: Frank Reizenstein; Music Director: John Hollingsworth; Camera: Len Harris; Production Manager: Don Weeks; Hairstyles: Henry Montsash; Costumes: Molly Arbuthnot; Egyptology Advisor: Andrew Low; Assistant Director: John Peverall; Assistant Director: Chris Barnes; Filmed at Bray Studios; 88 minutes

Peter Cushing (*John Banning*), Christopher Lee (*Kharis, the Mummy*), Yvonne Furneaux (*Isobel Banning/Princess Ananka*), Eddie Byrne (*Insp. Mulrooney*), Felix Aylmer (*Stephen Banning*), Raymond Huntley (*Joseph Whemple*), George Pastell (*Mehemet Bey*), John Stuart (*Coroner*), Michael Ripper (*Poacher*), Harold Goodwin (*Pat*), Dennis

The Mummy

Shaw (*Mike*), George Woodbridge (*Police Constable*), Willoughby Gray (*Dr. Reilly*), Stanley Meadows (*Attendant*), Frank Singuineau (*Head Porter*), Frank Sieman (*Bill*), Gerald Lawson (*Irish Customer*), John Harrison, James Clarke (*Priests*), David Browning (*Sergeant*)

Universal, still basking in the glow of the huge success of the Dracula subject, basically opened up their coffers and offered Hammer carte blanche to do any film from their library, so it was only natural that after a Frankenstein and Dracula film, the next one in line would be *The Mummy*. (*Midnight Marquee* #47, Dick Klemensen)

The story of love through the ages is told Hammer style with the customary beautiful Bernard Robinson sets and, of course, features the current titans of terror, Peter Cushing and Christopher Lee.

"Hammer Films have made the most distinguished of English horror films..." — *The London Times*

"Spectacular." — *The Kinematograph Weekly*

"While not Hammer's greatest horror, it is close behind *Dracula*." — *Hammer Films*

"One of Hammer's most visual productions, the film contains many impressive moments..." — *Hammer, House of Horror*

The Hellfire Club

"Hammer's most exotic horror fantasy to date..."—*A History of Horrors*

"Fisher's surrealist use of colour, at its most unforgettable in the nightmarish scenes of the mummy's death in the swamps and in the opening sequence set in ancient Egypt, together with his unnerving sense of camera position and cutting, give the movie a genuinely macabre poetry..."—*The Encyclopedia of Horror Movies*

"...lively Hammer reworking of the classic mummy material."—*The Motion Picture Guide*

THE HELLFIRE CLUB (1960)

Released in England by Regal International in March 1961; Released in the U.S. by Embassy in September 1963; Color; A New World Production; Photographed, Produced and Directed by Robert S. Baker and Monty Berman; **Screenplay:** Leon Griffiths and **Jimmy Sangster; Story: Jimmy Sangster**; Music: Clifton Parker; Music Conducted by Muir Mathieson; Art Director: Ray Simon; Editor: Fred Wilson; Sound: Bill Daniels; 93 minutes

Keith Michell (*Jason*), Kai Fischer (*Yvonne*), Adrienne Corri (*Isabel*), Peter Arne (*Thomas*), David Lodge (*Timothy*), Bill Owen (*Martin*), Peter Cushing (*Merryweather*), Francis Matthews (*Sir Hugh*), Desmond Walter Ellis (*Lord Chorley*), Denis Shaw (*Sir Richard*), Tutte Lemkow (*Higgins*), Peter Howell (*Earl of Chatham*), Bernard Hunter

Do You Want It Good or Tuesday?

(*Marquis de Beauville*), Michael Balfour (*John the Juggler*), Miles Malleson (*Judge*), Jean Lodge (*Lady Netherden*), Andrew Faulds (*Lord Netherden*), Martin Stephens (*Jason as a Boy*), Rupert Osborne (*Thomas as a Boy*), Skip Martin (*Joey the Dwarf*)

An 18th-century story of debauchery among the aristocracy. An heir returns to fight for his property.

"...a colourful historical extravaganza whose title is misleading for the Hellfire Club is barely featured for most of the movie... aided by an enterprising Sangster script, but its style is piecemeal and only a few touches distinguish it from other Baker/Berman historical nonentities."—*A Heritage of Horror*

THE BRIDES OF DRACULA (1960)
Released in England by Rank; Released in the U.S. by Universal-International; A Hammer Production; Associate Producer: Anthony Nelson-Keys; Executive Producer: Michael Carreras; Produced by Anthony Hinds; Directed by Terence Fisher; **Screenplay: Jimmy Sangster**, Peter Bryan and Edward Percy; Photography: Jack Asher (Technicolor); Music Composed by Malcolm Williamson; Music Supervisor: John Hollingsworth; Production Designer: Bernard Robinson; Art Director: Thomas Goswell; Makeup: Roy Ashton; Special Effects: Syd Pearson; Costumes: Molly Arbuthnot; Continuity: Tilly

The Brides of Dracula

From Hammer Films to Hollywood! A Life in the Movies

195

Day; Hair Dresser: Frieda Steiger; Supervising Editor: James Needs; Editor: Alfred Cox; Assistant Director: John Peverall; Camera Operator: Len Harris; Sound Recordist: Jock May; Sound Editor: James Groom; Filmed at Bray Studios; 85 minutes

Peter Cushing (*Dr. Van Helsing*), Freda Jackson (*Greta*), Martita Hunt (*Baroness Meinster*), Yvonne Monlaur (*Marianne Danielle*), Miles Malleson (*Dr. Tobler*), Henry Oscar (*Herr Lang*), David Peel (*Baron Meinster*), Victor Brooks (*Hans*), Mona Washburn (*Frau Lang*), Michael Ripper (*Coach Driver*), Fred Johnson (*Cure*), Andree Melly (*Gina*), Fred Johnson (*The Priest*), Norman Pierce (*The Innkeeper*), Vera Cook (*Innkeeper's Wife*), Marie Devereux (*Village Girl, Vampire*), Harold Scott (*Severn*), Michael Mulcaster (*Man in Black*)

Christopher Lee did not wish to reprise his Dracula role, so the first vampire sequel to *Dracula* was basically Draculaless. David Peel appears as a decadence loving youth who is stricken by vampirism, here treated as a disease. Peter Cushing reprises his Dr. Van Helsing role. The exciting climax is one of Hammer's better efforts.

"*The Brides of Dracula* is one of Hammer's best horrors and is one of the great vampire movies."—*Hammer Films*

"...the results still contained some excellent moments and, as in the sequel to Frankenstein, a greater assurance in dealing with the paraphernalia of the myth..."—*A Heritage of Horror*

"Fisher's direction is effective, with his customary lingering camera movements, but the overall result is decidedly uneven."—*The Encyclopedia of Horror Movies*

"Chilling special effects highlight a rather gory production."—*Motion Picture Guide*

"A Gothic tour de force with a real Brothers Grimm atmosphere to it..."—*Hammer, House of Horror*

THE SIEGE OF SIDNEY STREET (1960)

Mid-Century/United Producers; Photographed, Edited, Produced and Directed by Robert S. Baker and Monty Berman; **Screenplay: Jimmy Sangster** and Alexander Baron; **Story: Jimmy Sangster**; Music: Stanley Black; Art Director: William Kellner; Set Designer: Freda Pearson; Special Effects: Cliff Richardson; Makeup: Jill Carpenter; 93 minutes

Donald Sinden (*Insp. Mannering*), Nicole Maurey (*Sara*), Kieron Moore (*Yoska*), Peter Wyngarde (*Peter*), Godfrey Quigley (*Blakey*), Leonard Sachs (*Svaars*), Tutte Lemkow (*Dmitrieiff*), George Pastell (*Brodsky*), Angela Newman (*Nina*), T. P. McKenna (*Lapidos*), Maurice Good (*Gardstein*), James Caffrey (*Hefeld*), Harold Goldblatt (*Hersh*), Christopher Casson (*Police Commissioner*), Harry Brogan (*Old Harry*), **Jimmy Sangster (Winston Churchill)**

A historical drama centering on a group of Russian anarchists in London. The group profits from robberies and murder.

"The story is laid out matter-of-factly, making it too pedestrian and not very interesting. The acting isn't bad, however, and the final sequence makes up for the rather straightforward handling of the rest of the film."—*The Motion Picture Guide*

THE CRIMINAL (1960)

Anglo-Amalgamated/A Merton Park Production; U.S. title: *The Concrete Jungle*; Produced by Jack Greenwood; Directed by Joseph Losey; Screenplay: Alun Owen; **Story: Jimmy Sangster**; Photography: Robert Krasker; Music: Johnny Dankworth; Editor: Reginald Mills; Production Design: Richard MacDonald; Art Director: Scott MacGregor; Costumes: Ron Beck; 97 minutes

Stanley Baker (*Johnny Bannion*), Sam Wanamaker (*Mike Carter*), Gregoire Aslan (*Frank Saffron*), Margit Saad (*Suzanne*), Jill Bennett (*Maggie*), Rupert Davies (*Mr. Edwards*), Laurence Naismith (*Mr. Town*), John Van Eyssen (*Formby*), Noel Willman (*Prison Governor*), Derek Francis (*Priest*), Redmond Phillips (*Prison Doctor*), Kenneth J. Warren (*Clobber*), Patrick Magee (*Chief Warder, Barrows*), Kenneth Cope (*Kelly*), Patrick Wymark (*Sol*), Jack Rodney (*Scout*), John Molloy (*Snipe*), Brian Phelan (*Pauly Larkin*), Paul Stassino (*Alfredo Fanucci*), Jerold Wells (*Warder Brown*), Tom Bell (*Flynn*), Neil McCarthy (*O'Hara*), Keith Smith (*Hanson*), Nigel Green (*Ted*), Tom Gerard (*Quantock*), Larry Taylor (*Chas.*)

Criminal Johnny Bannion plans a robbery when in prison and proceeds with the plot when he is released only to have the plan backfire. He lands in prison again before breaking out and meeting a dire end.

"Something is missing from this otherwise crackling film."—*The Motion Picture Guide*

THE TERROR OF THE TONGS (1960)

Released in England by British Lion on September 29, 1961; Released in the U.S. by Columbia in October 1961; A Hammer Film Production; Filmed at Bray Studios; Associate Producer: Anthony Nelson-Keys; Executive Producer: Michael Carreras; Produced by Kenneth Hyman; Directed by Anthony Bushell; **Screenplay: Jimmy Sangster**; Photography: Arthur Grant (Color); Music: James Bernard; Music Director: John Hollingsworth; Production Designer: Bernard Robinson; Editor: Eric Boyd-Perkins; Supervising Editor: James Needs; Camera Operator: Len Harris; Makeup: Roy Ashton; 79 minutes

Geoffrey Toone (*Jackson*), Christopher Lee (*Chung King*), Yvonne Monlaur (*Lee*), Brian Worth (*Harcourt*), Richard Leech (*Insp. Dean*), Marne Maitland (*Beggar*), Ewen Solon (*Tang How*), Burt Kwouk (*Ming*), Barbara Brown (*Helena*), Bandance Dao Gupta (*Anna*), Michael Hawkins (*Priest*), Marie Burke (*Maya*), Milton Reid (*Guardian*), Charles Lloyd Pack (*Doctor*), Roger Del Gado (*Wang How*), Eric Young (*Confucius*), Johnny Arlen (*Executioner*), Santso Wong (*Sergeant*), Andy Ho (*Lee Chung*), Arnold Lee (*Spokesman*)

Oriental crime drama with Christopher Lee as Chung King, the leader of a gang of drug/slave marketers.

"...a tightly plotted tale of revenge."—*A History of Horrors*

The Terror of the Tongs

"...a nasty entry in Hammer's move from Gothic horror to costume adventure."—*Hammer Films*

"Violent and gory but full of action."—*The Motion Picture Guide*

"...audience reaction was mostly indifferent and... the film is little revived today, despite such ripe dialogue as, 'Have you ever had your bones scraped?'"—*Hammer, House of Horror*

TASTE OF FEAR (1961)

Columbia; A Hammer Film Production; American title, *Scream of Fear*; Executive Producer: Michael Carreras; **Screenplay and Produced by Jimmy Sangster**; Directed by Seth Holt; Photography: Douglas Slocombe; Music: Clifton Parker; Music Supervisor: John Hollingsworth; Production Designer: Bernard Robinson; Supervising Editor: James Needs; Editor: Eric Boyd-Perkins; Production Manager: Bill Hill; Assistant Director: David Tomblin; Camera: Desmond Davis; Sound Recordist: Leslie Hammond; Sound: Ted Mason and Len Shilton; Continuity: Pamela Mann; Sound Editor: James Groom; Makeup: Basil Newall; Hair Stylist: Eileen Bates; Wardrobe: Dora Lloyd; Filmed at A.B.P.C. Studios, Elstree; 90 minutes (England), 81 minutes (U.S.)

Susan Strasberg (*Penny Appleby*), Ronald Lewis (*Bob*), Ann Todd (*Jane Appleby*), Christopher Lee (*Dr. Gerrard*), John Serret (*Insp. Legrand*), Leonard Sachs (*Spratt*), Anne Blake (*Marie*), Fred Johnson (*Father*), Bernard Brown (*Gendarme*), Richard Klee (*Plainclothes Sergeant*), Mme. Lobegue (*Swiss Air Hostess*)

Taste of Fear

Susan Strasberg stars as a woman confined to a wheelchair who is investigating mysterious goings on at her father's estate.

"...contrived but expertly executed mystery shocker."—*Variety*

"...certainly the best of the group [of Hammer psychological thrillers]"—*Hammer Films*

"The perfect film to show those people that always seem to figure out the ending after the first half hour."—*The Motion Picture Guide*

"...a truly spooky film, suspenseful, and well-made."—*Videohound's Golden Movie Retriever*

"...benefits greatly from Douglas Slocombe's beautiful monochrome photography."—*A Heritage of Horror*

"It delivers its mixed bag of chills with professional grace."—*A History of Horrors*

"...one of the best scripts by Sangster."—*Hammer, House of Horror*

"...excellently directed Holt movie."—*The Encyclopedia of Horror Movies*

THE PIRATES OF BLOOD RIVER (1961)
Released in England by British Lion on August 13, 1962; Released in the U.S. by Columbia in July 1962; A Hammer Film Production; Executive Producer: Michael Carreras;

The Pirates of Blood River

Produced by Anthony Nelson-Keys; Directed by John Gilling; Screenplay: John Gilling and John Hunter; **Story: Jimmy Sangster**; Photography: Arthur Grant (Color); Music: Gary Hughes; Musical Director: John Hollingsworth; Production Designer: Bernard Robinson; Editor: Eric Boyd-Perkins; Supervising Editor: James Needs; Special Effects: Les Bowie; Camera Operator: Len Harris; Makeup: Roy Ashton; Filmed at Bray Studios; 87 minutes

Kerwin Mathews (*Jonathan*), Glenn Corbett (*Henry*), Christopher Lee (*LaRoche*), Marla Landi (*Bess*), Oliver Reed (*Brocaire*), Andrew Keir (*Jason*), Peter Arne (*Hench*), Michael Ripper (*Mac*), Jack Stewart (*Mason*), David Lodge (*Smith*), Marie Devereux (*Maggie*), Diane Aubrey (*Margaret*), Jerold Wells (*Commandant*), Dennis Waterman (*Timothy*), Lorraine Clewes (*Martha*), John Roden (*Settler*), Desmond Llewelyn (*Blackthorne*), Keith Pyott (*Silas*), Richard Bennett (*Seymour*), Michael Mulcaster (*Martin*), Denis Shaw (*Silver*), Michael Peake (*Kemp*), John Colin (*Lance*), Don Levy (*Carlos*), John Bennett (*Guard*), Ronald Blackman (*Pugh*)

Christopher Lee stars as pirate LaRoche on a search for buried treasure. Directed by the versatile John Gilling. Also stars swashbuckler Kerwin Mathews of *The Seventh Voyage of Sinbad*.

"...thrilling story, robust characterization, hectic highlights."—*The Kinematograph Weekly*
"The cast is one of the best Hammer assembled. This is one of Hammer's most satisfactory all-around films."—*Hammer Films*
"Good production values and cast help this otherwise ordinary adventure."—*The Motion Picture Guide*

THE SAVAGE GUNS (1962)
MGM/Capricorn/Tecisa; Released in the U.S. in 1959; **Produced by Jimmy Sangster** and Jose Maesso; Directed by Michael Carreras; Screenplay: Edmund Morris; Photography: Alfredo Fraille (Metrocolor and Metro Scope); Music: Anton Garcia Abril; Editors: David Hawkins and Pedro Del Rey; Art Director: Francisco Canet; Makeup: Paco Puyol; 84 minutes

Richard Basehart (*Steve Fallon*), Don Taylor (*Mike Summers*), Alex Nicol (*Danny Pose*), Paquita Rico (*Franchea*), Maria Granada (*Juana*), Jose Neto (*Ortega*), Fernando Rey (*Don Hernan*), Felix Fernandez (*Paco*), Antonio Fuentes (*Capt. Baez*), Sergio Mendizabal (*Mayor*), Rafael Albaicia (*Gonzalez*), Jose Manuel Martin (*Segura*), Victor Bayo (*Sanchez*), Pilar Caballero (*Sanchez's Wife*)

Richard Basehart does the cowboy thing recovering from a gunshot wound. He eventually goes to the aid of ranchers threatened by an evil cattle baron. Basehart had appeared in *He Walked by Night* (1948) *and Moby Dick* (1956).

"...the less said the better."—*Hammer, House of Horror*
"Shot in Spain, this is an offbeat western that offers some interesting characterizations but doesn't vary too much from an old western formula."—*The Motion Picture Guide*

TO HAVE AND TO HOLD (1963)
Merton Park/AA; Produced by Jack Greenwood; Directed by Herbert Wise; **Screenplay: John Sansom [Jimmy Sangster]**; Based on the novel *The Breaking Point* by Edgar Wallace; 71 minutes

Ray Barrett (*Sgt. Fraser*), Katherine Blake (*Claudia Lyon*), Nigel Stock (*George Lyon*), William Hartnell (*Insp. Roberts*), Patricia Bredin (*Lucy*), Noel Travarthen (*Blake*), Richard Clarke (*Charles Wagner*)

Another variation on the *Double Indemnity* theme as Ray Barrett is persuaded by the lovely Katherine Blake to do away with her husband.

"...vaguely entertaining..."—*The Motion Picture Guide*

MANIAC (1963)
Released in the U.S. by Columbia; Released in England by BLC; A Hammer Film Production; **Screenplay and Produced by Jimmy Sangster**; Directed by Michael Carreras; Photography: Wilkie Cooper (Megascope); Art Director: Teddy Carrick; Assistant Art Director: Jean Peyre; Supervising Editor: James Needs; Editor: Tom Simpson; Production Design: Bernard Robinson; Music: Stanley Black; Makeup: Basil Newall; Production Manager: Bill Hill; Assistant to the Producer: Ian Lewis; Sound Editor: Roy Baker; Camera: Harry Gilliam; Sound Recordist: Cyril Swern; Hair Stylist: Pat

Maniac

Do You Want It Good or Tuesday?

McDermott; Continuity: Kay Rawlings; Wardrobe: Molly Arbuthnot; Filmed at MGM Studios, Elstree, and on location in France; 87 minutes

Kerwin Mathews (*Geoff Farrell*), Nadia Gray (*Eve Beynat*), Donald Houston (*"Georges" Beynat*), Liliane Brousse (*Annette Beynat*), George Pastell (*Insp. Etienne*), Arnold Diamond (*Janiello*), Norman Bird (*Salon*), Justine Lord (*Grace*), Jerold Wells (*Giles*), Leon Peers (*Blanchard*)

A man sentenced to an insane asylum after killing the man who raped his young daughter is helped to escape by his wife and an American artist.

"A plot of extraordinary cunning, not particularly well performed."—*The New York Times*

"It takes a while for *Maniac* to get moving, but the film's second half is as good as any of Hammer's psycho-thrillers."—*Hammer Films*

"Could have been an interesting thriller, but it is marred by a plot that is hard to follow and a routine ending."—*The Motion Picture Guide*

"...director Carreras and the cast do little to bring the plot's convoluted twists and turns to life."—*Hammer, House of Horror*

PARANOIAC (1963)

Released in the U.S. by Universal; Released in England by Rank; A Hammer Film Production; Associate Producer: Basil Keys; Produced by Anthony Hinds; Directed by Freddie Francis; **Screenplay: Jimmy Sangster**; Photography: Arthur Grant; Production Designer: Bernard Robinson; Art Director: Don Mingaye; Music: Elizabeth Lutyens; Music Supervisor: John Hollingsworth; Supervising Editor: James Needs; Production Manager: John Draper; First Assistant Director: Ross MacKenzie; Continuity: Pauline Wise; Sound: Ken Rawkins; Makeup: Roy Ashton; Hairdresser: Frieda Steiger; Wardrobe Supervisor: Molly Arbuthnot; Special Effects: Les Bowie and Kit West; Wardrobe Mistress: Rosemary Burrows; Camera Operator: Moray Grant; Filmed at Bray Studios; 80 minutes

Janette Scott (*Eleanor Ashby*), Oliver Reed (*Simon Ashby*), Liliane Brousse (*Francoise*), Alexander Davion (*Tony Ashby*), Sheila Burrell (*Aunt Harriet*), Maurice Denham (*John Kossett*), John Bonney (*Keith Kossett*), John Stuart (*Williams*), Colin Tapley (*Vicar*), Harold Lang (*RAF Type*), Laurie Leigh, Marianne Stone (*Women*), Sydney Bromley (*Tramp*), Jack Taylor (*Sailor*)

A woman questions her sanity after seeing her dead brother at her parents' memorial service. The bizarre family situation turns into a *Psycho*-style thriller.

"Hammer Productions has now come tantalizingly close to the bullseye."—*The New York Times*

"*Paranoiac* was an impressive debut [for Freddie Francis] and might be his best effort for the company."—*Hammer Films*

"*Paranoiac*, while nothing like its inspiration [*Psycho*], ranks as one of the best of these efforts."—*The Motion Picture Guide*

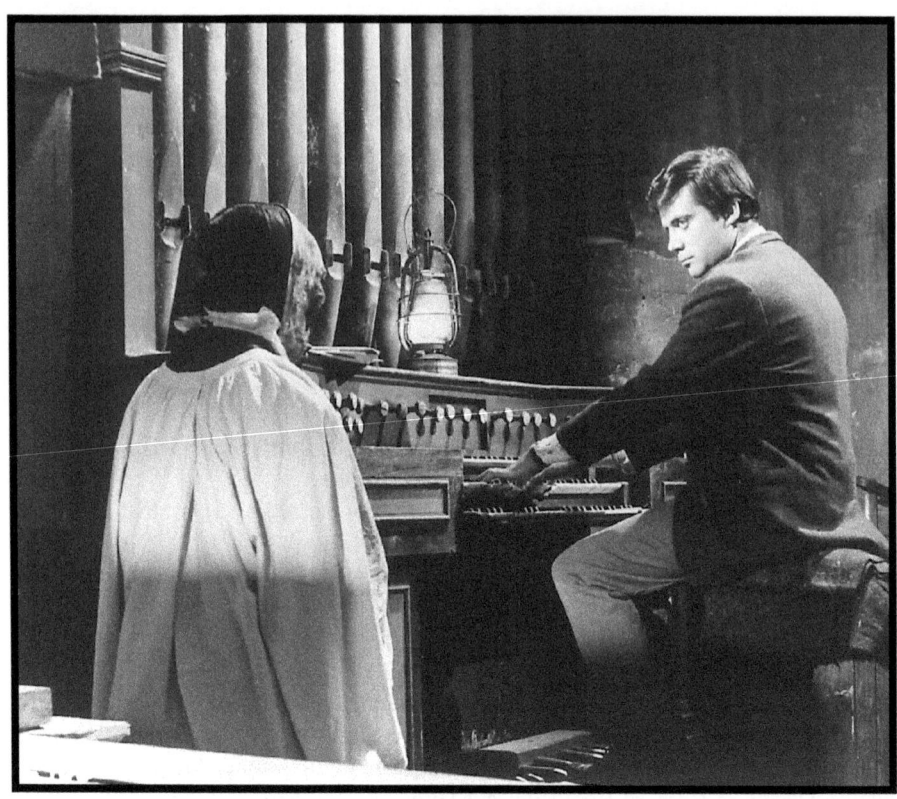

Paranoiac

"...thanks to the inventiveness of Sangster's script the results, though formulaic, are still pretty diverting." — *Hammer, House of Horror*

NIGHTMARE (1964)

Released in England by the Rank Organization on April 19, 1964; Released in the U.S. by Universal; A Hammer Film Production; **Screenplay and Produced by Jimmy Sangster**; Directed by Freddie Francis; Photography: John Wilcox (Hammerscope); Music: Don Banks; Music Supervisor: John Hollingsworth; Production Designer: Bernard Robinson; Art Director: Don Mingaye; Editor: James Needs; Makeup: Roy Ashton; Production Manager: Don Weeks; Special Effects: Les Bowie; Filmed at Bray Studios; 82 minutes

David Knight (*Henry Baxter*), Moira Redmond (*Grace*), Brenda Bruce (*Mary*), Jennie Linden (*Janet*), George A. Cooper (*John*), Irene Richmond (*Mrs. Gibbs*), John Welsh (*Doctor*), Timothy Bateson (*Barman*), Clytie Jessop (*"Woman in White"*), Hedger Wallace (*Sid*), Julie Samuel (*Maid*), Elizabeth Dear (*Janet as a Child*), Isla Cameron (*Mother*)

Also known as *Here's the Knife, Dear, Now Use It*. A woman (Jennie Linden) is tortured by people trying to drive her insane.

Nightmare

"Though it has been undervalued, it is more than passable entertainment." — *Hammer Films*

"...despite the familiarity of its ingredients, the film manages to work up a certain degree of tension and remains one of the better examples of its kind." — *Hammer, House of Horror*

"A routine suspense film..." — *The Motion Picture Guide*

THE DEVIL-SHIP PIRATES (1964)

Released in the U.S. by Columbia; Released in England by Associated British-Warner-Pathe; A Hammer Film Production; Produced by Anthony Nelson-Keys; Directed by Don Sharp; **Screenplay: Jimmy Sangster**; Photography: Michael Reed (Technicolor and Hammerscope); Production Design: Bernard Robinson; Art Director: Don Mingaye; Supervising Editor: James Needs; Music: Gary Hughes; Production Manager: Don Weeks; Assistant Director: Bert Batt; Special Effects: Les Bowie; Musical Director: John Hollingsworth; Makeup: Roy Ashton; Filmed at Bray Studios; 86 minutes

Christopher Lee (*Capt. Robeles*), John Cairney (*Harry*), Barry Warren (*Manuel*), Ernest Clark (*Sir Basil Smeeton*), Natasha Pyne (*Jane*), Suzan Farmer (*Angela*), Andrew Keir (*Tom*), Duncan Lamont (*Bosun*), Michael Ripper (*Pepe*), Charles Houston (*Antonio*), Harry Locke (*Bragg*), Michael Newport (*Smiler*), Peter Howell (*Vicar*), Jack Rodney (*Mandrake*), Philip Latham (*Miller*), Leonard Fenton (*Quintana*), Barry Linehan (*Gus-*

tave), Bruce Beeby (*Pedro*), Michael Peake (*Grande*), Johnny Briggs (*Pablo*), Joseph O'Connor (*Don Jose*), Annette Whiteley (*Meg*), June Ellis (*Mrs. Blake*)

Christopher Lee once again takes to the high seas as a pirate. This time he is terrorizing an English town.

"Impressively mounted adventure meller." — *Variety*

"*The Devil-Ship Pirates* shows Hammer at its best, using its production expertise to give the film a look equal to many times its cost." — *Hammer Films*

"Well-done Hammer swashbuckler..." — *The Motion Picture Guide*

"...a straight-forward romp." — *Hammer, House of Horror*

HYSTERIA (1964)

MGM/A Hammer Film Production; **Screenplay and Produced by Jimmy Sangster**; Directed by Freddie Francis; Photography: John Wilcox; Production Design: Edward Carrick; Supervising Editor: James Needs; Music: Don Banks; Music Supervisor: Philip Martell; Production Manager: Don Weeks; Camera: David Harcourt; Continuity: Yvonne Axworthy; Sound Recordist: Cyril Swern; Sound Editor: Roy Hyde; Makeup: Alex Garfath; Hairstyles: Alice Holmes; Wardrobe: Maude Churchill; Assistant Director: Basil Rayburn; Titles: Chambers and Partners; Filmed at MGM/EMI Elstree Studios; 85 minutes

Robert Webber (*Mr. Smith*), Anthony Newley (*Dr. Keller*), Jennifer Jayne (*Gina*), Maurice Denham (*Hemmings*), Lelia Goldoni (*Denise*), Peter Woodthorpe (*Marcus Allen*), Sandra Boize (*English Girl*), Sue Lloyd (*French Girl*), John Arnatt, Marianne Stone, Irene Richmond, Kiwi Kingston

Hysteria

Another in the psycho-thriller films from Hammer. A man with amnesia searches for the identity of the woman using a photograph in his possession.

"...suffering mainly from the lack of a more charismatic star."—*Hammer Films*
"A taut shocker with chilling psychological undertones."—*The Motion Picture Guide*

FACE OF A STRANGER (1964)
Merton Park/AA; Produced by Jack Greenwood; Directed by John Moxey; **Screenplay: John Sansom [Jimmy Sangster]**; Based on a Novel by Edgar Wallace; 56 minutes

Jeremy Kemp (*Vince Howard*), Bernard Archard (*Michael Forrest*), Rosemary Leach (*Mary Bell*), Philip Locke (*John Bell*)

An ex-prisoner impersonates his cellmate, trying to learn the whereabouts of the cellmate's hidden stash.

"...an interesting programmer."—*The Motion Picture Guide*

THE NANNY (1965)

Released in the U.S. by 20th Century-Fox; Released in England by Warner-Pathe; A Hammer-Seven Arts Production; Executive Producer: Anthony Hinds; **Screenplay and Produced by Jimmy Sangster**; Based on the Novel by Evelyn Piper; Directed by Seth Holt; Photography: Harry Waxman; Music: Richard Rodney Bennett; Music Supervisor: Philip Martell; Production Design: Edward Carrick; Supervising Editor: James Needs; Editor: Tom Simpson; Production Manager: George Fowler; Assistant Director: Christopher Dryhurst; Continuity: Renee Glynn; Makeup: Tom Smith; Filmed at MGM/EMI Studios, Elstree; 93 minutes

Bette Davis (*Nanny*), Wendy Craig (*Virgie Fane*), Jill Bennett (*Penelope*), James Villiers (*Bill Fane*), William Dix (*Joey*), Pamela Franklin (*Bobby*), Jack Watling (*Dr. Medman*), Maurice Denham (*Dr. Beamaster*), Alfred Burke (*Dr. Wills*), Nora Gordon (*Mrs. Griggs*), Sandra Power (*Sarah*), Harry Fowler (*Milkman*), Angharad Aubrey (*Susy*)

The incomparable Bette Davis, still a stellar movie presence, dominates this story of a Nanny with deep dark secrets and psychotic tendencies. A boy blamed for the death of his sister knows the death was caused by the Nanny (Davis). He tries to make people believe him but has no luck. He is only saved when the Nanny realizes what she has done to his sister. She packs her bags and leaves.

"Bette Davis gave what is probably the best performance by an actress in a Hammer film."—*Hammer Films*

"This spotty film is often frightening but is at times clumsy, though Davis' performance is noteworthy."—*The Motion Picture Guide*

"...highly accomplished version of above average Jimmy Sangster script."—*A Heritage of Horror*

"Without doubt the best psychological thriller Hammer ever made, and certainly comparable with the work of Hitchcock in this field."—*Hammer, House of Horror*

DRACULA—PRINCE OF DARKNESS (1966)

Released in England by Warner-Pathe; Released in the U.S. by 20th Century-Fox; A Seven Arts-Hammer Film Production; Executive Producer: Anthony Hinds; Produced by Anthony Nelson-Keys; Directed by Terence Fisher; **Screenplay: John Sansom [Jimmy Sangster]**; From an Idea by John Elder [Anthony Hinds]; Photography: Michael Reed (Color and Techniscope); Production Designer: Bernard Robinson; Art Director: Don Mingaye; Music: James Bernard; Music Supervisor: Philip Martell; Supervising Editor: James Needs; Editor: Chris Barnes; Special Effects: [Les] Bowie Films Ltd.; Assistant Director: Bert Batt; Makeup: Roy Ashton; Produced at Bray Studios; 90 minutes

Christopher Lee (*Count Dracula*), Barbara Shelley (*Helen Kent*), Andrew Keir (*Father Shandor*), Francis Matthews (*Charles Kent*), Suzan Farmer (*Diana Kent*), Charles Tingwell (*Alan Kent*), Thorley Walters (*Ludwig*), Philip Latham (*Klove*), Walter Brown (*Brother Mark*), George Woodbridge (*Landlord*), Jack Lambert (*Brother Peter*), Philip Ray (*Priest*), Joyce Hemson (*Mother*), John Maxim (*Coach Driver*)

A group of weary travelers stops at a lonely castle where their host offers them his hospitality. Unfortunately, the hospitality comes at a high price. Barbara Shelley

Dracula—Prince of Darkness

is wonderful as a proper English matron who turns into a savage seductress under the spell of Dracula (Christopher Lee).

"...an extremely well-made example of classic ghoulish horror." — *The Kinematograph Weekly*

"Terence Fisher has directed it with his usual know-how." — *Variety*

"...a superior horror package." — *Hammer Films*

From Hammer Films to Hollywood! A Life in the Movies

209

"...routine scare production..."—*The Motion Picture Guide*

"The best thing about *Dracula—Prince of Darkness* is the prologue."—*A History of Horrors*

"...any defects the narrative might have are at least shored up by some strong performances."—*Hammer, House of Horror*

DEADLIER THAN THE MALE (1967)

Universal; Produced by Betty Box, Sydney Box and Bruce Newberry; Directed by Ralph Thomas; **Screenplay: Jimmy Sangster**, David Osborn and Liz Charles-Williams; **Story: Jimmy Sangster**; Based on the Character Created by H. C. McNeile ("Sapper"); Photography: Ernest Steward (Color); Editor: Alfred Roome; Music: Malcolm Lockyer; 98 minutes

Richard Johnson (*Hugh Drummond*), Elke Sommer (*Irma Eckman*), Sylva Koscina (*Penelope*), Nigel Green (*Carl Peterson/Weston*), Suzanna Leigh (*Grace*), Steve Carlson (*Robert Drummond*), Virginia North (*Brenda*), Justine Lord (*Miss Ashenden*), Zia Mohyeddin (*King Fedra*), Lee Montague (*Boxer*), Yasuko Nagazumi (*Mitsouko*), Laurence Naismith (*Sir John Bledlow*), George Pastell (*Carloggio*), Milton Reid (*Chang*), Leonard Rossiter (*Bridgenorth*)

Richard Johnson portrays famous detective Bulldog Drummond.

"...overlong and silly."—*The Motion Picture Guide*

THE ANNIVERSARY (1967)

Released in the U.S. by 20th Century-Fox on February 7, 1968; Released in England by Warner-Pathe; on February 18, 1968; A Hammer-Seven Arts Film Production; **Screenplay and Produced by Jimmy Sangster**; Directed by Roy Ward Baker; Based on a Play by Bill MacIlwraith; Photography: Harry Waxman (Technicolor); Art Director: Reece Pemberton; Supervising Editor: James Needs; Editor: Peter Weatherly; Music Supervisor: Philip Martell; Assistant Director: Bert Batt; Makeup: George Partleton; Filmed at MGM/EMI Studios, Elstree, England; 95 minutes

Bette Davis (*Mrs. Taggart*), Sheila Hancock (*Karen Taggart*), Jack Hedley (*Terry Taggart*), James Cossins (*Henry Taggart*), Elaine Taylor (*Shirley Blair*), Christian Roberts (*Tom Taggart*), Timothy Bateson (*Mr. Bird*), Arnold Diamond (*Head Waiter*), Albert Shepherd, Ralph Watson (*Construction Workers*), Sally Jane Spencer (*Florist*)

Bette Davis is the mother-from-Hell who tries to control the fate of her bizarre family.

"A vehicle for the extravagant tantrums of Bette Davis."—*Variety*

"[Director] Baker didn't quite rise to the challenge and made an adequate if unambitious film out of producer-screenwriter Jimmy Sangster's straightforward adaptation of the play."—*Hammer, House of Horror*

"Davis is great, but the film suffers from the staginess of the play on which it was based."—*The Motion Picture Guide*

The Anniversary

CRESCENDO (1970)

Released in England by Warner Pathe; Released in the U.S. by Warner Bros./Seven Arts; A Hammer Production; Produced by Michael Carreras; Directed by Alan Gibson; **Screenplay: Jimmy Sangster and Alfred Shaughnessy**; Photography: Paul Beeson (Color); Editor: Chris Barnes; Music: Malcolm Williamson; Music Performed by the London Symphony Orchestra; Art Director: Scott MacGregor; Production Manager: Hugh Harlow; Assistant Director: Jack Martin; Camera: John Wilbolt; Filmed at MGM-EMI Studios, Elstree, and on location in France; 95 minutes (England), 83 minutes (U.S.)

Stefanie Powers (*Susan Roberts*), James Olson (*Georges/Jacques*), Margaretta Scott (*Danielle Ryman*), Jane Lapotaire (*Lillianne*), Joss Ackland (*Carter*), Kirsten Betts (*Catherine*)

Stefanie Powers visits a family with hidden secrets and finds a madman locked in an attic.

"Scripted by Jimmy Sangster and Alfred Shaughnessy, the film is almost rabid in its borrowings, yet director Alan Gibson manages to give the familiar proceedings a certain visual style."—*Hammer, House of Horror*

Crescendo

"...not worth the wait."—*Hammer Films*
"...not one of Hammer's better efforts."—*The Motion Picture Guide*

HORROR OF FRANKENSTEIN (1970)

Released in England by Anglo-EMI; Released in the U.S. by Continental; A Hammer Film Production; **Produced and Directed by Jimmy Sangster; Screenplay: Jimmy Sangster and Jeremy Burnham**; Photography: Moray Grant (Color); Music: Malcolm Williamson; Music Supervisor: Philip Martell; Art Director: Scott MacGregor; Production Manager: Tom Sachs; Editor: Chris Barnes; Assistant Director: Derek Whitehurst; Makeup: Tom Smith; Filmed at MGM-EMI Elstree Studios; 95 minutes

Ralph Bates (*Victor Frankenstein*), Kate O'Mara (*Alys*), Veronica Carlson (*Elizabeth*), Dennis Price (*Bodysnatcher*), Joan Rice (*His Wife*), Graham James (*Wilhelm*), Bernard Archard (*Professor*), Jon Finch (*Officer*), Dave Prowse (*Monster*)

The Frankenstein legend is updated by Hammer with a darkly comedic script. Ralph Bates, being groomed for Hammer stardom, is cast as Victor Frankenstein.

"...a shocking and up-to-date rendition of the age-old plot."—*Videohound's Golden Movie Retriever*
"...it is difficult to defend the film on any level."—*Hammer Films*

Do You Want It Good or Tuesday?

Horror of Frankenstein

"The first hour is not only painless, but also fun."—*The New York Times*

"...feeble attempt by Hammer..."—*The Motion Picture Guide*

"By all accounts it was fun to make, but that was where the fun ended."—*A History of Horrors*

"A sorry mess indeed..."—*Hammer, House of Horror*

LUST FOR A VAMPIRE (1971)

Released in the U.S. by American Continental Films (Levitt-Pickman); Released in England by Associated British Picture Corp.; A Hammer Film Production; Produced by Harry Fine and Michael Style; **Directed by Jimmy Sangster**; Screenplay: Tudor Gates; Based on the Characters Created by J. Sheridan Le Fanu; Photography: David Muir (Color); Art Director: Don Mingaye; Music Supervisor: Philip Martell; Assistant Director: David Bracknell; Editor: Spencer Reeve; Makeup: George Blackler; Music: Harry Robinson; Filmed at MGM-EMI Studios, Elstree; 95 minutes

Ralph Bates (*Giles Barton*), Barbara Jefford (*Countess Karnstein/Heritzen*), Suzanna Leigh (*Janet Playfair*), Michael Johnson (*Richard LeStrange*), Yutte Stensgaard (*Mircalla/Carmilla*), Mike Raven (*Count Karnstein/Dr. Froheim*), Helen Christie (*Miss Simpson*), David Healy (*Raymond Pelley*), Michael Brennan (*Landlord*), Pippa Steele (*Susan Pelley*), Luan Peters (*Trudi*), Christopher Cunningham (*Coachman*), Judy Matheson (*Amanda McBride*), Eric Chitty (*Prof. Hertz*), Christopher Neame (*Hans*),

Lust for a Vampire

Harvey Hall (*Insp. Heinrich*), Caryl Little (*Isabel Courtney*), Jack Melford (*The Bishop*), Erica Beale, Jackie Leapman, Melita Clarke, Patricia Warner, Christine Smith, Vivienne Chandler, Sue Longhurst, Melinda Churcher (*School Girls*)

The second film in the Hammer Karnstein trilogy. Ralph Bates stars as a demented schoolmaster seeking immortality from the vampire Mircalla (Yutte Stensgaard). A teacher at the school (Michael Johnson) falls in love with Mircalla.

"...moody and erotically charged, with an impressive ending."—*Videohound's Golden Movie Retriever*

"Part of the trilogy of Karnstein pictures, it glorified the worst excesses of its predecessor while lacking any of that film's positives."—*Hammer Films*

"Whatever rich Gothic flavor this material may have had is totally destroyed by Sangster's annoying direction which relies heavily on leering zooms and garish color. To make matters worse, what should be highly-charged erotic scenes are ruined by deplorably bad songs."—*The Motion Picture Guide*

"Sangster's direction is much less assured than in *Horror of Frankenstein*."—*A History of Horrors*

"...the results are more often than not embarrassing."—*Hammer, House of Horror*

FEAR IN THE NIGHT (1971)

Released in England by Anglo/EMI; Released in the U.S. by International Co-Productions/ Pisces; A Hammer Film Production; **Produced and Directed by Jimmy Sangster**; **Screenplay: Jimmy Sangster** and Michael Syson; Photography: Arthur Grant (Technicolor); Editor: Peter Weatherley; Production Manager: Christopher Neame; Music: Don McCabe; Musical Director: Philip Martell; Filmed at MGM/ EMI Elstree Studios; 96 minutes

Judy Geeson (*Peggy Heller*), Joan Collins (*Molly Carmichael*), Ralph Bates (*Robert Heller*), Peter Cushing

Fear in the Night

(*Michael Carmichael*), Gillian Lind (*Mrs. Beamish*), James Cossins (*Doctor*), John Brown, Brian Grellis (*Policemen*)

Peter Cushing stars as a headmaster of a private school. Joan Collins is the evil wife who tries to drive another woman insane so she will kill Cushing.

From Hammer Films to Hollywood! A Life in the Movies

215

"...suspenseful tale of murder."—*Videohound's Golden Movie Retriever*

"...too long and might have worked better as an hour-long television play."—*Hammer Films*

"...watchable but basically tired hokum."—*Hammer, House of Horror*

"...far-fetched to say the least."—*The Motion Picture Guide*

WHO SLEW AUNTIE ROO? (1971)

AIP/A Hemdale Production; Produced by Samuel Z. Arkoff and James H. Nicholson; Directed by Curtis Harrington; **Screenplay: Jimmy Sangster**, Robert Blees, and Gavin Lambert; Story: David Osborn; Photography: Desmond Dickinson (Color); Music: Kenneth V. Jones; Editor: Tristam V. Cones; Art Director: George Provis; Makeup: Eddie Knight and Sylvia Croft; Assistant Director: Colin Brewer; Sound: Ken Ritchie and Nolan Roberts; English title: *Whoever Slew Auntie Roo?*; 89 minutes

Shelley Winters (*Rosie Forrest*), Mark Lester (*Christopher*), Ralph Richardson (*Mr. Benton*), Lionel Jeffries (*Insp. Willoughby*), Judy Cornwell (*Clarine*), Michael Gothard (*Albie*), Hugh Griffith (*Mr. Harrison*), Chloe Franks (*Katy*), Rosalie Crutchley (*Miss Henley*), Pat Heywood (*Dr. Mason*), Jacqueline Cowper (*Angela*), Richard Beaumont (*Peter*), Charlotte Sayce (*Katherine*), Marianne Stone (*Miss Wilcox*)

The excellent Shelley Winters stars as Rosie Forrest driven over the edge by the death of her young daughter. The black comedy also stars Mark Lester, who would go on to appear in *Oliver!*

"[Director] Harrington tends to overdo the Grand Guignol sequences."—*The Encyclopedia of Horror Movies*

"...walks a fine line between good and bad taste, manipulating audience expectation and loyalties gleefully and shamelessly."—*The Motion Picture Guide*

The Legacy

THE LEGACY (1979)
Universal; Directed by Richard Marquand; Produced by David Foster; **Screenplay: Jimmy Sangster**, Patric Tilley and Paul Wheeler; **Story: Jimmy Sangster**; Photography: Dick Bush and Alan Hume (Technicolor); Music: Michael J. Lewis; Editor: Anne V. Coates; Production Designer: Disley Jones; Costumes: Shura Cohen; Special Effects: Ian Wingrove; 100 minutes

Katharine Ross (*Maggie Walsh*), Sam Elliott (*Pete Danner*), John Standing (*Jason Mountolive*), Ian Hogg (*Harry*), Margaret Tyzack (*Nurse Adams*), Charles Gray (*Karl*), Lee Montague (*Jacques*), Hildegard Neil (*Barbara*), Marianne Broome (*Maria*), William Abney (*Butler*), Patsy Smart (*Cook*), Mathias Kilroy (*Stable Lad*), Reg Harding (*Gardener*), Roger Daltrey (*Clive*)

Katharine Ross stars in this devil-worship film as the reincarnated woman who is to lead the cult.

"...death and demons abound."—*Videohound's Golden Movie Retriever*
"...dry, dull, and terribly predictable."—*The Motion Picture Guide*

PHOBIA (1980)

Paramount/Spiegel-Bergman Films; Directed by John Huston; Produced by Zale Magder; **Screenplay: Lew Lehman, Jimmy Sangster and Peter Bellwood**; Story: Gary Sherman and Ronald Shusett; Photography: Reginald H. Morris (Color); Music: Andie Gagnon; Editor: Stan Cole; Art Director: David Jaques; 94 minutes

Paul Michael Glaser (*Dr. Peter Ross*); John Colicos (*Insp. Barnes*); Susan Hogan (*Jenny*); Alexandra Stewart (*Barbara*); Robert O'Ree (*Bubba*); David Bolt (*Henry*); David Eisner (*Johnny*); Lisa Langlois (*Laura*); Kenneth Welsh (*Sgt. Wheeler*); Neil Vipond (*Dr. Clegg*); Patricia Collins (*Dr. Toland*); Marian Waldmar (*Mrs. Casey*); Gwen Thomas (*Dr. Clemens*)

The great John Huston directed *Phobia*, his only horror venture. A psychologist tries to treat criminals by forcing them to confront their fears.

"...cunningly well-crafted in a self-effacing style." — *The Encyclopedia of Horror Movies*

"Stupid and unpleasant story that lasts too long and probably should never have started." — *Videohound's Golden Movie Retriever*

"a simpleminded script that will leave most viewers bored after the first 15 minutes." — *The Motion Picture Guide*

THE DEVIL AND MAX DEVLIN (1981)

Buena Vista; Produced by Jerome Courtland; Directed by Steven Hilliard Stern; Screenplay: Mary Rodgers; **Based on a Story by Mary Rodgers and Jimmy Sangster**; Photography: Howard Schwartz (Color); Music: Buddy Baker; Editor: Raymond A. de Leuw; Art Directors: John B. Mansbridge and Leon R. Harris; Music: Marvin Hamlish and Carole Bayer Sager; 96 minutes

The Devil and Max Devlin

Elliott Gould (*Max Devlin*), Bill Cosby (*Barney Satin*), Susan Anspach (*Penny Hart*), Adam Rich (*Toby Hart*), Julie Budd (*Stella Summers*), David Knell (*Nerve Nordlinger*), Sonny Schroyer (*Big Billy*), Charles Shamata (*Jerry*), Deborah Baltzell (*Heidi*), Ronnie Schell (*Greg*), Jeannie Wilson (*Laverne*), Stanley Black (*Counterman*), Ted Zeigler (*Billings*), Vic Dunlap (*Brian*), Reggie Nalder (*Chairman*)

Elliott Gould and Bill Cosby star in this Disney film. Gould must acquire three pure souls for the devil (Cosby).

"Despite an encouraging start, the film degenerates into typical Disney sentimentality."—*The Motion Picture Guide*

"Good cast wanders aimlessly."—*Videohound's Golden Movie Retriever*

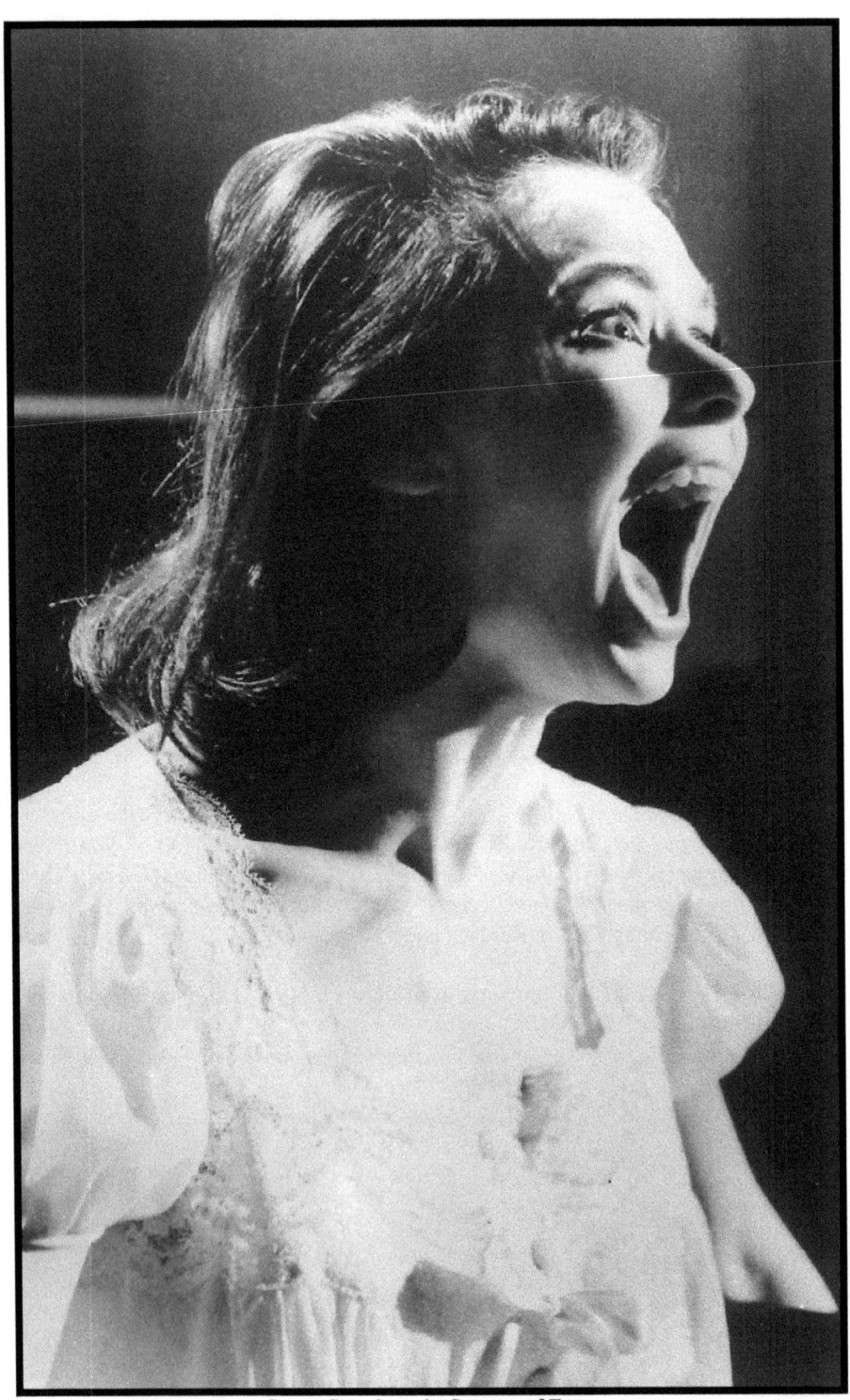

Susan Strasberg in *Scream of Fear*

TECHNICAL and TELEVISION CREDITS and NOVELS

EARLY TECHNICAL CREDITS

Carlton Hill Studios
Camera Assistant on wartime documentaries

Ealing Studios
The Captive Heart (1946) — 3rd Assistant Director
Pink String and Sealing Wax (1950) — 3rd Assistant Director

Mario Zampi Production
Third Time Lucky (1950) — 3rd Assistant Director

Brighton Studios
The Adventures of Jane (1949) — Assistant Director

Hammer
2nd Assistant Director
Celia (1949)
Dick Barton Strikes Back (1949)
Dr. Morelle (1949)
Meet Simon Cherry (1950)
The Adventures of PC 49 (1950)

Assistant Director
The Lady Craved Excitement (1950)
The Man in Black (1950)
Room to Let (1950)
Someone at the Door (1950)
What the Butler Saw (1950)
Cloudburst (1951)
The Black Widow (1951)
The Rossiter Case (1951)
To Have and To Hold (1951)
Death of an Angel (1952)

The Last Page (1952) (USA — *Man Bait*)
Whispering Smith Hits London (1952) (USA — *Whispering Smith vs. Scotland Yard*)
Wings of Danger (1952)
The Flanagan Boy (1953) (USA — *Bad Blonde*)
The Saint's Return (1953) (USA — *The Saint's Girl Friday*)
Spaceways (1953)
36 Hours (1954) (USA — *Terror Street*)

From Hammer Films to Hollywood! A Life in the Movies

221

What the Butler Saw

Murder by Proxy

Do You Want It Good or Tuesday?

The Stranger Came Home

Blood Orange (1954) (USA—*Three Stops to Murder*)
Face the Music (1954) (USA—*The Black Glove*)
Five Days (1954) (USA—*Paid to Kill Us*)
Murder by Proxy (1955) (USA—*Blackout*)
The House Across the Lake (1954) (USA—*Heat Wave*)

Production Manager
Mask of Dust (1954) (USA—*A Race for Life*)
Men of Sherwood Forest (1954)
The Stranger Came Home (1954) (USA—*The Unholy Four*)
Break in the Circle (1955)
Third Party Risk (1955) (USA—*Deadly Game*)
Women Without Men (1956)

Writing Credits
UK Television
The Big Wheel—Armchair Theatre (1958/59)
I Can Destroy the Sun—Armchair Theatre (1958/59)
The Killers—four-part serial (1958/59)
Motive for Murder—four-part serial (1958/59)

Men of Sherwood Forest

US Television
Wrote and Produced
Spy Killer (Private I)—ABC Movie of the Week (1969)
Foreign Exchange—ABC Movie of the Week (1970)

Wrote
Movie of the Week
Good Against Evil
No Place to Hide (1975)
Northbeach and Rawhide (1985) CBS
Once Upon a Spy
Scream Pretty Peggy (1973) ABC
Taste of Evil (1971) ABC
The Billion Dollar Adventure
The Toughest Man in the World (1984) CBS

Pilots
Ebony, Ivory and Jade (wrote and produced)
Murder in Music City (wrote and produced) (1979) NBC
The Concrete Cowboys (wrote and produced) (1979) CBS
Young Dan'l Boone (series producer) (9/12/77-10/4/77) CBS

Series
Believe It or Not—ABC (wrote and directed the first year) (1982)

Story Edited and/or Scripted
Over 100 hours of American episodic TV including:
B.J. and the Bear (1979) NBC
Banacek (1972-74) NBC
Bronk (1975-76) CBS
Cannon (1971-76) CBS
Columbo (1971-78) NBC
Ghost Story (1972-73) NBC
Ironside (1967-75) NBC
Kolchak, The Nightstalker (1974-75) ABC
McCloud (1970-77) NBC
Movin' On (1974-76) NBC
Six Million Dollar Man (1974-78) ABC
The Magician (1973-74) NBC
Wonder Woman (1976-77) ABC

Novels
Blackball (1987)
Foreign Exchange (1968)
Hardball (1988)
Private I (1967)
Snowball (1986)
Touchfeather (1968)
Touchfeather, Too (1970)
Your Friendly Neighbourhood Death Pedlar (1971)

The Brides of Dracula

Do You Want It Good or Tuesday?

INDEX

Do You Want It Good or Tuesday?

ACKNOWLEDGMENTS

The terrible thing about writing a list of acknowledgments is the fear that you'll forget somebody. I'd far rather just say "thanks to you all." and mention no names. But that would be chickening out. So, apologizing in advance to those I might have forgotten, let me thank Tom Johnson and Deborah Del Vecchio for writing *Hammer Films: An Exhausive Filmography* (published by McFarland) and Denis Meikle for his exhaustive and compelling book on *Hammer: A History of Horrors* (published by Scarecrow Press). Both these books told me things about my career that even I didn't know. Also thanks to Eric Caidin, Wayne Kinsey, John Parnum, Linda J. Walter, and Tom Weaver.

Two other people who deserve thanks are Ernie Frankel for checking the manuscript from time to time and Ron Lyon for doing the same.

Also thanks to Jo Carreras for being around and Ruth Alley for being Ruth Alley.

But my real thanks must go to Michael Carreras, who is no longer with us, and to Anthony Hinds, who most certainly is (though I wish he was around more often). Without these two there would have been no Hammer, I probably wouldn't have ended up a writer, and you wouldn't be reading this autobiography.